The Clarion Call

THE SOUL AND SERVICE TRILOGY

By Susan S. Trout, PhD

Born to Serve: The Evolution of the Soul Through Service

The Awakened Leader: Leadership as a Classroom of the Soul

The Clarion Call: Leadership and Group Life in the Aquarian Era

The Clarion Call

Leadership and Group Life in the Aquarian Era

By Susan S. Trout, PhD

THREE ROSES PRESS ◆ ALEXANDRIA, VIRGINIA

Portions of this book were first published in *Born to Serve: The Evolution of the Soul Through Service* and *The Awakened Leader: Leadership as a Classroom of the Soul.*

Published by Three Roses Press, P. O. Box 320245, Alexandria, VA 22320
Printed in the United States of America

ISBN: 978-0-9625386-4-3
Library of Congress Catalog Card Number: 2008907653

Cover and book design by Jane Perini
Thunder Mountain Design & Communications

Take the hand
of tomorrow
for the yesterday
is no more.

– SUSAN S. TROUT

To Alitah Kay

TABLE OF CONTENTS

Part Two
SOUL-INSPIRED LEADERSHIP

Part Four

PRACTICES FOR LIVING AN AQUARIAN WAY

LIST OF FIGURES

LIST OF TABLES

APPRECIATION

My heart settles into a bevy of joy as I extend my gratitude to Peggy Tabor Millin, editor of the three books of *The Soul and Service Trilogy*. Long ago, it seems, Peggy and I agreed to join in purpose on behalf of *The Trilogy's* message, mindful that the books were to be written to ease the uncertain and delicate soul journey of humankind. Spanning forty years, our writer-editor partnership and our friendship have evolved into an expression of Aquarian ideals—we strive to work from the aspect of the mind that dwells in the heart, that esteems beauty, and that loves all sentient beings without distinctions.

ACKNOWLEDGMENTS

True to the spirit and values of the Aquarian Era, many have contributed to the teachings in *The Clarion Call*. I liken my decades of experience with individuals, leaders, groups, teams, and organizations to the process of alchemy, the power of transforming something common into something extraordinary. In the Aquarian Era, we create group consciousness by mastering alchemy.

I am forever indebted to the faculty and graduate students of the Department of Learning Disabilities at the University of the Pacific Medical Center in San Francisco, California, and to the board, volunteers, and participants at the Institute for the Advancement of Service in Alexandria, Virginia, for the opportunity to fully live the challenges and gifts of leadership and group life. To have eventually recognized my life and its work as a classroom for my soul has brought me limitless freedom and blessed my life in countless ways.

I feel especially honored to have had the opportunity to participate in the Institute's destiny and to have had the freedom to develop a template for leadership and group life that is grounded in soul development. For nearly thirty years, members of the Institute and I have joined in striving to evolve a philosophy, an organizational design, a leadership style, and psychospiritual practices that open the door of group cooperation and consciousness. The two tenets of our vision and mission have kept us focused and steadfast in our purpose: the participation in our healing process (self-transformation) and the willingness to extend unconditionally that healing to others (service).

To those who financially supported the writing of *The Clarion Call,* I extend my highest esteem and gratitude: Cornelius Bennhold, John Blum, Carolyn Ducca, Shirley Fine, Myra Jackson, Teresa Peterson, Maggie Scobie, Rod Smith, Scottie Wiest, and Iris Williams. The integrity of *The Clarion Call* was ensured by superb critical readers: Ann Benvenuto, Wayne Caskey, Carolyn Ducca, Wendy Glaubitz, and Scottie Wiest.

Finally, I am indebted to the group of teachers on the inner planes who have shown themselves to be capable, intentional, generous, and unconditional. As my spiritual book committee, they have been ever present and ever wise during the twelve years of writing *The Soul and Service Trilogy.*

PROLOGUE

We stand precariously at the midpoint of the transition from the Piscean Era to the Aquarian Era. No longer having a foothold in the past, we step onto uncharted land. Old organizational structures and belief systems collapse around us as new ones emerge. Conflict between the old and new, the known and unknown, arises as we struggle to adjust to the necessity of change and to develop new models of leadership and group life.

Subtle Aquarian energies first appeared on planet Earth around the year 1760. Predictions suggest that by the year 2260 Piscean energies will have yielded to Aquarian energies. *The Clarion Call: Leadership and Group Life in the Aquarian Era* addresses the anticipated challenges and needs in leadership and group life between 2008—the midpoint of the five-hundred-year transition—and the year 2025.

The Clarion Call is the third book of *The Soul and Service Trilogy* that began in 1997 with *Born to Serve: The Evolution of the Soul Through Service* and continued in 2005 with *The Awakened Leader: Leadership as a Classroom of the Soul.* Rooted in the questions I had about my own service and the common challenges I observed in others, *Born to Serve* provides a roadmap to guide individuals and groups in deepening their consciousness of the relationship between their motives for serving and the quality of their service. The foundation for *The Awakened Leader* formed as my awareness of leadership as soul lessons grew and as I examined my personal experiences and the common difficulties I observed in other leaders. I discovered that what we as leaders do not resolve and develop within ourselves is acted out with adverse effects in our personal life and in our leadership.

The last chapter of *The Awakened Leader* introduced the transition from the Piscean Era to Aquarian Era and addressed one aspect of this transition, the feminine face of leadership. Readers told me that the book left them with the question, "And then what?" In response to this feedback, I realized I was to write a trilogy. I soon understood that the third book would use the perspective of the Piscean-Aquarian transition to expand on the aspects of soul development in service, leadership, and group life introduced in the first two books.

* * *

The new reality opening to us is an era of conscious leaders and conscious groups. This era promises to imbue the world with an energy that unites masculine mind (clarity, order, practicality, knowledge, and words) with feminine heart (cooperation, beauty, synthesis, connectedness, poetry, art, and tenderness). We awaken by deepening and unifying our inner lives. Then, as awakened leaders and groups, we can transform our organizations and communities so that they truly support their members and those they serve. We harvest the good from where we have been and welcome change as new models unfold. We call on the wisdom of the universe to help us with the practical application of that knowledge. We deepen our collective understanding of what wants to emerge in the world. Taking a step through the Aquarian doorway, we move out of the personal into the collective and out of duality into wholeness. We choose to articulate a new template for the evolution of soul-inspired leadership and group consciousness.

* * *

Early in 2007 at the hush of dawn, the word "clarion" crept unobtrusively into my thoughts. A clarion, I learned, was a medieval trumpet used between the twelfth and fourteenth centuries to call men to battle and to announce royalty. The shrill tone of a clarion heralds a clear call to action. Post-fourteenth century poets and spiritualists have used the clarion's trumpet as a metaphor for a call to life and a call to return Home. A once-unused word in my vocabulary, I began incorporating "clarion" in my writings and conversations.

I soon recognized that the third book of *The Soul and Service Trilogy* is a clarion call—a call to life and a call to action. We are called to make a choice at the midpoint between the Piscean and Aquarian eras, to choose between the old and the new, between what was and what will be, between faith and knowing, and between religiosity and spirituality. We are called to practice cooperation and to live as one global family. As leaders and groups, we are called to manifest the Aquarian values of partnership and consciousness.

An inspired message came to me that articulated the profound spiritual meaning of clarion call and why it needed to be the focus and title of my third book.

Imagine it is 2025. A crisis of epidemic proportions blankets the world. No one, yes, no one has imagined the nature of the manifold events that now shatter our reality. Years before some had heard and accepted the call to make the strong stronger and prepared themselves physically, psychologically, and spiritually to be helpers rather than those needing help. Even so, whether consciously forewarned and prepared or not, no one is exempt from the life-altering experience. Together, we enter into the darkness of bewildering inner and outer chaos. Our psyches, our homes, our lands, and our modes of operating in the world dim into a barren blend of mist and smoke.

THE CLARION CALL

Most of what once was cannot be reconstructed or revived. The phoenix of the Aquarian begins to rise from Piscean ashes. Tucked among the ashes are durable Piscean remnants and cherished Aquarian seeds that still vibrate with life.

A door of sacred fortune opens before us and we cross a threshold. What our ears no longer silence, we now can hear—the irrepressible clarion call of life, a call sounded at the beginning of time, when we forgot who we were and why we had come. Hearing a clarion blast, we awaken to our injured world. We decide to answer the call—together. Together we had left our Source and entered a world of vast disconnection and discontent; now we choose to cooperate as a global family and join a world of One.

Susan S. Trout, PhD
Alexandria, Virginia
November 19, 2008

INTRODUCTION

Welcome to Aquarian Life

In opening *The Clarion Call,* you join the increasing number of sincere individuals, leaders, and groups who are aware of being in the midst of an intense adaptation to an Aquarian way of being in the world. You undoubtedly feel the urgency of this planetary transformation and seek creative ways to participate.

You can immediately champion Aquarian values by combining vision and action to manifest cooperation and group consciousness. If you fuel this active imagination with excitement and enthusiasm, your passion during the transition will energize and inspire others to work together for the greater good of all people and the planet.

The Clarion Call supports your desire to be part of the change that is coming by providing a spiritually centered holographic template as a guide. This template offers the structure and flexibility that enable you as an individual, whether leader or group member, to redirect your life and wholeheartedly commit to the unfoldment of the Aquarian future.

Holographic models reflect the Aquarian emphasis on connectedness and on synthesis of parts into the whole. A hologram is a three-dimensional image created by interacting light sources whose individual parts contain the entire image within them, although each from a slightly different perspective. Holographic models contrast with the more familiar linear models that reflect the Piscean emphasis on cause and effect and on analyzing the whole into disparate parts. Communicating a holographic model presents the challenge of illustrating and talking about a circular, fluid, and three-dimensional model within the confines of the linear, static, and two-dimensional world of written words.

To read *The Clarion Call* from a holographic perspective, you are asked to shift your mode of reading and learning. The information in this book is like a thread that spirals up from where you are in the current moment to the next level. The importance of the spiral image is that a spiral builds in layers, holding past, present, and future in one thread. A spiral opens up in a funnel shape. Where the spiral carries you depends on where you begin–not where the book begins, but where you are when you begin to read and work with the material.

Your purpose during this transition is to practice living from the heart in whatever situation you find yourself. *The Clarion Call* empowers you with the knowledge and tools to take responsibility for your thoughts and actions during the Piscean-Aquarian transition.

The book invites repeated study over time. You will be at a different point of development each time you enter the book; therefore, you will experience the material differently. Your progress in understanding and applying the teachings in *The Clarion Call* will be facilitated if you have read *Born to Serve* and *The Awakened Leader,* the first two books of *The Soul and Service Trilogy.*

Further assistance in comprehending the material in *The Clarion Call* is provided for you in two supportive ways. First, the core teachings of *The Soul and Service Trilogy* are assembled in the "Guiding Principles for Aquarian Leadership and Group Life" section between Parts Two and Three. Second, the table of contents with a list of figures and tables; a glossary; a bibliography; and an index will assist you in your study.

The Hologram of the Foundational Teachings of *The Clarion Call*

As the third book in *The Soul and Service Trilogy, The Clarion Call* shares the same holographic template as *Born to Serve* and *The Awakened Leader.* Each book and its contents reflect a different perspective of the author's philosophical construct of the evolutionary stages of soul development. *Born to Serve* discusses the stages of the soul as an evolution of the motives for serving and the quality of service. *The Awakened Leader* looks at the stages and how they relate to leadership. *The Clarion Call* describes the stages in terms of leadership and group life in a time of planetary transition.

The philosophy and practices in *The Clarion Call,* as in the other books of *The Trilogy,* are holographic because each component 1) represents the purpose, vision, mission, and philosophy of the whole from a different point of view and 2) supports the growth of individuals and groups, and thus supports the parallel growth of the whole. A holographic model responds to the people supporting it. A hologram becomes more alive and vibrant when increasing numbers of individuals share its common vision and take responsibility for the whole as well as for their individual piece.

Figure 1 on the following page illustrates a holographic model that can be adapted for use by any spiritually centered organization, group, or project.

A holographic model used in a spiritual context is represented as a ship's wheel with concentric circles interconnected by spokes. The circles identify aspects of the philosophy of the entity being represented. These aspects of the philosophy and their relationship to one another must be in place before the spokes can fully develop. The distance between the circles allows for readability and has no other significance. Imagined as a spiral,

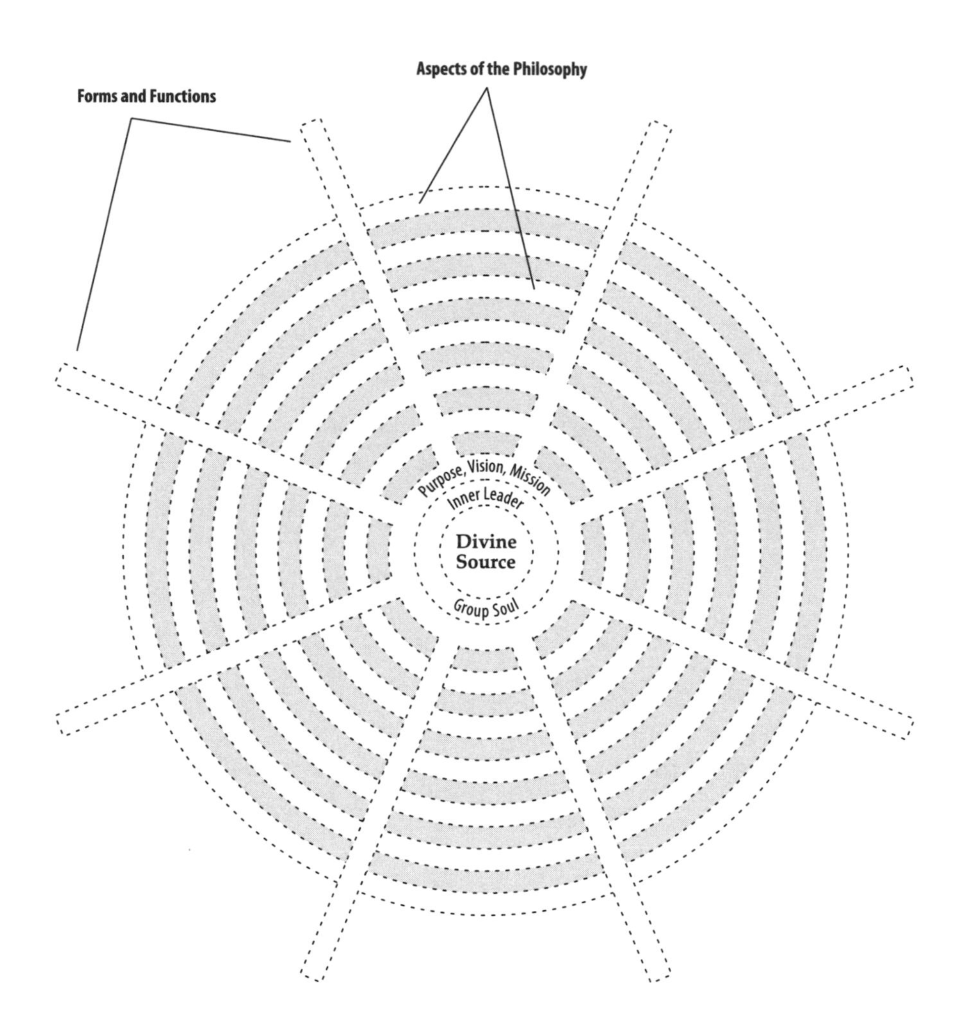

Figure 1: A Spiritually Centered Holographic Model *is diagrammed as a ship's wheel with concentric circles interconnected by spokes. The Divine Source at the center provides the energy that flows through the entire hologram. The philosophy, comprised of universal truths and diagrammed as concentric circles, permeates all the forms and functions, which are diagrammed as spokes. This circular, open design reflects an Aquarian model of reality rather than the linear and hierarchical construct used in the Piscean Era.*

Drawing by Randal Pride

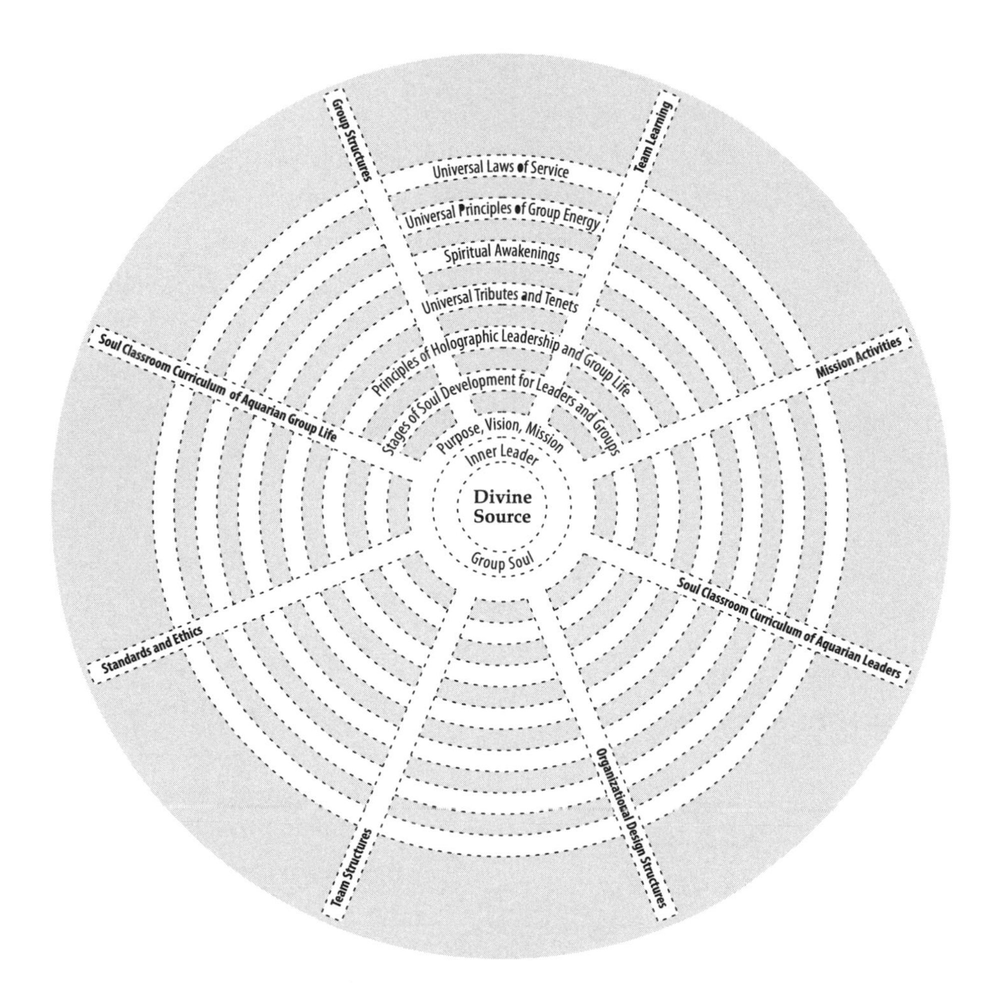

***Figure 2: The Hologram of the Foundational Teachings of* The Clarion Call** *illustrates that The* Clarion Call *reflects the philosophy of soul development in every part of the soul curriculum for individuals, leaders, and groups, including every universal principle and law and every form and function. The components are listed separately below in Table 1.* Drawing by Randal Pride

the circles connect and become part of a continuum that expands and contracts. One place on the spiral is related to and organically connected with every other place. The spokes represent different functions or services through which the philosophy is expressed. The nature of the boundaries of both circles and spokes is permeable. This allows for fluidity of creative energy and receptivity to inner guidance inspired by the Divine Source as the shaft of the wheel.

Figure 2 represents the foundational holographic model of *The Clarion Call*. The diagram conveys the book's unified philosophy. The circles identify universal truths that comprise that philosophy. The spokes

Table 1: Components of the Hologram of the Foundational Teachings of *The Clarion Call*

Circles (listed from the inside out)	Radiating Spokes
Divine Source	Soul Classroom Curriculum of Aquarian Leaders
Inner Leader – Group Soul	Organizational Design Structures
Purpose, Vision, Mission	Team Structures
Evolutionary Stages of Soul Development for Leaders and Groups	Standards and Ethics
Principles of Holographic Leadership and Group Life	Soul Classroom Curriculum of Aquarian Group Life
Universal Tributes and Tenets Spiritual Awakenings	Group Structures
Universal Principles of Group Energy	Team Learning
Universal Laws of Service	Mission Activities

identify forms and functions, such as structures, guidelines, curriculum, and activities that derive from the foundational teachings. Spokes and circles on a hologram have their own hologram. For example, holograms exists for Mission Activities, the Laws of Service, and so on.

The energy of the Divine Source radiates through all parts of the hologram as the energy guiding the purpose, vision, and mission of *The Clarion Call*. As part of *The Soul and Service Trilogy*, *The Clarion Call* reflects the philosophy of the whole. The philosophy is the understanding and articulation of the structure of the universe and humanity's relationship with the Divine Source. All forms and activities are invited to emerge from the life-giving energy of the Divine Source. The philosophy of *The Trilogy* flowing through *The Clarion Call* creates the medium in which service, leadership, and group life exist. Everything within the hologram has a role to play in the whole. Nothing can be excluded, denied, or ignored.

Conclusion

As you proceed on the path laid out by *The Clarion Call*, you will meet intellectual and spiritual challenges. Your fervor, exuberance, and devotion will define the journey that will take you through the book and on to the future you envision. Change and its challenges hang in the air as you climb the steep steps toward attaining Aquarian values in your leadership and groups. To accept this opportunity requires that you be willing to engage in personal and group effort. Your willingness opens the soul gate of opportunity. Bringing forward the gifts of the Piscean Era and welcoming those of the Aquarian ensure that opportunity will be met with steady wisdom. With confidence, you begin your walk with many others toward a shared vision of wholehearted unity.

Part One

Emerging Templates of Leadership and Group Life

The Aquarian spreads before us as
an age of possibility. To fulfill that
potential requires humility, diligence,
and the deepening of consciousness,
particularly while we continue
traversing the challenging years
of the transition.

Susan S. Trout

INTRODUCTION

The purpose of Part One is to illustrate where we have been historically and energetically and to shine a light on the changes necessary in leadership and group life to fulfill the destiny of the Aquarian Era. The Aquarian spreads before us as an age of possibility. To fulfill that potential requires humility, diligence, and the deepening of consciousness, particularly while we continue traversing the challenging years of the transition. To proceed through *The Clarion Call* necessitates an understanding of astrology as the framework for the discussion.

The discipline of astrology—the study of celestial alignments and their influence on human activities—provides a useful container for examining millennial history. In the context of this book, astrology provides a way to discuss different levels of reality—the universal and individual, the spiritual and material—in terms of distinct cycles of growth and modes of expression. When astrology is related to history, the two disciplines offer us a long and wide view of planet Earth and the human experience.

Astrologically in 2008, Earth reached the midpoint of the five-hundred-year transition between the Piscean and the Aquarian Eras. The two-thousand-year astrological cycle of the Piscean Era has been dominated by the characteristics of the element of Water—emotions, idealism, and devotion to authority. In the Western world, Christianity and the Christian Church encapsulated Piscean thought. Four of the major traits that illustrate the Piscean character are compassion, a worldview based on unquestioning faith, creativity through beauty and invention, and individualism.

The Aquarian characteristics of the element of Air—the mind, cooperation, and consciousness—began appearing during the Age of Enlightenment in the mid-eighteenth century. Four of the major traits that illustrate the Aquarian character are mental focus, a worldview based on intellect and experiential proof, creativity combined with technology, and group cooperation.

The Aquarian Era, like all other astrological cycles, spans 2,120 years. Each astrological cycle is the result of a precession of the equinoxes. As-

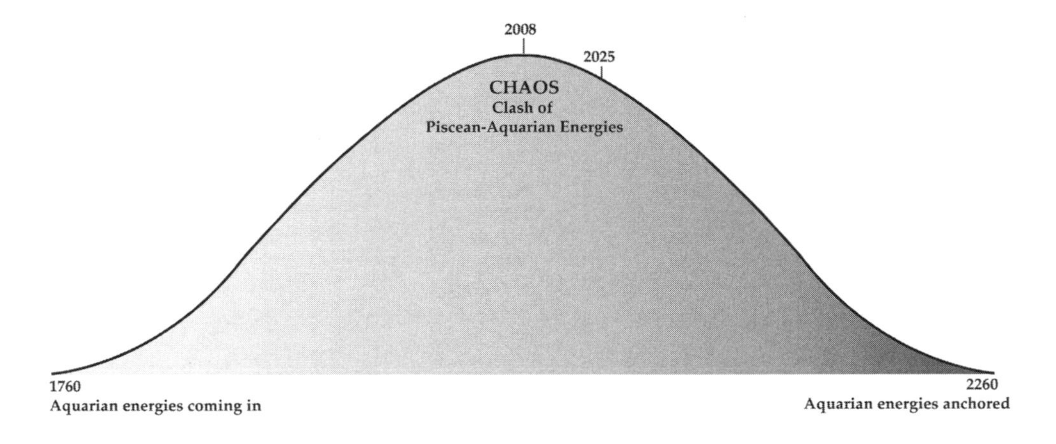

Figure 3: The Span of the Transition from the Piscean to the Aquarian Era: Piscean Model *is presented as a linear, two-dimensional, bell-shaped curve. This curve spans 500 years, showing the Aquarian Era's initial arrival in 1760, the midpoint of its arrival in 2008, and its full arrival in 2260.*[1] *As the Aquarian Era gradually arrives, the Piscean gradually withdraws.* Drawing by Ginger Graziano

1 This drawing of the five hundred overlapping years of the Piscean and Aquarian eras is based on the writings of Nostradamus scholar John Hogue; Master Djwhal Khul, who dictated the Ageless Wisdom teachings to Alice Bailey; and Torkom Saraydarian, author and Master of Ageless Wisdom. These writers vary slightly in the specific span of years they report. John Hogue's designated years are used here because his work documents references to history, literature, and metaphysics.

tronomy and astrology identify these cycles, also referred to as eras or ages, by the movement of a grouping of stars called a "sign" of the zodiac. The eras differ in their consciousness, realm of experience, field of activity, and source of power.

The transition from the Piscean Era to the Aquarian can be explained using preferred scientific styles from each era. Figure 3 shows the overlap drawn from the Piscean perspective, which prefers static and linear models, whereas Figure 4 shows the overlap through Aquarian eyes, which prefer a fluid and wholistic model.

On an individual level, the sign under which individuals are born is their sun sign. Although many other planets influence their astrological chart, their sun signs align with their destiny—what they are on Earth to do. As a result, individuals share the common destiny of their era along

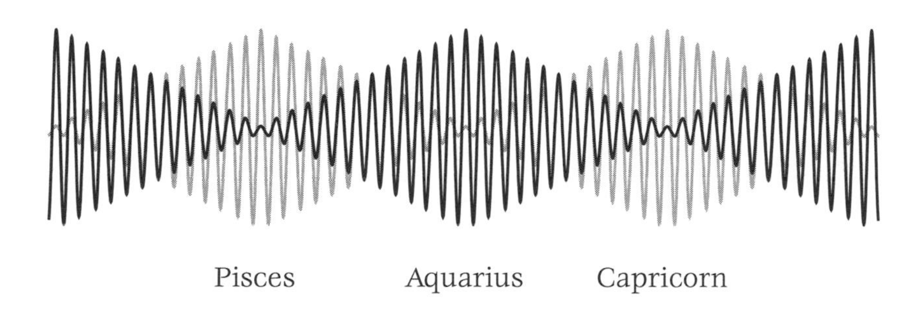

Pisces Aquarius Capricorn

Figure 4: The Span of Transition from the Piscean to the Aquarian Era: Aquarian Model *is presented as fluid, three-dimensional, overlapping spirals that convey a pattern of movement. Such patterns resemble poet William Butler Yeats's drawings of gyres. A gyre has precise, constant movements that quicken or dwindle. A gyre's pattern of movement is one way to explain the Piscean-Aquarian evolutionary shift. The gyre moves from the total dominance of the Piscean over the Aquarian, through an increasing mixture of the Aquarian with the Piscean, until the minimum of the Piscean pattern and the maximum of the Aquarian pattern is reached.* Drawing by Randal Pride, adapted from drawings by Neil Mann, http://YeatsVision.com. Used with permission.

with their personal destiny. The sun signs and the natural elements with which they are associated influence the traits and worldviews of the individual and the era. The four elements and their corresponding Zodiac signs are: Fire—Aries, Leo, and Sagittarius; Earth—Taurus, Virgo, and Capricorn; Water—Cancer, Scorpio, and Pisces; and Air—Gemini, Libra, and Aquarius.

From the astrological perspective, the world is emerging from deep water into thin air.

From the astrological perspective, the world is emerging from deep water into thin air. Stephen Arroyo in *Astrology, Psychology, and The Four Elements* characterizes water signs as having force and power. Water can destroy the other elements by washing away earth, saturating air, and extinguishing fire. Arroyo associates air signs like Aquarius with the life force that materializes ideas on Earth and brings thought into action. People born in air signs can feel burdened by the emotions of water signs like Pisces, whereas people born in water signs can feel intimidated by the intellect of air signs. Air uses rational, objective thought *to let the obstacles pass by,* whereas Water *moves around obstacles.*

Understanding the complementary and opposing traits of both Pisces and Aquarius provides a way to gain perspective on the past, to examine current reality, and to predict the rewards and challenges of the future.

Part One includes:

Chapter One: The Foundations of Change provides the basis for understanding the traits and shadow tendencies of the Piscean and Aquarian eras by examining four major traits illustrated with examples from history. Historic examples also exemplify the interplay between the two energies since the Aquarian began emerging in the mid-eighteenth century while we lived out the end of the Piscean Era.

Chapter Two: Setting the Stage examines how to educate and prepare ourselves by understanding the stages of change, the differences between Piscean and Aquarian values, and the templates of leadership and group life in the Aquarian Era.

Chapter Three: The Challenges at the Threshold covers various challenges that will contribute to the inevitable turbulence of transition. These include the fear of change and polarization; the astrological meaning of the change from Water to Air; the return of the Divine Feminine and the initiation of a true partnership of feminine and masculine energies; the arrival of the Millennial Generation; and the paradox of technology.

CHAPTER ONE
THE FOUNDATIONS OF CHANGE

Introduction

Change occurs when two or more opposing factors come together: health and illness, peace and war, food and famine. The outer changes in the environment, economy, energy, and ideologies demand internal shifts in problem solving, attitudes, worldview, and consciousness. To make these shifts, we must first understand the mechanisms at work during this time when Piscean and Aquarian energies are dancing together. The Piscean seeks to maintain the lead, the Aquarian to take its rightful role. Occasionally the dance is harmonious, but increasingly conflict erupts.

This chapter explores the traits and shadow tendencies of both the Piscean and the Aquarian eras. One purpose of the exploration is to dispel two common misconceptions: the polarization of Aquarian and Piscean characteristics into good/bad and right/wrong, and the belief that the "Age of Aquarius" will descend like a magical, starlit blanket to bring peace and light without demanding any effort on our part. Another purpose of the exploration is to present the lessons of history in the context of Piscean and Aquarian traits and shadow tendencies, grounding theory in reality.

Piscean Traits and Shadow Tendencies

As is true with individuals, each astrological era exhibits both positive traits and shadow tendencies related to its sign. Among the positive traits of the Piscean to take forward through the difficult transition ahead are compassion, the work ethic, and the appreciation of beauty.

The shadow of any quality reveals itself as the opposite quality projected out into the world. For example, a minority group that feels powerless may project power by exhibiting prejudicial behavior against another minority. When left unrecognized, the shadow will play itself out to the extreme and become visible, forcing the individual, group, or nation to notice it so they can take conscious action. At any time during the transition or afterward, an unresolved shadow issue can reemerge. Currently, the shadow of the Piscean appears very dark because unresolved shadow tendencies have swung to the extreme and become visible. This phenomenon illustrates the inevitable darkness before the dawn. It alerts us individually to the need for change and awakens us globally to the transformation of the Aquarian Era.

Table 2 (see opposite page) delineates four major Piscean traits and their associated shadow tendencies.

History grounds this discussion for us, providing examples of how the traits and shadow tendencies appeared during the Piscean Era between the first and mid-eighteenth centuries in Western Europe. Neither traits nor shadow responses occur in isolation and more than one is usually at work in any single example.

Trait: Compassion
Shadow: Idealism and Fanaticism

The onset of the Piscean Era over two thousand years ago is identified with the spiritual teachings of Jesus, a radical Jewish rabbi in Jerusalem in the first century, identified as the Christ or Messiah by segments of the Jewish people of his time. After his crucifixion in approximately 30 CE, his apostles and relatives spread his teachings through the Greco-Roman world. His teachings exemplified the true nature of the Piscean heart and were

Table 2: Piscean Traits and Shadow Tendencies

Piscean Traits	Piscean Shadow Tendencies
Compassion Expressed through the emotions, charity, and good works	**Idealism and fanaticism** Use of power to oppose and control, to establish either/or, right/wrong rules, and to discredit the emotions and heart, resulting in degradation of the feminine
Worldview is faith-based Expressed through dependence on outer authority, including a personified God "out there"	**Escapism and optimism** Dependence on hope instead of action; avoidance of taking action based on early warning signs; lack of curiosity; denial of current reality
Creativity expressed through beauty and invention Expressed through the creative arts, scientific advances, and mechanical inventions	**Emphasis on the creative result rather than on artistic and scientific free expression** Denial that the artist as creator is connected to the Divine as the Creator; misappropriation of art, science, and invention by those in authority to advance their own agendas
Individualism Expressed through a striving for personal freedom, world exploration, and discovery; the group fulfills the individual's need	**Ignoring the good of the whole group** Decisions based on rights of individuals or special interest segments of the group; exploitation of people and nature for the sake of wealth and power

imparted with a vibration of spiritual love and wisdom, loving acceptance, inner peace, inclusiveness, intelligent conviction, and service.

Initially persecuted for their faith, Christians prevailed through love and compassion, and the teachings increasingly gained acceptance. Eventually, the Roman Emperor Constantine legalized Christianity in 313 CE. Jesus's message became interpreted and codified into church dogma. The shadow tendencies of compassion began to polarize into rigid right/wrong rules, and fanaticism led to ethnic cleansing and other acts of terror. On the premise that Eve was created second to Adam and subsequently led him into sin, church authorities debased women and discredited the feminine by denying the importance of emotions and the heart.

Even as the Church used power to oppose individual expression and to control behavior, it also provided security, community, and ministry. For example, monasteries and convents provided necessary charitable support for the poor and infirm during the many wars, famines, and changes in political structures. Despite the often reprehensible actions of the Church and the unChrist-like behavior of some of the clergy, the faithful held to the ideal of Jesus's teachings. Those teachings validated their emotional yearnings and their hearts' longing for certainty in an uncertain world.

Trait: Faith-Based Worldview
Shadow: Escapism and Optimism

Generally throughout the Piscean, people were obedient to religious teaching and social standards, depending on the outer authority of the Church and the governing individual or group for physical safety. They approached life on faith without questioning the reasons behind their assumptions or actions. The necessities of the agrarian life and a desire to be good and faithful servants of the Lord led people to develop a strong work ethic.

The shadow of their faith-based view led to escapism and unfounded optimism. People were at the mercy of the judgment of a personified Father God who resided outside them. Until the Reformation in the sixteenth century, they believed God could be reached only through the intercession of priests and the sacraments. To counter the arbitrariness of what they interpreted as God's retribution in the form of famine, illness, and war, they relied on the optimism of hope and escapism by denying their current reality. Their hope lay in their salvation through Jesus the Christ's forgiveness and his promise of eternal life. They hoped, prayed, and waited on the will of heaven.

In order to be protected by the safety of an outer authority, whether Church, king, employer, or God, people surrendered the curiosity that might have caused them to question the premise on which the authority stood. By giving away the responsibility of their lives to someone above them in the hierarchy, they avoided assessing their current reality for the early warning signs that would have compelled them to action. Until the Enlightenment in the eighteenth century, hierarchical religious and governmental structures held absolute authority. Curiosity and taking action against authority could lead to conflict, and in some instances, death.

Historically, the Inquisition within the Roman Catholic Church, particularly between the twelfth and sixteenth centuries, presents a prime example of the shadow of the faith-based worldview. The following are more modern examples of people holding on to optimistic beliefs despite warnings:

- The German people denied the warning signs of the inevitable outcome of the rise to power of the Nazi Party.
- The United States government and its people clung to the belief, against concrete evidence, that the United States could not be attacked on its own soil. Consequently the tragedy of September 11, 2001, not

only occurred, but also led to the unprovoked invasion of Iraq.

- Despite more than thirty years of warnings about the limitations of fossil fuels, the health of the ocean, and the dangerous level of the water supply, the United States trails most other industrialized nations in taking decisive action to develop alternative energy sources, to combat global warming, and to conserve natural resources.

Trait: Creativity Through Beauty and Invention
Shadow: Emphasis on the Creative Result Rather Than on Artistic and Scientific Free Expression

During the Middle Ages between the fifth and sixth centuries, individual talents, viewed as gifts from God, were expressed in religious forms. Art, music, and architecture expressed the faith of the artists, who were given little if any credit for their work. For artists, the shadow of the faith-based worldview and dependence on authority meant that the art itself was prized while the artist's soul as conduit was dismissed. The stained glass windows, flying buttresses, and intricate stonework of Gothic cathedrals still speak eloquently of both the acumen of the anonymous craftsmen and the emotional yearning of their hearts to creatively express their love of beauty and of God.

The Renaissance (ca. 1400–1600 CE) created a cultural shift across Europe that inspired new themes and modes of art and expanded the study of human knowledge. In 1441, Johannes Gutenberg's invention of a printing process that used movable type, metal molds and alloys, a special press, and oil-based inks allowed the mass production of printed books. The availability of books spread literacy across Europe and led to the founding of schools where noblemen's sons were introduced to the humanistic education being imported from Italy. During the two hundred years—some say three hundred fifty years—of the Renaissance period, the Church gradually relaxed restrictions on the subject matter available for study. Students and artists pursued previously forbidden interests in the classics, ancient languages, mythology, and the sciences, particularly astronomy and medicine. These changes produced phenomenal results, among them mechanical inventions like clocks and the flush toilet and scientific inventions like eyeglasses and telescopes.

Freed from centuries of imposed restrictions, artistic and scientific creativity leapt toward freedom of expression, but the shadow of Piscean creativity continued, impacting science and medicine.

Throughout Europe, but especially in Italy, the Church sponsored artistic expression in all its many forms. Art and architecture gave way to a style reflective of classical antiquity with an emphasis on symmetry, proportion, and geometry. Artists were allowed to study and incorporate classical motifs and explore nonreligious subjects, although they still depended on sponsors for financial support and were limited by their patrons' commissions. To this day the world esteems the works of the Italians, Michelangelo, da Vinci, and Raphael, as well as Renaissance artists from the Netherlands, France, and Spain.

The availability of books opened the door to informed study and inquiry, which greatly impacted the science of medicine. Ancient Greek theories were tested. Whereas Michelangelo once dissected corpses in secret at the risk of his life, the Church eventually allowed dissection of human corpses and the printed illustration of body parts. Expeditions to Africa, Asia, and the Americas returned with new herbs and medicinal recipes that aided in developing new medicines such as laudanum, which reduced pain. Some physicians began to investigate the spread of infectious diseases and others modernized surgical procedures.

Freed from centuries of imposed restrictions, artistic and scientific creativity leapt toward freedom of expression, but the shadow of Piscean creativity continued, impacting science and medicine. Galileo escaped death during the Inquisition only by recanting his finding that Earth revolved around the sun instead of the sun around Earth. In the late eighteenth century, thousands of women died of childbed (puerperal) fever because fellow physicians would not accept Alexander Gordon's evidence that washing their hands could reduce the spread of infection. Refusal to see beyond faith in their own beliefs, to accept current reality, and to accept the full humanity of women all contributed to intensifying the shadow. The misappropriation of art, science, and invention by authority figures for their own purposes is easily exemplified by the use of captive labor. Some African slaves in America were accomplished artists of the metal and woodwork seen today around southern cities like Charleston and Savannah, and Jewish scientists were forced to contribute their expertise to the Nazi war machine as slaves in German factories.

Trait: Individualism
Shadow: Ignoring the Good of the Whole Group

In 1517, after years of studying the New Testament in the original Greek, Martin Luther, a German monk, declared that people did not need the Church to mediate for them, that their salvation was a free gift from God, dependent only on repentance and faith in Jesus the Christ as the Messiah. Luther translated the Bible into German, making it available to thousands and beginning the Protestant Reformation. In 1611, the *King James Version of the Bible* was published in England. Luther's proclamation contributed to the expansion of human knowledge, appreciation of beauty, and value of creative endeavors, opening the way for the rise of individualism and the questioning of the absolute power bestowed both on church and governmental leaders.

The rise of the individual threatened the power of the Church, while at the same time Pisceans clung to their dependence on outer authority and their faith-based view of the world. Piscean individualism served the group in exchange for the group's protection. Too great a departure from group rules or defiance of the leaders led to being shunned, exiled, or worse. In sixteenth and seventeenth century England, religious dissenters abounded and factions developed. Many sects, among them the Congregationalists and the Quakers, created non-hierarchical organizational structures. The development of disparate individualistic groups, even though still primarily Christian in theology, challenged the societal order and the power of Church and civic leadership. Many monarchs reacted with force, killing dissidents or forcing them to flee, some to the promise of the New World in America.

The exploration that led to the discovery of North America and to European colonization around the world illustrates one aspect of Piscean individualism. Sea travel provided the opportunity for adventure, and even glory for individual feats. Exploration, however, was dependent on funding from monarchs, trading companies, or wealthy individuals. Lands, resources, and treasures were claimed for countries, not for individuals. The individual served his immediate group without regard for a greater good, which led to the shadow expressing itself in nationalism and territorialism. This narrow view meant that if other groups, nature, or resources were destroyed, the consequences were not considered. Each group felt God was on their side and had given them the right to kill or enslave natives and to use natural resources at will.

Exploration brought prosperity and new ideas along with new foods and goods. Colonization led toward imperialism. The very Piscean structures being bolstered—monarchy, hierarchy, Church—were coming under scrutiny. Beliefs and values long held began to be questioned. The gap opened through which the Aquarian would enter. Its entry paralleled the playing out of the unresolved shadow of the Piscean through increasing polarization, religious fundamentalism, and the breakdown of social and civic groups in favor of individual rights and needs.

By the early eighteenth century, Europeans were questioning the status quo with increasing urgency. During what became known as the Age of Enlightenment, thinkers across Europe emphasized "reason" as the tool to solve humanity's problems and unlock nature's secrets. Dr. Gerhard Rempel, professor of history at Western New England College, defines the Enlightenment as "an age of reason based on faith, not an age of faith based on reason." He goes on to say that it was this period, not the Reformation or the Renaissance, "that dislodged the ecclesiastical establishment from central control of cultural and intellectual life... [and] rendered possible the autonomous evolution of modern culture."

Aquarian Traits and Shadow Tendencies

Astrology associates Aquarian energy with mental clarity, practicality, and intellect combined with compassion, cooperation, intuition, and connectedness. We do not yet know how these and other Aquarian traits and their shadow tendencies will exhibit themselves. This section focuses on the Enlightenment, during which Aquarian traits arrived and began influencing Western cultures, including the Americas. Some shadow elements are already visible as are conflicts with Piscean thought. Aquarian traits and shadow tendencies are explained throughout this book in relation to soul development, leadership, and group life (see Table 3).

The Age of Enlightenment was simultaneously a response to the shadow

Table 3: Aquarian Traits and Shadow Tendencies

Aquarian Traits	Aquarian Shadow Tendencies
Mental focus Expressed through reason and finding compatible modes for sharing intellectual competence, abstract ideas, and theories	**Arrogance, devaluation of emotion** Refusal to test ideas to see if they work; eccentric and/or fanatical because of intellectual prowess; avoidance of the emotions
Worldview based on inner knowing validated by experiential proof Expressed as reliance on intellectual knowledge, inner wisdom, and the interconnection and equality of all things	**Avoidance of interpersonal relationships, misuse of technology** Replacement of face-to-face encounters with technology; dependence on technology leads to mechanical, automatic solutions; denial of a relationship with inner wisdom because "I can do it alone"
Creativity combined with technology Expressed through problem solving of both practical problems of global concern and practical problems in creating new art and music forms; employing systems thinking	**Technology negating reason, heart, and creating from the soul** Unintended consequences occur when mind problem solves without heart; technological creations lack soul and reduce brain's access to imagination and play
Group cooperation Expressed through an objective and rational approach without unnecessary emotional involvement; what is good for the group is good for the individual; good social skills because group members objectively appreciate one another's thoughts; possibility of developing group consciousness	**Negation of the individual, spiritual pride, misunderstands inclusiveness** Fears of not being recognized for individual contributions; assumption of levels of spiritual advancement not yet attained; assumption of ability to maintain a group without a leader or structure; sentimental; wants to include everyone, whether or not they share the group vision

of the Piscean Era and the entry of the Aquarian Era. Enlightenment thinkers, sometimes called philosophes, replaced the emotional, heart-based Piscean with the Aquarian traits of mental focus expressed through reason and group cooperation for the sharing of intellectual competence, abstract ideas, and theories. According to Rempel, enlightenment figures such as Voltaire, Hume, and Kant considered themselves to be among a "cosmopolitan solidarity of enlightened intellectuals." They imagined a world filled with independent free thinkers who slowly added pieces to the puzzle until the whole picture unfolded. They thought that if enough information were amassed and subjected to sound thinking, everything could be understood. Though arrogant about their intellectual prowess, the philosophes believed they could benefit the greater good by replacing or moderating the faith-based worldview with one founded on natural laws discerned through careful observation, research, and proof.

Enlightenment thinkers, sometimes called philosophes, replaced the emotional, heart-based Piscean with the Aquarian traits of mental focus expressed through reason and group cooperation for the sharing of intellectual competence, abstract ideas, and theories.

In France, many philosophes rejected religion as superstitious. In England, Germany, and elsewhere, however, these thinkers often portrayed rationality as complementary or neutral to religion. These two approaches—one that rejected religion in favor of science and one that saw the two as noncompeting, if not complementary—fostered tension between advocates of scientific inquiry and the Church still evident today. The conflict can be framed as the Piscean shadow of idealism insisting on an either/or, right/wrong duality opposing the Aquarian worldview that honors interconnection and seeks equality in both/and nonduality. Whatever the general attitude to religion, there was a tendency to question the hierarchical authority of both church and state. In all cases, Enlightenment thinkers assumed one set of universal truths and believed that those truths were generally attainable through reason and observation.

In America, many of the framers of the United States Constitution, notably Benjamin Franklin, Thomas Jefferson, Thomas Paine, and George Washington, embraced the Enlightenment movement. They integrated the language into the American spirit when they referred to natural law, inherent freedoms, equality, and self-determination. The Age of Enlightenment planted the seeds for changes in religion, politics, and social structures that would take a century to come to fruition through the establishment of representational government and the demise of monarchies, the condemnation and end of slavery, and the separation of church and state. The faith-driven, heart-centered Piscean culture organized by top-down hierarchies leading obedient, loyal, and devoted individuals began confronting the reason-driven, mind-centered Aquarian energy that would gradually demand different group and leadership models. This confrontation was most evident in the evolution of the United States.

America became the frontier for the individual—the outcasts and outlaws, the dissidents and free thinkers. Its vast wilderness offered a seemingly endless supply of natural resources to be exploited through capitalistic ventures. On a new continent, new social structures, foods, tools, machines, and attitudes evolved. Among those new attitudes were a growing reliance on the right of people to govern themselves through a democratic process and the need to uphold individual freedom of worship by separating the secular state from religious affiliation. Until late in the drafting of the Constitution, the founders assumed that their new government would include a state-approved religion. The fact that it did not was an outgrowth of the Enlightenment's emphasis on individual conscience and the questioning of religious authority.

Piscean/Aquarian Overlap

From the mid-eighteenth century until the present time, Piscean and Aquarian energies have coexisted. The Piscean dominates because the energy is well entrenched and because the threat posed by the Aquarian causes the Piscean shadow to become darker and stronger. In this section, examples from history prior to 1960 illustrate the overlap in terms of the four traits and shadow tendencies of the Piscean and the Aquarian.

Heart and Mind

The great democratic experiment in the United States tested the Enlightenment's belief in the individual's ability to reason and be guided by conscience. Still, the Piscean organizational model persisted in which people depend on the leader—whether monarch or mill owner—like a father. In eighteenth-century Britain, the innovations in agriculture increased productivity and led to population growth. This enabled people to move to cities and helped drive the Industrial Revolution, bringing prosperity and mechanization. In the nineteenth century, imperialism expanded, as did its shadow in the form of slavery, decimation of indigenous people, pollution, and destruction of natural resources. In Western European imperialistic countries, the poor, particularly women and children, were marginalized.

Christians integrated the heart of Piscean compassion with Aquarian mental focus when they formed grassroots groups with the shared vision of applying Jesus's teachings to the creation of a common good. The Method-ists in England united religious people against slavery, a cause also taken up by the Quakers in the United States. The use of social activism designed to inspire legal solutions to societal problems spread from the issue of slavery to poverty, crime, temperance, and disease. Women, expected to be the leaders in the Aquarian Era, became crucial in all of these campaigns as both the primary motivators and the hands-on workers. They acted not only as abolitionists and supporters of temperance laws, but established tuberculosis sanitariums, maternity hospitals for the poor, social welfare agencies, and schools. With the organizational skills learned from these endeavors, women united to fight for women's suffrage.

With stronger central governments, tremendous resources, increased religious tolerance, and scientific notions of human activity, both Christian and Jewish organizations addressed social ills by integrating religion and science. The ethic of giving paralleled the emergence of an aristocracy of wealth in America. Philanthropy, as we think of it, was born when steel baron Andrew Carnegie challenged his peers to donate to social causes. People like John D. Rockefeller and Margaret Olivia Slocum Sage responded, and with others established a legacy of charitable foundations unaffiliated with organized religion.

In addition, national volunteer associations emerged as men's business groups and women's social meetings turned their groups toward public service. The Piscean individualism that used the group to meet its own needs gave way to groups of individuals formed to meet a greater good. Groups still operated within restricted territories, social rules still defined behavior, and larger organizations of business and government remained hierarchical and male-dominated. Church affiliation and class stratified American society and groups were divided along religious as well as cultural, racial, and gender lines.

Worldview

At the beginning of the twentieth century, World War I shifted the societal structures of Western and Eastern Europe, the Soviet Union, and the United States. Colonized countries around the world demanded independence and this led, most notably, to the decline of the British Empire. Because of England's debt after the war, the world's financial center shifted from England to the United States. The Aquarian worldview of mental focus and rational thought was being increasingly integrated. People no longer felt confined to socially defined roles. Though still faith-based in outlook, they also wanted some measure of self-determination and equality. Women cut their hair and raised their hems in defiance of social norms. The working class men and women who had been fully employed during the war did not return to their former roles of subordination to the aristocracy. Gradually wealth became more equally distributed across social classes. This equalization extended to the right of women to vote throughout most of the European countries following the war and in the United States in 1920.

The Piscean faith-based worldview that avoided responsibility and overlooked current reality and action in favor of belief and hope could not meet the needs of this expanded world.

The end of the First World War accelerated changes already under way and created hardships and instability in Germany, the Balkans, and the Soviet Union that people were not equipped to meet. Countries like France and Germany lost their next generation of leaders on the battlefields. The United States suddenly had world leadership thrust upon it, a responsibility its people, an ocean away from the turmoil, were ill prepared to accept. The Piscean faith-based worldview that avoided responsibility and overlooked current reality and action in favor of belief and hope could not meet the needs of this expanded world. Mental focus, practical problem solving, and action based on reason and research were needed. As nations tried to adjust to a new reality none wanted to accept, political, social, and economic instability increased in Europe, creating fertile ground over the next thirty years for the conflict that led to the Second World War.

American participation in World War II brought the Depression to an end. Many Americans opposed involvement in the war. The war years exemplified the strengths of the Piscean character as, after the Japanese attacked Pearl Harbor, people joined together to support the war effort and protect America. This group behavior arose from the Piscean faith-based view and materialized as idealism—patriotism, self-righteousness, polarization, and optimism—tempered by compassion. The denser shadow of Piscean idealism—nationalism, authoritarianism, and persecution—revealed itself in the philosophies and actions of the German, Italian, and Japanese governments.

At the war's end in 1945, Germany, Japan, and England were in ruins and France had to recover from Nazi occupation. Protected by oceans, the United States was spared physical destruction. Energized by national pride, America found itself not only an economic and political world leader, but also guardian of the Free World. England and other imperialist nations began the dismantling of their colonial empires, while France attempted to maintain control over Algeria and Vietnam.

The creation of the United Nations promised a new era of international cooperation, an Aquarian concept the world had not been able to accept after World War I when President Woodrow Wilson suggested the League of Nations. Wilson's dream of peaceful cooperation was left unfulfilled because the Piscean shadow had not been fully acknowledged and resolved. The schism caused by polarized thinking regarding World War II resulted in increasing conflict. The United States and the European allies differed greatly in vision and ideology from the Soviet Union, which had helped them win the war. The apportioning of postwar administration among Allied nations resulted in the split of Germany into East and West and to the eventual creation of the physical Berlin Wall and the metaphorical Iron Curtain that divided the European continent. While the United States converted West Germany and Japan to democracy, the Soviet Union forced socialism on East Germany and the other central and eastern European countries under their administration.

Mounting tensions between the United States and the Soviet Union fed by rampant idealism and competition for world power eventually led to the buildup of nuclear armaments and the spread of communism. Armed with nuclear warheads, economic means, and international political power, the two countries became world superpowers on opposing sides of the Cold War. Conflict broke out around the world. In China, communist forces established the People's Republic of China on the mainland and nationalist forces retreated to Taiwan. In Greece, royalist forces defeated the communists. War also broke out between North and South Korea. The European imperialist powers, economically exhausted by the war, began surrendering their holdings, acquiescing, usually peacefully, to the Aquarian-influenced demands of indigenous people for self-determination. The United States and their Western allies joined the struggle on behalf of South Korea while the Soviet Union backed North Korea. Although the Korean War stopped in 1953, Korea remains divided and the conflict is unresolved.

Creativity

After World War II, despite the conflict around the globe, the specter of the "communist threat," and the fear of nuclear annihilation, Americans recreated their lives using the results of their creative wartime endeavors in medicine, manufacturing, and military science. The Aquarian use of creativity expressed through technology had also emerged as part of the war effort. The United States imported German nuclear and aeronautical scientists, some of whom had been active Nazi sympathizers, into the armament and space programs.

There was a pervading faith-based sense that good had prevailed and God was on the side of the righteous. Women who had worked during the war years returned to their roles in the home in order to open jobs for returning service members. The GI Bill enabled many veterans to go to college. Universities also created programs in the allied medical and helping professions to meet the care needs of the war wounded. As the economy prospered, the huge advances made during the war in medicine, psychology, psychiatry, neuropsychology, audiology, and in physical, speech, and occupational therapies encouraged more government funding for research and training grants in these fields and in allied areas like special education. Women had shown their merit as productive workers during both world wars. By the mid-1950s, some women seized the opportunity to obtain advanced degrees in helping professions, successfully combining Piscean compassion and Aquarian intellect and bringing more feminine energy into the work world. Although many other fields were still closed to women, the increased status of the helping professions gave women opportunities they had never had before.

By the mid-1950s, some women seized the opportunity to obtain advanced degrees in helping professions, successfully combining Piscean compassion and Aquarian intellect and bringing more feminine energy into the work world.

Outside the United States, Soviet neurologist Aleksandr Luria and two Canadians, neurosurgeon Wilder Penfield and neuropsychology researcher and physician Lamar Roberts, were among those doing groundbreaking work on brain function, neurological dysfunction, and traumatic brain injury. Advances in technology allowed the Soviets to put the Sputnik satellite into orbit in 1957, and America responded with improved programs in math and science in order to compete in the Space Race. In medicine, the use of antibiotics and the polio vaccine reduced childhood mortality rates. The fifties also saw the first organ transplant, the first heart and lung machine, and the first pacemaker.

Individualism and Groups

The Piscean Era focused on creating an orderly and secure life through faith in outer authority, being on the side of "right," and individualism expressed through hard work and inventiveness. As prosperity increased, people also coped with urbanization, capitalism, corporate business, and the stress of suburban living and commuting. Piscean individualism was based on the group meeting the needs of the individual. In earlier times, the group provided physical protection and economic stability along with religious structure and community. In the fifties, the shadow of hierarchy depersonalized business life, resulting in a sense of alienation. Large hierarchical corporations did not meet the individual's need for community, and the individual was too far removed from any "group good" to feel connected to it. Money and power were the main rewards for work in large, impersonal organizations. Religious groups still played an important role in sustaining community, but increasing numbers of people felt spiritually bereft and found little in religion to fill their emptiness.

After the war, images of the victims of the Holocaust filling *Life* and

Time magazines validated the sacrifices Americans had made and enhanced America's heroic image of itself. The idealism of the Piscean character tended to deny the country's internment of Japanese- and German-American citizens or the consent it gave to Stalin's demands to expel German civilians from within the Soviet Union's new borders. The latter policy was undertaken to suppress ethnic violence by creating ethnic homogeneity. It resulted in the deaths of as many as two million people.

Denial of the shadow of the United States over centuries had veiled the realities of the treatment of native peoples, African Americans, Jews, coal miners and other laborers, foreign migrant workers, women, and the poor. As awareness of inequities grew, assisted by radio and television, people found it harder and harder to sustain the myth of America as the land of opportunity, freedom, and equality. They began to examine the truth of their prideful patriotism, unquestioning faith in God, and idealistic view of the American way.

Despite America's standing abroad, citizens at home began to see the national shadow in the divisions along ethnic, religious, gender, economic, and class lines. Evidence of this shadow was apparent in the reaction to the intense fear of communism brought about by the rise in power of the Soviet Union. Urged by Senator Joseph McCarthy, the House Un-American Activities Committee targeted members of the Communist Party and other left-wing political groups, as well as movie stars, scientists, artists, and ordinary citizens, for investigation. Many people were interrogated and suffered personal and economic ruin as a result of the government's witch-hunt tactics.

The discrepancy between America's image and her reality widened further as events in the South reverberated across the nation, revealing the depth of the nation's shadow of racial injustice. The civil rights movement gained momentum with the 1954 Supreme Court decision in

Brown vs. Board of Education that began the desegregation of schools; the Montgomery, Alabama, bus boycott of 1955–56; and the Civil Rights Act of 1957, which aimed to ensure the voter registration rights of Africa-Americans. Riding the same wave, the Chicano movement established the Mexican- American Political Association in 1958 to promote the rights of Mexican-Americans. These responses to social problems heralded another step toward Aquarian group life by increasing the grassroots activism that laid the foundation for Aquarian groups.

In 1961, in his last speech as president, Dwight D. Eisenhower expressed concerns for the future of the United States. Some of those concerns are summarized as follows:

- Crises, great or small, would tempt us "to feel that some spectacular and costly action could become the miraculous solution to all current difficulties."
- Failure to guard against "unwarranted influence, whether sought or unsought," exerted by the military-industrial complex would ultimately lead to "the disastrous rise of misplaced power."
- Technology and research would become dominated, and therefore limited, by government control, and/or "public policy could itself become the captive of a scientific technological elite."
- Americans would collapse under "the impulse to live only for today, plundering, for our own ease and convenience, the precious resources of tomorrow," and this mistake would lead democracy to "become the insolvent phantom of tomorrow."

Nearly fifty years later, we can list the ways in which Eisenhower's concerns have been validated by choices and events. These negative consequences resulted from the American inability to face its own suffering and to recognize its own shadow. The shadow in action is both Piscean and Aquarian. Both energies are present now, so both shadows are present as well.

The Piscean shadow tendencies included are: the tendency to support authority without inquiry; to manipulate technological and scientific "research" in order to maintain power and control; to avoid individual responsibility by dependence on authority; to ignore warning signs; to look to the group for protection; to focus on the immediate territory without global concern and thereby misuse natural resources for economic gain; to deny current reality and therefore delay action; and to rely on faith-based solutions.

The Piscean was an age of unshakeable faith, idealism, and optimism in which people looked to outside authority and social institutions to define themselves.

Aquarian shadow tendencies related to the concerns include: forgetting that technology is a tool of creativity rather than the generator of theories or ideas; failing to test a theory's viability or a technology's applicability; ignoring inner wisdom out of arrogance; overlooking human compassion and the common good; allowing the fear of losing individuality to overshadow the knowledge that what is good for the group is good for the individual; and forgetting to share the vision with the global community.

As Eisenhower left office, the forces of change were already at work that would shake the foundations of the United States and the world. The seeds of dissent sown in the fifties were ready to burst forth as the transition to the Aquarian Era neared the midpoint.

Conclusion

Examining the Piscean Era in terms of some of its traits and shadow tendencies and their role in shaping historic events shows us where we have been. The Piscean was an age of unshakeable faith, idealism, and optimism in which people looked to outside authority and social institutions to define themselves. The Piscean character is devotional, filled with fiery zeal, sincere, and humble. Its aspiration to be loyal, earnest, and ethical holds the potential for the true use of heart energy exemplified by a will toward good.

Delineating the Aquarian traits and shadow tendencies and their emerging influence projects where we are going and the challenges we will meet. In its highest form, the Aquarian could be an age of peace, equality, inner wisdom, and group consciousness. Manifesting these noble qualities will occur only with great effort, individual and group shadow work, and alignment with the Soul.

CHAPTER TWO
SETTING THE STAGE

Introduction

In this chapter, the geographic focus used in the historic examples narrows to the United States primarily because this country was born from the Aquarian principles of the Enlightenment into a Piscean world. Although it has embodied and propagated the shadow side of the Piscean, the American culture has never totally abandoned the Aquarian vision that is centered on the development of the mind, cooperation among equal partners, and the development of consciousness. As the Aquarian Era emerges more completely, humankind will be called to shift attention from trying to control the outer world to understanding how alignment with the inner world and with the Soul can manifest in the organizations and groups needed to create positive and lasting change.

Creative Tension

Robert Gilman, a leader in the field of sustainable culture and cofounder of Context Institute, suggests that cultural change occurs in three basic stages. Gilman delineates these stages as preparation, transformation, and elaboration. He defines culture as a combination of learned behavior patterns and the beliefs, values, and symbols that a given group of people share. A third element of culture is its natural and social environment.

A culture changes when something impacts its stability, something like a new technology (the computer), a new philosophy (*A Course in Miracles*), or

It is only when a critical mass is present on the side of innovation that the culture reaches a tipping point, the place of climactic transformative change.

a new scientific construct (quantum physics). The culture responds, either by reacting and attempting to revert to old ways or by changing in a way that allows the culture to adapt.

The push/pull between these two disparate responses can be seen in terms of "creative tension." According to Peter Senge, organizational specialist and author of *The Fifth Discipline: The Art and Practice of the Learning Organization*, creative tension is the force generated by "the juxtaposition of vision (what we want) and a clean picture of current reality (where we are relative to what we want)." As the gulf widens between those pulling to go back to the old way (reversion) and those pushing to go toward the new reality (innovation), the tension increases. If the impact on a culture's stability occurs suddenly rather than gradually, a crisis of dramatic proportions develops and forces the culture to lean in the direction of the greatest mass. It is only when a critical mass is present on the side of innovation that the culture reaches a tipping point, the place of climactic transformative change.

The following chart shows the shifts leaders and groups need to make in behavior and beliefs to move from Piscean to Aquarian values. Some of these shifts are well under way while others are just beginning. Each pair of values holds creative tension between reversion and innovation.

To move into the Aquarian Era, leaders and groups will need to choose the innovative response and leave behind old values and social structures. They then will articulate and manifest an unprecedented model of leadership and group life. A model based on the Aquarian values of inner authority, partnership, group consciousness, and the synthesis of masculine and feminine energies will replace the Piscean leadership model of

Table 4: Comparison of Piscean and Aquarian Values

Piscean	Aquarian
Dependence on an outer leader	Dependence on the individual's inner leader
Competition	Cooperation
Hierarchical decisions	Shared decision making or decision by an inspired leader
Separation from leader and one another	Partnership with leader and one another
Separation	Unity
Territorial priorities	Global priorities
Superiority	Equality
Homogeneity	Diversity
Idealism	Thought brought into practical action
Self-discovery	Group discovery
Personal vision	Shared vision
Individual needs	Group needs
Outer authority	Inner authority
Faith and hope	Knowledge and wisdom
Responsibility vested in others	Self-responsibility
Problem solving by addressing effects	Problem solving by addressing cause
Analysis	Systems thinking
Separation of personality and soul	Soul-infused personality
Separation of spirituality and essence	Integration of spirituality and science
Brotherhood	Sisterhood and brotherhood; humanity
God the Father	God, Goddess, All That Is
Superiority of masculine energy	Partnership of masculine and feminine energy
Duality	Nonduality

hierarchical, masculine-energy-dominant relationships.

Aquarian leadership and group life require inner awareness, relatedness, and synthesis as their driving forces. Leaders and groups educate themselves about the heart and mind and their relationship to action in the world. Women and men share responsibility for decisions and participate equally in matters of national and international importance. Unity within diversity, spiritual attainment, and world peace are potential fruits of the 2,100-year span of the Aquarian Era. These fruits will be the proof of our ability to use creative tension to take steps toward translating our inner work into outer action in a fully conscious way.

Since the Enlightenment in the eighteenth century, humankind has been preparing for the Aquarian Era. During the time of preparation, small components of the new culture were developed and implemented, ready for the true transformative crossroads. The basic needs, values, and potential of humanity have not changed in the past one hundred thousand years, while expression of those needs and values have altered. "We do what we have the 'tools' to do—spiritually, mentally, emotionally and physically," writes Gilman. "Thus the most effective way to genuinely change a culture is to create new ways to address basic needs." The nonviolent challenges to civil rights in the midfifties illustrated the effectiveness of this way of change and provided the seeds that led us into the crisis and instability at the transformative crossroads of the sixties.

The Crossroads of Transformation

The Sixties

The first half of the twentieth century, with America's three wars and sudden rise to world dominance, prepared the way for cultural revitalization. During the 1950s, stress and tension induced by rapid social and cultural changes and an atmosphere of fear brought us to the crossroads of cultural transformation embodied in the sixties, historically framed as 1962–1973. As is often the case with major social change, young people who could see with clearer eyes set forth to recall the country to its Aquarian birth. They voiced their belief that the institutions and mental constructs of "the way things are" no longer met the physical and spiritual need of society's soul. They named the institutions and mental models that were not working and rebelled against the homogenization of their world. They refused to conform and demanded the right to make their own decisions and to create the world in which they wanted to live.

Whereas the decade after the war offered a reactionary revitalization of "doing the old way harder," the sixties presented radical change, innovative revitalization that insisted those still blind to the current reality make the choice to see. Many inspiring and impassioned leaders like Jean Shinoda Bolen, Betty Friedan, Jesse Jackson, John F. Kennedy, Robert Kennedy, Martin Luther King, Jr., and Gloria Steinem stepped forward. Change rippled out across the nation as three major social-political movements intersected: civil rights, women's rights, and the anti-Vietnam War protest.

The turbulence of the time was evidenced in closely juxtaposed events of victory and tragedy. On June 11, 1963, President John F. Kennedy proposed legislation that would become the Civil Rights Act of 1964, which guaranteed basic civil rights to all Americans regardless of race. The following day, June 12, Medgar Evers, civil rights activist and NAACP field secretary, was assassinated. In August 1963, two hundred fifty thousand people engaged in the March on Washington for Jobs and Freedom, the first demonstration to have extensive television coverage. President Kennedy was assassinated the following November. Other civil rights leaders assassinated were Malcolm X (February 1965), Martin Luther King,

Jr. (January 1968), and Robert Kennedy (June 1968). The midsixties saw riots in Detroit and Watts in Los Angeles. The United States seemed to be disintegrating over the issue of civil rights for African-Americans, but that was not the only battle being waged.

American women had long fought for equal rights and equal pay. Now their voices gained force and support as they protested and staged their own marches on Washington, DC. Beginning with the approval for sales of birth control pills in 1961, the next decade saw tremendous changes in the rights of women, including fair hiring practices, paid maternity leave, affordable child care, and the establishment of the President's Commission on the Status of Women and the Equal Employment Opportunity Commission (EEOC). The publication of Betty Friedan's *The Feminine Mystique* in 1963, the reshaping of *Cosmopolitan* by Helen Gurley Brown in 1965, and the founding of the National Organization of Women (NOW) in 1967, followed by the publication of *Ms.* magazine in 1971, liberated women to make independent personal choices. The women's rights movement made possible the choices that young women today take for granted—participation in school athletic programs, reproductive freedom, enlistment in the armed forces, choice of academic field and career, and much more. Through the women's rights movement, women found new ways and stronger voices to support issues that women have always upheld—social and health services for the poor, children, and women; education; and peace. Many women took to the streets, not only for themselves and their African-American neighbors, but in protest of the United States war in Southeast Asia.

Lasting from 1959 to 1975, the Vietnam War—never an officially declared war—was the longest military conflict in U.S. history. Fifty-eight thousand Americans died and 304,000 were physically wounded. More than thirty years later, as the effects of Agent Orange contamination and post traumatic stress disorder (PTSD) continue to affect the health of that war's veterans, Americans are aware of an additional number of wounded not counted at the time. The antiwar protest brought together disparate groups for a common cause. Norman Cousins, editor of the *Saturday Review,* pediatrician Dr. Benjamin Spock, and writer and activist Tom Hayden were among early leaders of the movement. College students, religious groups, labor unions, middle-class mothers, and government workers became allies. Because this movement crossed political, racial, and cultural lines like no other ever had, it exposed deep economic and social inequalities and challenged the patriotic- and duty-bound values of the late Piscean Era.

The obvious cultural changes at the end of the sixties were in attitudes and laws regarding racial minorities and women, the rejection of accepted social structures and organizations, and the increased distrust of government and business.

After the Tet Offensive in January 1968 and the My Lai Massacre later that year, the war protest movement swelled. President Johnson soon announced he would not seek reelection. In 1969, men walked on the moon and sent back photographs of Earth so startlingly jewel-like that they inspired tenderness and deep longing for peace around the world. Suddenly the words "global" and "small world" took on new meaning. By April 1971, an antiwar protest in Washington, DC, attracted seven hundred fifty thousand people. Slowly, the road to peace, pushed forward by public opinion, was paved.

Transformational passages are unstable and usually span alternating periods of turmoil and rest, each taking us closer to the climactic tipping point that profoundly changes all three elements of culture: behaviors, beliefs, and environment. Things must fall apart before they can be reintegrated. Studies of individual creativity reveal that commonly new insights occur following relaxation, recreation, or when the mind is distracted by a task unrelated to the problem at hand. The sixties was a time of disintegration, yet it planted the seeds of consciousness-raising to be nurtured during the period of rest in the seventies.

The obvious cultural changes at the end of the sixties were in attitudes and laws regarding racial minorities and women, the rejection of accepted social structures and organizations, and the increased distrust of government and business. People no longer felt compelled to follow social rules that confined them to certain behavior. Men wore their hair long and grew beards; women wore jeans and gave up hats, gloves, and bras—actions unheard of in the fifties. Many people, especially those in their twenties and thirties, turned away from the churches of their childhood and sought out Eastern spiritual traditions like Zen Buddhism and Transcendental Meditation, introduced in 1958 by Maharishi Mahesh Yogi and one of the first widely taught meditation techniques in the United States. Many experimented with hallucinogenic drugs like LSD and peyote, hoping to induce transcendent experiences and raise their consciousness. Young people flocked to India to study with gurus, hitchhiked around the world, and joined the Peace Corps.

In San Francisco, amidst all of the exploration and change, the early holistic and human potential movement appeared. Many of the psychologists, writers, and scientists involved in the movement taught at Esalen, a retreat center at Big Sur on the California coast that became a laboratory for experimentation with a wide range of philosophies, religious disciplines, and psychological techniques. The work at Esalen developed what the English writer Aldous Huxley called "a new ethic," one that focused on awareness of personal experience, the sharing of that experience, and attentively listening to feedback. Esalen participants attended facilitated experiential workshops instead of lectures. These workshops created a format still used today to explore personal and spiritual growth and group dynamics.

These new concepts encouraged people to look within rather than without for understanding and inspiration. Those still anchored in Piscean values correctly perceived this change in vision as a rejection of the outward orientation of the past two thousand years and reacted with fear and disparagement. Audiences booed and mocked professionals speaking on new paradigms of medicine and education. Newspaper and magazine articles spoke negatively about meditation and organizations like Esalen and the Erhardt Seminar Trainings (*est*). The term "New Age," which referenced the coming astrological Aquarian Era, received particular criticism because it was associated with the perceived free love, irresponsibility, and unorthodox spiritual practices of the hippie subculture. By the end of the sixties, the time of rest and integration was at hand, a time that would advance consciousness.

Rest and Integration

The Seventies

Although from the outside it appeared that during the seventies people simply turned from activism to entertainment, drugs, and sexual freedom, it was soon evident that a different journey was under way—one that led inward. Prior to the sixties, engaging in psychological and psychiatric therapies could result in social shame or ostracism, as could admission of alcoholism or having a mentally disabled child. In the seventies, people ignored these social conventions and, as the saying went, "let it all hang out." They joined support groups, went to therapy, attended personal growth workshops, learned meditation, and read the newly published *A Course in*

Miracles. As a response to the depersonalizing aspects of modern society, increasing numbers turned to yoga, meditation, Eastern philosophical and religious systems, and transpersonal psychologies. There was even wider interest in altered states of consciousness, induced by drugs or by shamanistic and meditation practices. In medicine, physician Carl Simonton and clinical psychologist Stephanie Simonton presented research to affirm that visualization and attitude could positively impact the course of disease. Studies of high-performing people in business and other fields affirmed that individuals could create their own realities by clear visualization of goals accompanied by conscious intention to achieve the desired outcome.

Two social movements, environmentalism and feminism, broadened cultural awareness and planted seeds for further transformation. In 1970, U.S. Senator Gaylord Nelson of Wisconsin established Earth Day in order to place the environment on the national agenda. The environmental movement, supported by advocacy organizations like the Sierra Club and Greenpeace, succeeded in raising awareness and changing laws. The feminist movement continued addressing unofficial inequalities like salary differences and the need for coeducation at the university level. Other successful advocacy programs affected child care and child health, improvement in children's television programming, and led the way to the banishment of cigarette advertising on television and radio.

While the "Me Generation" focused on its inner search, support for American institutions and organizations, from the nuclear family to religion and government, deteriorated. The Watergate scandal and subsequent resignation of President Richard Nixon deflated the country and further increased distrust of government authority. More women joined the workforce in professional positions. Civil rights laws required country clubs, businesses, and all other groups to open opportunities to Jews, African-Americans, and other minorities. Neighborhoods ceased being centers of community life and church membership and involvement in schools, civic activities, and voting declined. As divorce rates rose so did the number of single parent households. The Ten Commandments as the foundation of a civil and godly society began to be ignored. The chasm widened between those bound by Piscean ideals and those on the new path of individual self-exploration and self-expression. Tension increased.

The United States experienced a serious economic recession and an oil crisis that raised public awareness of American dependence on foreign oil. Colonial imperialism had ended, and a new middle class appeared in the developing world. The seventies was also the decade technology entered private lives in a new way with the development of fiber optics, video games, the barcode, and the personal computer. The world was on its way to globalization of all aspects of life.

The economic base of the country moved from manufacturing and agriculture to technology alongside a reactionary revitalization attempt in the form of a revival of religious and conservative ideology.

The Eighties

With the advent of the eighties, the world seemed to spin through change faster than ever. In 1980, Marilyn Ferguson published *The Aquarian Conspiracy: Personal and Social Transformation in the 1980s,* defining the approaching paradigm shift of consciousness. Interest in consciousness deepened. The availability of alternative health care approaches like acupuncture and Reiki energy healing expanded from coastal regions into the Midwest and South. Elisabeth Kübler-Ross opened a national conversation on death and dying, starting a hospice movement across the country. New Thought churches founded in the 1920s, like

Unity and Religious Science, prospered, attracting people who wanted to study how to "create their own reality" and to apply the principles to creating prosperity and health.

Groups offering spiritual growth and personal healing abounded. Not all groups were led by well-trained or trustworthy teachers. The emphasis on philosophies of love and acceptance created great confusion over personal boundaries. This confusion resulted in people giving away their power to teachers and engaging in inappropriate behaviors within groups. The shadow of spiritual teachers and groups evidenced in misuse of sex, power, and money left many followers disenchanted. At the same time, physical and sexual abuse became topics on television talk shows, raising awareness, but also resulting in unfounded accusations that destroyed reputations and lives.

More and more people understood they could choose compassion, love, and self-knowledge over judgment, hatred, and blame.

In the outer world, American wealth and production began moving abroad for cheap labor and leaving empty factories and jobless workers behind. The economic base of the country moved from manufacturing and agriculture to technology alongside a reactionary revitalization attempt in the form of a revival of religious and conservative ideology. Toward the end of the decade, the Cold War between the United States and the Soviet Union came to an end, symbolized by the overthrow of communist regimes in central and eastern Europe and the fall of the Berlin Wall in 1989. Throughout the world, population growth soared, raising questions about future sustainability. Heightened awareness of HIV-AIDS enhanced the perception of Earth as a global village.

During the eighties, the environmental, peace, and women's movements was accepted as aspects of transformative change. Increasingly, people recognized that Western industrial society had led to global dilemmas, including the exploitation of natural resources, nonwhites, and women. The mass consciousness, however, focused on capitalism, increasing consumption, watching television, and amassing wealth. America and its citizens felt entitled to fulfill their desires at the expense of others. Paradoxically, the country was also becoming re-spiritualized and more grounded in self-realization, transcendent meaning, and self-responsibility. More and more people understood they could choose compassion, love, and self-knowledge over judgment, hatred, and blame. They also understood that all institutions in society, no matter how powerful, get their legitimacy from what people believe. The understanding grew of how marketing—of political, religious, consumer, and social information—influenced them and their world.

Spiritual approaches appeared in the business world. Peter Senge, Robert Greenleaf, Peter Drucker, and others introduced concepts to change beliefs about how businesses and organizations operate. Their work continues to be instrumental in reeducating hierarchical Piscean organizations to use a more Aquarian approach of fostering growth and empowering individuals and teams.

The Technological Revolution

The Nineties

The revolution caused by technology that began after World War II is an example of a shift in cultural stability so gradual that its full impact is not recognized in its earlier stages. What began with advances in television and the laying of the first submarine transatlantic telephone cable (TAT-1) in the fifties, grew by the nineties into the widespread use of personal computers, satellite communications, cordless phones, cell phones, the Internet, the World Wide Web, e-mail, and video-recording devices. When the United States responded militarily to the Iraqi invasion of Kuwait in 1990, Americans watched technological warfare as if it were a television series. New technologies also led to increased economic productivity that made some investors around the world very wealthy.

Business interests moved from national to international levels; now corporate headquarters as well as manufacturing plants could be anywhere on earth. International prosperity and ease of flying increased the numbers of Americans traveling abroad and exposed them to Eastern and African cultures. Immigration, particularly from Asia, India, and the former Soviet bloc countries, created a new ethnic and religious diversity in the United States that was enhanced by Internet communication. Political correctness forbade the acceptance of public bigotry and people embraced multiculturalism and Eastern religions. Technology resulted in tremendous advances in science. DNA identification, the Hubble space telescope, therapy for HIV, and the global positioning system, were only a few of the many advances of the nineties.

Technology allowed people to see the dire consequences of a world that breaks life into fragments. Those grounded in spiritual awareness could see that the wholeness they were creating within themselves would allow them to support the creation of a global community. They strengthened the beliefs and behaviors they felt would be necessary to change the environment. They no longer held the view that their journey was only about themselves; they knew it was for all humankind, Earth, and all sentient beings. Meanwhile, the masses quelled their fears and discomfort by engaging in reactionary responses—increased consumerism, obsession with the accumulation of wealth, and religious fundamentalism.

Scientists warned about global warming, overpopulation, nuclear proliferation, and world hunger. Although people could see where they might be going, they felt powerless to change direction. The prosperity of the present cocooned even those with conscious awareness from the need for revolutionary action. The culture relapsed into a restorative pose, planting seeds and storing up resources. But tensions were rising.

By the end of the decade, the chasm between those still grasping Piscean values and those reaching to embody Aquarian ones widened even further. With manipulation by the neo-conservatives led by George W. Bush, the split became a religious one that set conservative and fundamentalist Christians against other more moderate and liberal groups. Gilman writes that "the inherent conservatism in most cultures favors reactionary movements, and it is common for a culture to attempt a 'let's do the old way harder' revitalization as its first response to realizing that something must be done to get the culture back on track." The election of Bush to the presidency was just such an attempt.

The Twenty-First Century

People entered the new century hopeful. Those clinging to Piscean values hoped the neo-conservatives would return the country to core values of "family, God, and country." Those with an innovative approach knew that the seeds of a more conscious world were firmly planted and hoped to be able to continue to nurture a new paradigm with workable solutions. They were ready to take the next step.

On September 11, 2001, terrorists attacked the United States by guiding two airplanes into the World Trade Center towers in New York City, a third into the Pentagon, and crashing a fourth—as the result of interference by passengers—into a Pennsylvania field. Excluding the nineteen hijackers, 2,998 people died, most of them civilians, including nationals from over ninety different countries. Fifteen of the terrorists were from Saudi Arabia, two from the United Arab Emirates, one from Egypt, and one from Lebanon. Several of the terrorists were known to have ties to Osama Bin Laden and his terrorist organization, al-Qaida.

Before the September 11 attacks, plans had been formulated for an international war effort against al-Qaida and the Taliban in Afghanistan. American planes began bombing on October 7. After the attacks, a link between Iraqi dictator Saddam Hussein and al-Qaida was manufactured to justify a military invasion of Iraq. Because the culture was undergoing a reactionary revitalization, the response was to go to war with Iraq.

After the terrorist attack of 2001, America ground its way through crisis after crisis. It became obvious that the war with Iraq was not only entered into on the basis of misinformation, but that getting out would not be quick or easy. The economic expense of the war drove up the national deficit, and the loss of lives—military and civilian, American and Iraqi—lay heavily on the American conscience. Drought, floods, the melting ice cap, hurricanes, tsunamis, and earthquakes occurred with increasing frequency, incurring devastation beyond anything previously documented.

Former Vice President Al Gore, in his documentary *An Inconvenient Truth,* took a huge step towards vanquishing denials of the reality of global warming. Data collected by www.mindfully.org indicates that in the past two hundred years in the United States, 50 percent of the wetlands, 90 percent of the northwestern old-growth forests, and 99 percent of the tall-grass prairie have been destroyed. While the United States constitutes 5 percent of the world's population, Americans consume 24 percent of the world's energy and discard two hundred thousand tons of edible food each day. A single American consumes 149 gallons of water per day while a single member of more than half the world's population consumes twenty-five. The nation has entered a serious economic recession created by rising energy prices, overspeculation in the housing market, and use of credit to support the American addiction to consume everything from food to energy.

Earth is home to a mobile society that communicates through technology rather than personal contact. This society lives in a global economy in which countries are dependent on one another for fuel, food, and other natural resources. The United States' position as a superpower has eroded, and China waits to take its place. According to Bill Bishop, coauthor of *The Big Sort: Why the Clustering of Like-Minded America Is Tearing Us Apart,* the United States is increasingly divided into like-minded groups by lifestyle preferences rather than by civic involvement, religious belief, age, race, or gender. As a result, while the nation becomes more diverse and inclusive in some ways, it is becoming increasingly insular in that people have less and less contact with those who have lifestyles unlike their own.

All of these shifts are moving American culture from "current reality" closer to the "desired vision." Although living in a world of crisis, self-transformation continues as Aquarian values slip into the void left by failed Piscean structures. Globally, people demand "new ways to address basic needs." The inner work and spiritual focus of the past four decades is increasingly translated into service. Individuals and small groups are taking matters into their own hands. Rather than depend on government support or direction for help, when they see a problem, they simply set about solving it, whether the problem is in their neighborhood or in another country. Throughout the world, a quiet burgeoning of partnership models addresses the needs—irrigation in Africa, loans for women-run businesses in India, an antidrug campaign in Baltimore. People are increasingly motivated by a need to learn, to experience the inner fulfillment that comes from using their gifts to serve others, and to put their spirituality into action. More and more organizations and institutions are working toward

People are increasingly motivated by a need to learn, to experience the inner fulfillment that comes from using their gifts to serve others, and to put their spirituality into action.

this end as well. Just as the American economic, political, energy, and environmental crises have impacted the entire world, so has the concept that individuals are able to take responsibility for their own lives and for changing society. Women especially are taking up this call around the globe.

The realization that all life is connected is taking hold. Around the world, across all ages, races, nationalities, and socioeconomic classes, people are asserting their individual power to intervene on their own behalf to save the planet.

Gilman says, "It is only after the failure of a reactionary revitalization attempt that a culture is willing to risk fundamental innovation." That fundamental innovation, that tipping point, is at hand. The development of templates for new models of leadership and group life becomes imperative so that preparation is made to meet the crises ahead. The foundation of these templates is the preparation of consciousness, which includes attending to individual, group, and organizational soul development, development of the Inner Leader, strengthening intuition, and steadfast spiritual practice. With this foundation in place, leaders and groups can employ creative and innovative means to carry us through the three major interrelated crises related to environmental sustainability, energy resources, and population growth. This task must be implemented quickly to avert mass hysteria from famine, wars over water, further environmental devastation, and the proliferation of military dictatorships.

The Templates of Leadership and Group Life

Ageless Wisdom, visionaries, and scholars of cultural change anticipated humanity's shift in consciousness as it enters the Aquarian Era. In 1940, the writings of metaphysician Alice Bailey predicted that significant progress in soul development and global awareness would span two hundred years, beginning in the later years of the Piscean Era and extending into the early years of the Aquarian. In 1972, George Leonard wrote *The Transformation,* a book about his observations of a coming shift in social organization that he projected would happen worldwide. Other publications followed with similar projections: Marilyn Ferguson's *The Aquarian Conspiracy,* Fritjof Capra's *The Turning Point,* and Theodore Roszak's *Person/Planet.*

In their book, *The Cultural Creatives,* authors Paul Ray and Sherry Anderson in 2000 identified a fast-growing subculture within the United States that exemplifies Aquarian qualities. Based on thirteen years of survey research studies of more than one hundred thousand Americans and numerous focus groups and in-depth interviews, they identified three subcultures within the United States: traditionals, moderns, and cultural creatives. Traditionals, who represent a quarter of the American population, want to return to an America of the 1890-1930s, a time of predominately rural communities, stable friendships, and biblical values. Moderns represent approximately half of American citizens. Their lifestyle centers on the work ethic and business. They prefer conservative religions and conventionality. They include the upper, middle, and lower-middle class.

The cultural creatives have emerged since the sixties. In 2008, Ray reported that on the basis of further surveys done worldwide, the population of this subculture is increasing in developed countries. In the United States, their numbers have increased to 30 percent. In some countries, notably France, Holland, and Japan, they comprise at least 35 percent of the population. Ray says that most probably the cultural creatives evolve from the moderns and the moderns from the traditionals, but he cautions against oversimplification. He suggests that the Millennial Generation is also likely to contribute to the rise in numbers of cultural creatives.

Cultural creatives lead a soul-oriented life and care deeply about spirituality, self-actualization, self-expression, social justice, and ecology. The cultural creatives are wayshowers for bridging a Piscean way of life with an Aquarian one. Wayshowers of the emerging Aquarian consciousness convey specific qualities and values. The following is a summary of the qualities and values identified in the emerging leadership and group life templates for the Aquarian Era:

Leadership Template

The individual leader:

- Lives a soul-inspired life
- Recognizes an Inner Leader
- Views leadership as a classroom of the soul
- Synthesizes feminine and masculine energies
- Strives to develop a soul-infused personality
- Integrates spirituality into the workplace
- Integrates science and spirituality
- Combines unilateral authority with empowering participation
- Supports change that grows out of shared decision making and/or is leader-inspired
- Partners with nature
- Brings spirit into matter
- Manifests, plans, organizes, and creates order and perfects form
- Employs new evolutionary processes that can potentially transform humanity

- Problem solves by addressing causes of problems, not their effects
- Is simultaneously visionary and pragmatic and can put ideals into form
- Earns loyalty

Group Life Template

Group members:

- Live soul-inspired lives
- Recognize their personal Inner Leader and the Group Soul
- View the group as a classroom of the soul
- Synthesize feminine and masculine energies
- Strive to develop a soul-infused personality
- Are self-responsible for inner work and personal growth
- Practice cooperation, partnership, and group consciousness
- Make decisions based on the good of the group as a whole
- Educate themselves about the meaning and use of shared decision making
- Support change that grows out of shared decision making and/or that is inspired by the leader
- Respect and understand the leader's role
- Use a win/win approach as an antithesis to polarization
- Invest authority in an empowered individual and group
- Practice right human relations
- Respect the autonomy of others
- Assume responsibility for staying informed
- Support the growth, transformation, and creativity of all group members and the leader
- Employ foresight, accountability, and ethics

- Are willing to be flexible and use experimentation
- Prize innovation and diversity as well as cooperative endeavors
- Are simultaneously visionary and pragmatic
- Accept support for being self-responsible

Conclusion

At times during the Piscean Era, the veil of forgetfulness covering our divinity lifted to reveal the Divine Light. The revelation of Light is especially probable whenever catastrophe occurs. When individuals, groups, and countries acknowledge their common humanity and honor one another with compassion, the veil lifts. The immediate public responses to the September 11, 2001, terrorist attack in New York City and to the tsunami in Indonesia on December 25, 2004, are two recent examples.

To experience the Light, we first need courage to face and accept the truth. Then we use our energy to solve our problems and to love and forgive.

Glimpses of Divine Light appear in our individual lives when we experience a genuine heart connection with one another. Heart connections occur because ignorance—the cause of darkness—has dissipated and the hidden darkness has been faced and brought to the Light with integrity, understanding, and compassion. To experience the Light, we first need courage to face and accept the truth. Then we use our energy to solve our problems and to love and forgive. Finally, with compassion, the veil of forgetfulness drops completely and Light is all we see within ourselves and others.

In the final years of the Piscean Era, the dark seems to be getting darker at the same time that the Divine Light becomes brighter. The number of Lightworkers—spiritually evolved people who embody Divine Light—is increasing dramatically. Clearly we, individually and collectively, are at a point of significant choice in determining the survival of our planet.

CHAPTER THREE
CHALLENGES AT THE THRESHOLD

Introduction

Although the Piscean Era began with the arrival of the love and wisdom teachings of Jesus the Christ, the practice of these teachings deteriorated over the centuries into conflict and disregard for human and planetary life. The human tendency regarding its spiritual development is to become inert and relapse. Often only a catastrophe can serve as an impetus to move forward. Humankind is being given an opportunity to start anew in the Aquarian Era. Once again, wisdom teachings are being showered upon the planet. This infusion of Light elucidates a path toward increased consciousness through which, over the next two thousand Aquarian years, individuals as leaders and members of groups can choose to lead from and serve through soul-inspired lives.

Chapters One and Two have defined and contrasted the prominent characteristics of the Piscean and Aquarian eras. This chapter acknowledges the major variables and challenges of the transition between these two eras.

The Turbulence of Transition

Human survival depends on the shift to Aquarian consciousness because of the ecological devastation and the collapse of economic, social, and institutional structures in the Piscean Era. Despite clear advantages of this shift in consciousness, a conflict inevitably occurs when one type of energy subsides while another increases. The gradual ebbing of the

Piscean and rise of the Aquarian energy are creating anxiety among those resistant to change. Polarization and conflict among leaders, individuals, and groups are evidencing themselves around the globe.

Based on observations of the differences between Piscean and Aquarian energies thus far, conflict will be provoked as the transitions delineated in Table 5 occur.

The inevitable turbulence of these shifts will be evoked by (1) the prevalence of fear of change and polarization, (2) the elemental transition from Water to Air, (3) the return of the Divine Feminine and the initiation of true partnership of feminine and masculine energies, (4) the influence of the Millennial Generation, and (5) the paradox of technology.

Prevalence of Fear of Change and Polarization

Fear of Change

During the next quarter century, the shift from Piscean to Aquarian energy will be both dramatic and traumatic for the world as a whole. Resistance naturally occurs as old patterns dissolve and new ones come into being. The amount of resistance people feel will parallel the depth and extent of the new learning required. Healthy resistance enables us to take time to sort out the implications of this learning. The major challenge is in discerning whether and when resistance represses wisdom and clarity. If resistance leads to helplessness and despair, its value is questionable.

At the heart of fear of change is resistance to loss. When facing the challenge of questioning values and possibly giving up a way of life, people perceive loss rather than a new situation that may be better than the current one. They prefer to deny the need to make adjustments in their lives, or place the blame and the responsibility for solving the situation on someone else.

Table 5: Transitions Evoking Conflicts

From the Piscean	to	The Aquarian
Authority invested in leaders	→	Authority invested in individuals (i.e., individuals are acknowledged for having a firm basis for their own inner knowing and outer action and do not abdicate this responsibility to leaders
Hierarchical decisions	→	Shared decision making or decisions made by an inspired leader
Dependency on loyalty to outer leaders	→	Reliance on each individual's Inner Leader
Separation from leader	→	Partnership with leader
Competition	→	Cooperation
Predominance of male leaders	→	Equal numbers of women and men leaders
Territorial concern	→	Global care
Leading with an ego-led personality	→	Leading with a soul-infused personality
God the Father	→	God, Goddess, All That Is
Primacy of the welfare of humans	→	Equal care and consideration for humanity and nature
Win/lose worldview	→	Win/win orientation to life
Living in the past with fear of the future	→	Being in the present moment
Faith-based mindset	→	Scientific mindset
Believing something is true	→	Knowing what is true firsthand

Conflicting thoughts, emotions, and physical responses to change tend to be misinterpreted as a call to resist by defending as "right" old beliefs and ways of being. Those who embrace the change and expand their belief systems may overlook the validity of some old beliefs and discard a belief rather than integrate it into the new system.

It behooves leaders to understand the nature of resistance so that they are not tempted to back away from leading a group through change.

Leaders and groups who initiate the shift from the Piscean to Aquarian energies within their organizations will experience the impact of the fear of change and may be tempted to back away. Others will be asked for direction, protection, and order, and what they offer will likely be resisted. This resistance may be short-lived, or it may persist for a considerable time. It behooves leaders to understand the nature of resistance so that they are not tempted to back away from leading a group through change. In their book *Leadership on the Line,* Ronald Heifetz and Marty Linsky write that leaders need an extraordinary amount of "presence, time, and artful communication" when they mobilize change. Leaders can help people adjust to unrealistic expectations by not treating the change as though it were as simple a matter as adjusting to a different office or a new technology. Heifetz and Linsky encourage leaders to be resourceful during change, building new models rather than depending on approaches that worked in the past.

Polarization

Reactions to the gradual withdrawal of Piscean energy may give rise to a climate of polarized thought and behavior among individuals, leaders, and groups. When asked to question and redefine aspects of personal identity, people feel disloyal to the past and incompetent in the present. When the validity of their long-held habits, beliefs, and values are challenged, they perceive their psychological wellbeing as jeopardized and become defensive. Beginning in childhood, individuals try to make sense of their experiences and to devise ways to survive. They interpret their experiences and draw conclusions about what they observe and then make assumptions about every aspect of the world—themselves, others, nature, institutions, cultures, words, and concepts. These assumptions coalesce into mental models. Assumptions and mental models lie beneath the level of awareness and shape behavior. They escape examination and become rigidly entrenched within the psyche as absolutes. Absolutes manifest as right/wrong polarities. When individuals feel unsafe, they react rather than respond. When they react, they engage in right/wrong polarity thinking and behavior. They see a black/white, either/or world.

One example of polarity thinking that has emerged on the cusp of the Piscean-Aquarian shift involves the Aquarian view of leadership. The Aquarian Era asks people to accept and value their inner authority and share responsibility for creating and accomplishing tasks in partnership and in teams. Those who carry resentment toward the hierarchical style of Piscean leadership interpret this shift to co-responsibility as meaning there are to be no leaders in the Aquarian Era, thereby polarizing leadership into leader/no leader. What the Aquarian Era demands instead is a shift in the style, purpose, and form of leadership away from and different than that of the Piscean Era.

Having polarities questioned can destabilize the psyche and create a loss of certainty. A loss of certainty, for many, is equivalent to a loss of physical, psychological, and spiritual safety. Whenever individuals feel exposed and unsafe, they find a means to put the world together so that it makes sense and feels safe once again. They protect themselves by projecting blame onto others, feeling victimized by circumstances, suppressing curiosity, choosing economic needs over the earth's ecological wellbeing, and resisting change. They create rigid boundaries, problem solve effects rather than cause, and invest in male authority. Protection can take the form of war and sacrifice. At its most extreme, it is a me-or-you and a kill-or-be-killed attitude used against other people, nature, and animals.

The Elemental Transition from Water to Air

Pisceans evidence certain identifiable attributes of the water element. They are optimistic, earnest, devoted, and sincere. The planning and designing necessary to manifest ideas into form come easily to them because they value practicality. Motivated by deep and often unconscious emotional yearnings that range from one extreme to another, they experience all-encompassing love and overwhelming fears. They can be compulsive, irrational, and oversensitive because they fail to control or channel their emotions. In a faith-based era, Pisceans became addicted to their feelings and beliefs. This addiction led to ignoring warning signs until a problem had fully manifested, tempting them to solve it by addressing the symptoms rather than the cause.

Members of an Aquarian society have attributes that reflect their air sign. Because they value curiosity, learning, and flexibility of the intellect, air signs easily see different perspectives and move in new directions. They use reason to problem solve and are not confined by emotions and reservations. Their ability to detach from the worries or emotions of others enables them to excel in teamwork and cooperation and to develop group consciousness. They appreciate the thoughts of others and rise above conflict even when they strongly disagree.

Air signs are transformers of opposites. For example, they can trans-

Just as a move from country to city, or from one country to another, causes stress to the psyche because of unfamiliarity with the physical, energetic, and elemental territory, so does humanity as a whole experience stress when it moves from cycle to cycle because its mental models no longer fit its experience.

form hate into love, pride into humility, and separation into unity. Motivated to materialize ideas and bring thought into matter, air signs easily employ intuition and understand and use science and electronics. They can master the ability to materialize thoughts to serve others. As a mental sign, they risk becoming preoccupied with and even fanatical about their theories and concepts. They can sacrifice the higher values of the heart and become addicted to their intellect. This addiction can become such a force that they feel threatened when their opinions are ignored or when their intellectual judgment is not valued. They also can lack deep emotions and fail to accept limitations of the physical body.

Transitioning from a heart- and emotion-centered reality (Water) to that of a mind- and mental-centered reality (Air) presents challenges. Assumptions about both Piscean and Aquarian cycles can become identified as "reality" and used to determine how energy will be focused during the transition. Stress is produced by the simultaneous desire to eradicate the old and to start a new way of being and doing. Just as a move from country to city, or from one country to another, causes stress to the psyche because of unfamiliarity with the physical, energetic, and elemental territory, so does humanity as a whole experience stress when it moves from cycle to cycle because its mental models no longer fit its experience.

Any elemental transition marks a stressful period because it requires letting go of one reality and embracing new possibilities. The society of the Piscean water sign will devalue the Aquarian air sign, viewing it as lacking emotional depth and practicality. If viewed not as either/or but both/and, the transition from Water to Air brings values of the heart to values of the mind. By bringing heart values forward from the Piscean Era, Aquarians can develop and materialize ideas that serve others.

Return of the Divine Feminine and Initiation of True Partnership of Feminine and Masculine Energies

Intuitives, Lightworkers, and teachers of Ageless Wisdom, both past and present, speak of the return of the Divine Feminine energy at the dawn of the Aquarian Era. This return initiates a correction of the adverse effects that occurred in the evolutionary process with the separation into polarities of the Divine Masculine and Divine Feminine. International teacher and Lightworker Patricia Cota-Robles, teacher of Ageless Wisdom Torkom Saraydarian, and others refer to this separation as a fall from grace. When this separation of the Divine Feminine and Divine Masculine occurred, the Divine Feminine withdrew into the heart for safekeeping while a distortion of the Divine Masculine, called the patriarchy, prevailed and dominated beliefs, values, and activities in most cultures around the world.

Through the centuries, enlightened beings have incarnated as spiritual teachers in an attempt to awaken humanity to its true spiritual identity. Progress was slow and often nonexistent until the inception of the Piscean Era some two thousand years ago. At the beginning of this cycle, the path back to Oneness with the Divine intensified. Enlightened women and men teachers taught and modeled the path to Oneness. Cota-Robles views Jesus and Mary Magdalene as the man and woman who initiated the synthesis of the Divine Masculine and Feminine. Ramakrishna and Saradavi,

Aurobindo and The Mother, Teresa of Avila and John of the Cross, and Francis and Claire of Assisi represent other pairs who blended the Divine Masculine and Feminine.

The belief that humans are separated from their Source and thus from the unity of the Divine Feminine and Divine Masculine resulted in fear, violence, and a disconnection with nature. The related abuse of power manifested as greed, corruption, fanaticism, and a disregard for the reverence of life.

Throughout the Piscean cycle, the masculine obscured the role of the feminine. Both positive and negative masculine values drove the relationship between women and men. Masculine attributes of action, protection, and reason coexisted with weapons, brute force, and cruel justice. The negative masculine evolved into a patriarchy that valued power, production, wealth, achievement, and competition over feelings and emotional depth. When Piscean cultures devalued the position of women in society, the voices of women grew silent. The influence of the feminine in home, community, and world affairs diminished. Wounded and alienated from the feminine principle, women ceased questioning the relevance of the patriarchy, adopted its values as their own, and developed a wounded masculine principle. By professing patriarchal values and designating feminine attributes as inferior, men also developed wounded masculine and feminine principles.

Without a voice and relegated to less valued positions of authority and leadership, women failed to develop an understanding of their feminine psychology. Positive feminine values of relatedness, spontaneity, nurturance, and feeling brought them partial awareness. Over time, however, the feminine principle became deeply wounded by a loss of personal power. Women were expected to sacrifice personal preferences and yield to cultural norms. Not until the Piscean cycle bridged into the Aquarian did women as a group begin the long journey of confronting their feminine wounding and claiming their distinct psychology as women. Men, as a group, have yet to begin the journey of confronting their masculine wounding and claiming their distinct psychology as men.

To make the transition from Piscean to Aquarian, the current leadership model must transform from a hierarchical dynamic of parent/child and masculine-dominant relationships to a partnership dynamic of group consciousness and equal-masculine-and-feminine relationships. Aquarian leadership depends on reclaiming the feminine principle. Women leaders now have a distinct purpose: to lead humanity to a place it has not been before—into the Aquarian era.

Four waves of feminist activism have spanned the last hundred years. Each wave has brought women as a group closer to attaining their place as participants and leaders in the world. Women's suffrage in the early 1900s represented the first wave. The second wave achieved economic and legal rights in the sixties and seventies. In the nineties, in a third wave, the feminism of the seventies experienced a backlash from younger women. They tested and stretched the united front of "women's liberation" through individualist physical display. They flaunted their bodies in revealing clothes, sported navel rings, boasted openly of their sexual promiscuity, and relished using coarse language.

Aquarian leadership, regardless of gender, requires the feminine energy of relatedness and synthesis as its driving force.

Beginning in 2000, a fourth wave began that combines social justice with connection to the sacred. This new wave of activism is based not in anger but in optimism. It is outward focused on global issues rather than on issues of the individual. Women form interfaith circles to address political, economic, and religious differences with compassion and tolerance. They hold international conferences and establish worldwide networks of peace building. One example is an initiative with the purpose of engaging religious leaders in United Nations peace-building plans: the Global Peace Initiative of Women Religious and Spiritual Leaders was launched in Geneva, Switzerland, in 2002. In a second example, beginning in 2004, the International Council of Thirteen Indigenous Grandmothers began to meet annually because they believe that the teachings of their ancestors will light the way through an uncertain future.

Aquarian leadership, regardless of gender, requires the feminine energy of relatedness and synthesis as its driving force. In this leadership paradigm, leaders educate themselves about the heart and its relationship to the mind. They consciously define and implement a shift to balance positive masculine and feminine energies. Women and men leaders share responsibility for decisions and participate equally in matters of national and international importance. The shift to balanced masculine and feminine energies is critical in order to restore ecological equilibrium and to create new economic, social, and institutional structures.

The Arrival of the Millennial Generation

History repeats itself in cycles every eighty to one hundred years. According to William Strauss and Neil Howe in their book *The Fourth Turning*, four repetitive periods occur within each cycle: High (growth), Awakening (maturation), Unraveling (entropy), and Crisis (destruction). The third cycle of Unraveling is ending. As this occurs, the world will enter the Crisis cycle.

Four generations span each cycle, each having an archetype. Archetypes repeat themselves during any given cycle: those born during a Crisis cycle are heroes, during a High cycle are artists, during an Awakening cycle are prophets, and during an Unraveling cycle are nomads. In the United States at the beginning of the twenty-first century, the GI Generation (born between 1901 and 1924) fulfill the hero role, the Silent Generation (born between 1925 and 1942) are the artists, the Boomers (born between 1943 and 1960) are the prophets, and Generation X (born between 1961 and 1981) are the nomads. A new Crisis cycle will soon begin and its hero generation, born between 1982 and 2002, has been dubbed the Millennial Generation. Children born after 2002 will replace the Silent Generation as artists. They will not receive a generational name until their nature and behavior emerge in later years.

Strauss and Howe identify the Millennials as the next great generation. The Millennial Generation is the largest generation in history, the most affluent, most educated, and most diverse (36 percent white), and is

GENERATIONS

Artist	**???**	**2003-2023**
Hero	**Millennial**	**1982-2002**
Nomad	**Generation X**	**1961-1981**
Prophet	**Boomer**	**1943-1960**
Artist	**Silent**	**1925-1942**
Hero	**GI**	**1901-1924**

Figure 5. The Cycles of the Generations *as identified by William Strauss and Neil Howe in* The Fourth Turning: An American Prophecy. Figure by Ginger Graziano

destined to play a significant role in the early years of the Aquarian Era. The much smaller Generation X preceded the Millennials and are their coworkers, managers, and parents. Their bosses and parents may also be Boomers while their grandparents are Silents and great-grandparents are GI Generation.

The Millennials are the same hero archetype as the GIs. They follow a pattern common to the last four hero generations in the United States in that they arrived at a time of societal upheaval in values and culture following a generation widely viewed as disappointing. Early in life their Boomer parents treated the Millennials as special, overprotected them, and held them to high standards while never saying no. Having not received correction or been taught responsibility, Millennials have grown up feeling entitled and demanding continual affirmation. They cannot delay gratification and expect to be given, rather than to earn, the highest quality in everything.

Their parents' overprotection kept the Millennials from engaging in unstructured play and from exploring and relating to nature. They grew up primarily indoors with television, computers, and video games as entertainment. As adults, they are often addicted to technology. Their interaction with the outside world occurs primarily through organized sports and socializing in groups through clubs or at malls. While Millennials bring good social and collaborative skills to the workplace and are generally high achievers, they expect their employers to meet their physical and emotional needs. As they enter young adulthood, their courage and fortitude will be put to a test by a climactic time in history. Later in life, they will become an honored generation of civic heroes and will craft a modern early-Aquarian world.

The Millennials and Generation X play a major leadership role during the bridging of the Piscean and Aquarian eras. Contrasting these two generations reveals a dramatic shift of focus that has potential for conflict in leadership. Adjoining generations often compete with one another and are more comfortable with a generation once removed. For example, Generation X relates more closely to the Silent Generation than to the Millennials, and the Millennials relate to the Boomers better than to Generation X. In 2003, the Learning Café and American Demographics compared Generation X with the Millennial Generation as shown in Table 6.

Table 6: Characteristics of Generation X and the Millennial Generation

Generation X	Millennial Generation
Accept diversity	Celebrate diversity
Pragmatic/practical	Optimistic/realistic
Rely on themselves/individualistic	Invent themselves/realistic
Reject rules	Rewrite rules
Mistrust institutions	Institutions are irrelevant
Personal computer	Internet
Use technology as a tool	Assume technology as a fact of life
Multitask	Multitask fast
Latchkey kids	Nurtured kids
Friends, not family	Friends are family
Work as place to learn	Demand that workplace meet personal needs

The Millennial Generation have several Aquarian qualities and values. Their celebration of diversity welcomes race and gender relations, including feminine and masculine energies. Their commitment to cooperation and teamwork supports partnership with humanity and nature. They emphasize accountability and ethics, prizing innovation and diversity as well as cooperative endeavor. With a sense of community and global service, teamwork, and civic spirit, the Millennials use the Internet to mobilize volunteers for worthwhile causes. Because they take pride in teamwork and action, they will be instrumental in bringing about change in politics and the environment. Their visionary and pragmatic approach to life will allow them to put their ideals into form.

The Paradox of Technology

Challenges resulting from the rapid development of technology already significantly impact the world. Technology has made increased acquisition of knowledge and global awareness possible. It has created economic opportunities and provided considerable flexibility and speed in communication.

While it is true that technology allows for instant communication and global sharing, it also prevents people from truly experiencing life, including relationships with others and nature. Western culture has developed assumptions and mental models about technology that threaten the basic expression of human nature. For example, one commonly held assumption is that technology can be used to solve social and environmental challenges. This assumption leads people to expect quick technological answers and to overlook the simple, non-technical answers that arise from collaborative creativity. The focus on technological solutions can result in overlooking the underlying cause of problems. The more symptoms that occur, the more technologies are developed to address them.

Technology alone cannot adequately develop and provide the three essentials for happiness proposed by Piscean spiritual teachers, philosophers, and psychologists: contact with nature, freedom to choose, and feeling heard. Technology supports the freedom to choose and allows people to feel heard, but it cannot be a substitute for the growth that occurs during face-to-face human interactions and through a deep connection with nature. In fact, technology distracts people from the effort required to maintain physical, emotional, mental, social, and spiritual health; in addition, it allows them to avoid developing their human capacity for compassion and wisdom.

When technology is used as a substitute for knowledge and wisdom gained through direct experience, individuals and cultures cease developing their own power to advance their wellbeing.

When technology is used as a substitute for knowledge and wisdom gained through direct experience, individuals and cultures cease developing their own power to advance their wellbeing. An example occurred in the United States in 2007 and 2008 when overconfidence in a booming housing market devastated the nation's economy and the personal lives of many innocent individuals. Led by incremental greed, banks and securities dealers loaned money to unqualified buyers using computer models that lacked the historical data necessary for accurate analysis. No such historical data existed because the current circumstances had never occurred before. This crisis is an example of how dependence on technology without benefit of common sense and ethical standards can lead to disastrous results.

Technology negatively impacts physical health. Sitting indoors with machines results in back and wrist strain, obesity from lack of exercise, and loss of bone density and Vitamin D. Sustained interaction with technology numbs sensory sensitivity. Exposure to loud sounds, particularly through earphones, impairs hearing acuity. Reports indicate that in 2007 over 80 percent of children under two spent several hours a day watching videos and television. Child development specialist and author Joseph Chilton Pearce documented that these activities produce changes in children's neurological and intellectual development that reduce imagination, abstract thinking, and creativity.

Because of the plasticity of the brain, use of technology also affects adult neurology. The Internet reprograms the brains of frequent users so they can scan material quickly for relevant data, resulting in scattered attention and diffused concentration. Gradually, the ability to read, and therefore to think in depth, recedes, along with the wisdom that comes from the contemplation of ideas. In "Is Google Making Us Stoopid? What the Internet Is Doing to Our Brains," a 2008 article in *The Atlantic,* author Nicolas Carr quotes the prediction of playwright Richard Foreman: "As we are drained of our 'inner repertory of dense cultural inheritance,' Foreman concluded, "we risk turning into 'pancake people'—spread wide and thin as we connect with that vast network of information accessed by the mere touch of a button."

Technology also affects emotional development and health. Many people are addicted to communication devices as well as to television, e-mail, and video games. Technology fosters a sense of separation from direct human contact, resulting in the denigration and psychological abuse of others. Cyber-bullying, character assassination, financial scams, and unsolicited pornographic messages are examples.

Communication through machines rather than face to face enables us to ignore healthy boundaries. The speed of technology allows people to react impulsively instead of being thoughtful and responsible. Without taking time to consider the consequences, an e-mail message is sent that the sender would neither speak nor write in a letter, or misinformation is forwarded that can eventually impact tens of thousands of people. Technology provides multiple distractions, one of which is the compulsion to be in continuous contact with the cyber community. As a result, people develop unease for silence and solitude.

While technology is used to petition for environmental protections, to raise money to protect endangered animals and forests, and to educate others about climate change, the very technology used harms the environment. The short life span of technological devices translates into piles of nonbiodegradable discards with components that are toxic to the earth. Electrical and sonar waves permeate the atmosphere and oceans. Government and private space programs leave debris to float in space without full awareness of the possible consequences.

Psychological and spiritual growth in the Aquarian Era depends on the ability to deepen a sense of interconnection with nature and one another while using technology to assist, rather than direct, progress. In his book *Presence,* Peter Senge and his colleagues write: "One basic way to expand our efficacy is through modern science and technology. But another is through integrated (emotional, mental, physical, and spiritual) growth and enhanced wisdom. This means growing in our sense of connection with nature and with one another and learning to live in ways that naturally cultivate our capacity to be human."

Conclusion

In applying Aquarian values, we can learn from the failings of the Piscean Era by not repeating the same mistakes and by deepening awareness of our own and our country's shadows. The consequences of the rigidity that developed within the Piscean Era can happen again in the Aquarian Era. Any aspect of the leadership and group life template can become concretized and polarized. Order can become rigid, perfectionistic, and

Patience, tolerance, and the understanding of the evolutionary process will be paramount for leaders and groups in the Aquarian Era.

routine. Because of the Aquarian emphasis on group life, individuality may not be tolerated. Conformity may be confused with cooperation. The will may be used to force rather than allow the evolution of consciousness. The growing reliance on technology may increase, resulting in diminished human development and wisdom.

Patience, tolerance, and the understanding of the evolutionary process will be paramount for leaders and groups in the Aquarian Era. Facing what is, allowing what is, and sustaining their energies and focus in the present moment will ensure the psychological and spiritual cushion of safety for those in this two thousand year cycle.

Part Two

SOUL-INSPIRED LEADERSHIP

As leaders expand their consciousness and extend that consciousness into outer action, they naturally embody Aquarian values...Leaders can only lead from the level of their own soul development. They must continue to evolve in order to lead their groups forward.

Susan S. Trout

CHAPTER FOUR
FOUNDATIONS OF AQUARIAN LEADERSHIP

Introduction

To become Aquarian leaders requires conscious dedication to the development of the soul. Only through establishing a solid spiritual foundation within themselves, will leaders be able to assist and lead others. The stages of soul development provide a universal template for building this foundation. Leaders begin at the stage in which they currently find themselves. Identifying their current stage requires an honest personal assessment and provides a map for the individual and leadership journey. The journey itself is one of expanding inner consciousness while developing and applying skills in the outer world. The conscious interrelationship between the inner and outer worlds defines Aquarian leadership.

As leaders expand their consciousness and extend that consciousness into outer action, they naturally embody Aquarian values, such as dependence on their inner authority, nondual thinking, and synthesis of feminine and masculine qualities. In turn, they lead their groups toward group consciousness by beginning where the group and its members are in soul development and supporting their growth. Leaders can only lead from the level of their own soul development. They must continue to evolve in order to lead their groups forward.

This initial chapter of Part Two introduces the fundamentals of the stages of soul development as they apply to leaders. Chapter Five examines Stages One through Four, during which leaders are outer-directed, seeking their value from something or someone outside themselves in the world. Chapter Six examines Stages Five and Six, in which leaders are

Individuals evolve in a natural progression from a level of little or no conscious awareness of their divinity to a level of abiding in the Divine as an instrument of Divine Will.

inner-directed and seek their value from within through self-transformation. Stage Seven is also discussed in Chapter Six.

In Figure 6, the journey of soul development is illustrated as a spiral with the outer entrance to the spiral being the first stage of soul development and subsequent inward turns representing evolutionary steps toward eventual union with the Divine.

St. Teresa of Avila used the metaphor of the soul as a castle in which there are many rooms as well as many ways to be in the castle. The stages represent different places in the castle.

Individuals evolve in a natural progression from a level of little or no

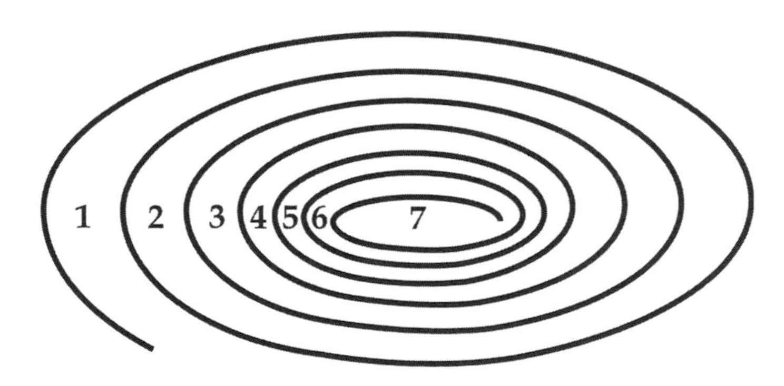

Figure 6: The Spiral of the Seven Evolutionary Stages of Soul Development *illustrates the individual's journey from searching for wholeness by looking to the outer world of human activity to searching for wholeness by looking within to the inner world of the soul.* Drawing by Ginger Graziano

conscious awareness of their divinity to a level of abiding in the Divine as an instrument of Divine Will. In Stages One through Four, they seek their value from something or someone outside themselves in the world and serve others to meet their personality needs. Moving closer to union with the Divine in the middle of the castle, those in Stage Five strive to purify obstacles to the awareness of Divine Presence and to balance care of self with the practice of service to others. Stage Six is in the heart of the castle where union with the Divine becomes a living experience. Those in Stage Six are devoted to being an instrument of Divine Will. Their self-identity and their work in the world are unified and exemplified as selfless service to humanity. Stage Seven represents the continuation of their soul's journey after physical death.

Evolutionary Stages of Soul Development

The stages of soul development, first described in *Born to Serve*, are summarized as follows:

- *Stage One: Awakening to Serve.* Those in this stage have little or no motivation to help others or to lead. Their primary focus is on caring for their own physical and material needs.
- *Stage Two: Work Ethic.* As doers, these individuals work to meet their physical and material needs and to bring order out of chaos. Their service is a natural extension of their work ethic.
- *Stages Three and Four: Missionary Attitude and Wounded Healer.* People in both of these stages serve with the often unconscious motive of having someone or something outside themselves meet their physical and emotional needs. Stage Three servers usually meet their needs through causes while Stage Four servers do so through relationships.

(transition from outer-directed to inner-directed)

- *Stage Five: Healing the Healer.* These individuals are self-responsible, doing inner work, and acknowledging the need to balance care of self with care of others, and to practice self-transformation through service.
- *Stage Six: Selfless Action.* Those in this stage have no attachment to the form and outcome of their service.
- *Stage Seven: Beyond the Physical.* After death, individuals' souls continue to serve in other dimensions.

Table 7: The Evolutionary Stages of Soul Development

Stage	Statement	Core Learning	Salient Fear	Primary Gift	
One: Awakening to Serve	Who am I?	Self-identity	If no one tells me who I am, I remain lost.	Emotional sensitivity	Surrender of self-absorption for purposeful activity
Two: Work Ethic	All my problems will be solved through action in the world.	Use of power	If I don't control the world, it will control me.	Productivity	Surrender of meeting individual needs for doing good in the world
Three: Missionary Attitude	What is best for me is best for all.	Humility	If I admit I don't have all the answers, I will be destroyed.	Social responsibility	Surrender of certainty in order to explore
Four: Wounded Healer	If I help others, I will get my emotional needs met.	Healthy boundaries	I am not enough.	Generosity	Surrender of self-deception for self-responsibility

(transition from outer-directed to inner-directed)

Stage	Statement	Core Learning	Salient Fear	Primary Gift	Transitional Shift
Five: Healing the Healer	The way out is the way in.	Willingness	I'll never achieve my goal.	Authenticity	Surrender of know-ing to not knowing
Six: Selfless Action	Service is the altar of devotion.	Being service	I remember fear, but I am fearless.	Steady wisdom	Surrender of the physi-cal body for service in a higher realm
Seven: Attaining Mastery	Beyond the physical	Attaining mastery	I remember doubt, but I trust the unseen.	Service to humanity	Surrender of self to Higher Self

Each stage is guided by the following:

- A **statement** that reflects the individual's worldview.
- A **core learning** that reflects the quality individuals can develop from the challenges of their life experiences within each stage and that is a gift to the self.
- A **salient fear** that reflects the underlying reason why individuals at this stage create obstacles to the soul's full expression.
- A **primary gift** that reflects the primary gift they offer the world.
- A **transitional shift** that reflects what orientation an individual must surrender in order to move from one stage to the next. These shifts lead one from a life with an outer focus to a life of inner contemplation at one with action.

Understanding the following parameters prevents misunderstandings concerning the stages of soul development:

- One developmental stage is not better than another. Rather, individuals bring what they have learned (i.e., their skills and wisdom) from one stage into the next. Because the stages are developmental (i.e., infancy through adulthood), it is not possible to skip a stage, although individuals sometimes attempt to bypass a stage out of personal woundedness.
- As people develop, they go through all of the stages. Therefore, all people have, to varying degrees, the wounds of each stage and also its lessons.
- People differ in how long they stay in a stage, but they are in only one stage at a time. Individuals can stay in one stage their entire life or can move through several stages. Personality, life circumstance, or woundedness all affect how, when, and if they choose to move forward in their personality integration and spiritual attainment. The shift from Piscean to Aquarian will depend on how readily people transition through the outer-directed stages and arrive at the inner-directed stages.
- Individuals may regress to an earlier stage under stress, and they may briefly experience a future stage as a glimpse of their potential.
- Stages are related to the motivation and level of consciousness of individuals and not to the form of service in the world. The level of consciousness of servers determines the essence of their service. For example, it is possible to be an activist from the third stage and view the world as black or white. It is also possible to be an activist from Stage Five and view the world as a classroom for psychospiritual learning and growth.

Because leadership is a form of service, these stages can be used as indicators of the soul development of leaders. The second book in *The Soul and Service Trilogy, The Awakened Leader,* describes how leaders move through each of these developmental stages and grow in psychological and spiritual awareness. Leaders can anticipate and meet their own growth needs and the needs of those they lead when they understand the nature of each stage and its gifts and shadow tendencies. *The Awakened Leader* posits that leaders view leadership as a classroom in which they learn five soul lessons: vision, right relations, analysis, synthesis, and to stand alone. Related topics discussed include boundaries, founder's syndrome, dangers, and feminine and masculine energies.

Leaders can anticipate and meet their own growth needs and the needs of those they lead when they understand the nature of each stage and its gifts and shadow tendencies.

In *The Clarion Call*, the study of soul development is applied to the understanding of leadership and group life in the early Aquarian Era. The following template of a leadership soul curriculum offers a congruent, stable, and spacious container through which to view leadership in the Aquarian Era in the context of soul development.

Leadership as a Classroom of the Soul: An Aquarian Curriculum

The soul classroom of leadership requires a unique curriculum during the transition from the Piscean Era to the Aquarian. This curriculum supports leaders and organizations as they face and respond to the challenges of this transition. The curriculum emphasizes the need to cultivate inner strength, creativity, practicality, and wisdom. It provides support at the physical, emotional, mental, and spiritual levels.

Those in different stages of soul development will experience this transition in varied ways and benefit from support and direction that matches their needs. In Chapter Five, leaders in the outer-directed stages receive instruction on the Inner Leader, providing guidance for their personal and leadership journey; the soul lessons that will strengthen and refine their leadership skills; and the feminine and masculine energies, the synthesis of which are required for true Aquarian leadership. In addition, the curriculum offers exploration of the shadow of leadership and organizations and the challenges of the Aquarian Era. In Chapter Six, leaders in the inner-directed stages are led through the same curriculum with two additional aspects that are specific to their stages of soul development: spiritual awakenings and tri-leadership.

The Inner Leader

The Aquarian Era requires leaders to shift from reliance on outside influences and authority to identification with the true power of their Inner Leader. According to Ageless Wisdom, an Inner Leader—also called Soul, Higher Self, Transpersonal Self, and Solar Angel—is depicted within the auric field about eight inches above the head. The auric field is comprised of three vibrational bodies—physical-etheric, emotional, and mental—that combine with the physical body to comprise the personality. The *sutratma* provides the energetic link between the human soul in the heart and the Soul. The *sutratma* descends from the Inner Leader and separates into two threads—the consciousness thread and the life thread. The consciousness thread goes to the brain and the life thread goes to the heart. This connection is also referred to as Self to self, Soul to soul, and Will to will.

As an extension of the Divine Source, the Inner Leader seeks contact with the human soul, initially through sudden thought impressions and dreams and later through words, symbolic visions, fragrances, and touches. The Inner Leader also uses the conscience to direct leaders toward

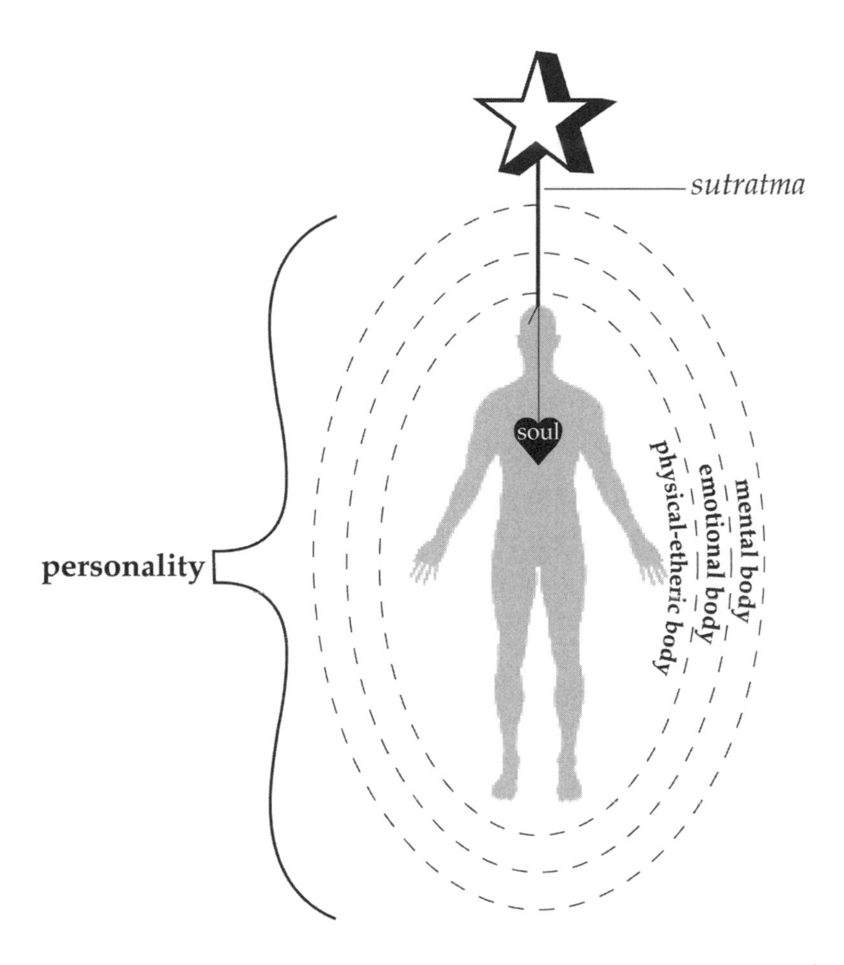

Figure 7: The Inner Leader *is always present and communicating. The individual can strengthen this communication through inner work, meditation, and contemplation.* Drawing by Ginger Graziano

what is right and just. It offers Itself as the most intimate guide on a path of perfection. Willingness and self-effort are required in order for leaders to receive protection, teachings, and reassurance from the Inner Leader. The Inner Leader guides leaders in their soul development and the lessons in the soul classroom in answer to their being self-responsible.

The Inner Leader is the true voice of inner authority and communicates through all activities and situations in daily life.

For the Inner Leader to help leaders realize their potential during an evolutionary shift, they need to educate themselves about Its nature, voice, and manifestation in the world. The Inner Leader is the true voice of inner authority and communicates through all activities and situations in daily life. As inner wisdom, the Inner Leader guides soul development. It expresses through the personality, inspires creativity, and enables leaders to translate their strength into action in the world.

The Inner Leader is a benevolent ally. Rising out of the silence within, it gives leaders the fuel to follow their *dharma*. Dharma is a term used in Eastern spiritual traditions and refers to two levels of duty. *Eternal Dharma* is a moral law of spiritual Truth applying to everyone and infusing every phenomenon. In Western thought, the obligation to love God with heart, soul, and mind is akin to Eternal Dharma. Leaders serve God or are *Dharmic* when they practice Eternal Truth in their lives. On the individual level, dharma is the practice of peace and service while doing their duty in the world from a place of right attitude. Leaders are dharmic when they follow their unique duty and function. Eternal Dharma articulates God's purpose, vision, and mission for individuals and for groups of individuals. In this way, a leader has dharma and groups or organizations have dharma.

Leaders may sense the Inner Leader alerting them not to go in a certain direction. They may choose to do so anyway and later realize their mistake. The Inner Leader may then say, "Now that you went that way, let's see if your choice/actions can bring you good fruit." The Inner Leader returns power to them in this way.

The vibration of the voice of the ego differs from that of the Inner Leader. The ego speaks against the soul's identity with the Divine in an effort to distract people from expressing their True Selves. Unfortunately, the ego's voice can attempt to guide, teach, and reassure. When the ego directs leadership, leaders can make choices that cause harm. Historically, and in daily life, examples of ego-driven leaders and their misuse of power abound. Fortunately, the Inner Leader's voice can reframe the ego's voice and guide leaders to learn from mistakes. Wise leaders are those who acknowledge their errors rather than hide them, and who gain strength from meeting adversity, whatever its origin.

Learning to discern between the voice of the Inner Leader and the voice of ego is critical to soul development in the inner-directed stages. Leaders can be certain they are hearing the voice of their Inner Leader if, over time, they feel increasingly peaceful regardless of their life circumstances, if others give them feedback that they look more peaceful, and if they increasingly see a world of unity instead of duality. They allow the wisdom of their Inner Leader to lead them. Always, they pause and choose the voice to which they grant leadership.

Soul Lessons

An Aquarian classroom for the soul is not modeled after the Piscean educational system with its emphasis on linear thinking, predetermined curriculums, accumulation of information, and competition. To the contrary, it is a setting or environment in which students learn from the inside out by translating inner experiences into outward expressions of words and actions. Learning from the inside out facilitates applying what students know. Interactions that show them the progress of the soul's learning become "tests," and acknowledgments, reactions, and suggestions from themselves and others function as "grades." Homework takes the form of inner work, reflection, and contemplation in the waking and dream states.

Leadership can arise from the personality or the soul. The most powerful and meaningful leadership arises when personality and soul fuse. When rigidly held dogmas, opinions, and belief systems fall away, the personality becomes a unique conduit of the expression of the soul. Established in this state of not knowing, the soul breathes and its deeper knowledge emerges. When the personality self opens to the gifts of the soul, it receives teachings that embody wisdom and understanding. The pouring in of soul force is then visible in the leader's every action, decision, and relationship.

Each soul lesson integrates experience with knowledge and has corresponding leadership challenges.

The leadership curriculum consists of five soul lessons. The first four lessons, mastered by the end of Stage Five, are vision, right relations, analysis, and synthesis. Once these lessons are mastered, the ultimate soul lesson of standing alone can be mastered in Stage Six. Each soul lesson integrates experience with knowledge and has corresponding leadership challenges. The level of commitment to the leadership curriculum allows leaders to engage in their classroom wholeheartedly and is what determines the depth and breadth of their learning. Over time they become the leader they were intended to become. Not the leader they thought, perhaps, or the leader others want them to be; rather, they become the leader they are meant to be.

Vision

Learning to formulate, sustain, and ground a **vision** is the bedrock underlying all soul lessons of leadership. This lesson gifts leaders with sustained energy to manifest the vision in the world.

The soul lessons in the vision curriculum include the ability to:

- Learn about vision
- Formulate a vision
- Ground the vision through the mission and organizational structure
- Acquire skill in the practical, day-to-day operations that ground the vision
- Translate personal vision into the slow, step-by-step creation of a shared vision
- Create shared vision with members of the organization while maintaining healthy working relationships with staff or with the population served
- Work with and appreciate diverse points of view while maintaining objectivity
- Maintain constant vigilance for needed organizational change in direction or structure

Right Relations

When leaders neglect their physical, emotional, and spiritual wellbeing and do not engage in continuous self-development, they are prime candidates to learn the second soul lesson, **right relations**. Learning how to be in proper relationship with self and others assures leaders that the highest good is served for all.

Soul lessons of right relations include the ability to:

- Acquire self-knowledge and identify obstacles to personal growth
- Attend to shadow issues

- Study the nature of the human psyche and healthy boundaries and implement this understanding in the workplace
- Apply communication skills and reframe mistakes as learning opportunities
- Seek and use wise counsel from helping professionals, mentors, and spiritual advisors

Analysis

Learning the soul lesson of **analysis** helps leaders distinguish between criticism and the ability to analyze. The energy of analysis promotes fairness and a nonjudgmental attitude. The energy of criticism is judgmental, accusatory, harsh, and attacking.

Soul lessons of analysis include the ability to:

- Assess a problem to determine accountability and address the solution without blame or condemnation
- Apply systems thinking by recognizing that a system is made up of dynamic interactions between parts that form a complex whole
- Appraise mistakes as opportunities to learn and to do a better job next time

Synthesis

Through the soul lesson of **synthesis**, leaders learn how to see the bigger picture and the destiny of their organization. They examine their willingness to serve as the "glue" that creates cohesiveness within their organization.

Soul lessons of synthesis include the ability to:

- Recognize every piece of the organization—person, information, idea, task, program, or event—as contributing to the creation of a shared vision and mission

- Perform all tasks in the spirit of service and maintain a holographic team and a holographic organization
- Apply both/and thinking and avoid polarization into right/wrong, black/white, either/or
- Engage intuition and imagination for problem solving
- Employ the Witness Self, that part of the mind that can stand back and observe without judgment

To Stand Alone

The ultimate soul lesson as leaders is to learn **to stand alone**. Leaders achieve this lesson when they learn to unconditionally love humanity and after they have mastered the four soul lessons of vision, right relations, analysis, and synthesis.

Soul lessons of standing alone include the ability to:

- Express self-confidence based on feeling connected to their spiritual essence
- Embody the spaciousness that comes with the acceptance of life as it is
- Face ambivalence about being a leader
- Discern attempts to compensate for ambivalent feelings about leadership by misplacing trust
- Acknowledge that they can stand alone only when they learn to love enough, regardless of the challenges and dangers experienced in the leadership role

Feminine and Masculine Energies

A unique characteristic of the human psyche, and thus of a leader, is the coexistence of two complementary energies, the feminine and the masculine. In Taoism, *yang*, or the masculine principle, is considered a complement to *yin*, the feminine principle. These energies exist in each person regardless of gender. Leaders degrade the value of both when they embrace one without honoring the other. The ultimate goal in the Aquarian Era is to have the masculine and feminine energies work in partnership and move into wholeness, a creative synthesis of opposites. When they reclaim feminine energy and use it in partnership with the masculine, leaders create conscious leadership.

The feminine generates the capacity for feeling and valuing, and for expressing emotional depth in the leadership role. Men and women experience the feminine through the qualities of the heart: relatedness, softness, tenderness, nurturance, and synthesis. The feminine knows when to listen, when to wait, when to keep still, what to choose, and when to act. The feminine provides a loving container for suffering and conflict, accepting life as it is without judgment. The feminine translates the theoretical by appraising the theory with the heart and selecting a heart-directed action. Preferred communication modes of the feminine are stories, humor, and art—modes reflecting spontaneity, receptivity, and reflection.

Masculine energy gives leaders the capacity to be productive, verbal, and orderly. Both genders experience the masculine through the qualities of the mind—discrimination, discernment, and predictability. The masculine enables leaders to analyze problems before taking action by questioning how something works, how well it works, and what it is used for. A drive to protect others is a major function of masculine energy. Masculine energy prefers a style of communication that is linear, analytical, rational, and impersonal, resulting in preferences for the political and scientific.

Woundedness of the feminine and masculine energies impacts leadership. In *From Wild Man to Wise Man: Reflections on Male Spirituality,* Franciscan priest Richard Rohr writes that a man who does not engage his feminine aspect lives from his head and uses his personality to function in the outer world as a mover, explainer, fixer, and manipulator. Reason preempts feelings. Conversely, a woman who does not engage her masculine aspect lives from her heart and becomes too inward and preoccupied with relationships. Her feelings are diffuse. She uses her personality to manipulate people and events to get what she wants and imposes her will by being over-responsible for meeting the needs of others.

Regardless of gender, leaders attain a synthesis of the feminine and masculine energies when they reach the inner-directed stages of soul development.

In order to be an Aquarian leader, **healing and synthesis** of the feminine and masculine energies are necessary. When leaders embody a synthesis of these energies, they attain wholeness. The qualities of heart and mind move beyond either/or and work in partnership. Leaders are not whole if they profess through words or actions that masculine energies are superior to feminine or vice versa. As a result, they neglect or degrade parts of their physical, emotional, mental, and/or spiritual selves and engage in oppositional thinking and behavior based on certain mental models—the beliefs and assumptions acquired in childhood as a means of making sense out of a chaotic and complex world. In the duality of the psyche, which thinks in terms of better than/worse than, right way/wrong way, and true/false, leaders hold mental models like "only men should be in the military" or "only women should be preschool teachers."

Regardless of gender, leaders attain a synthesis of the feminine and masculine energies when they reach the inner-directed stages of soul development. Only then are they comfortable with knowing and not knowing. The unity of being and doing allows them to express selfless action. Regardless of how they appear in the world, they possess calm self-confidence. Their dignity and authority emanate from within. Experiencing their wholeness they have no need to dress in a certain style, express a certain joy, or act a certain way. They no longer defend, deny, ignore, or judge. They are androgynous in the sense that they can, as Rohr says, be masculine in a womanly way and feminine in a manly way.

Shadow of Leadership and Organizations

Humanity cannot move into Aquarian consciousness without individuals engaging in shadow work. The shadow is the part of the psyche that attempts to hide the duality of dark and light. The shadow's darkness holds the neglected, undeveloped, unlived, negative, and destructive aspects of the psyche, as well as the shameful and unacceptable desires and emotions. Its light—the shadow's gold—contains unrealized potential for positive and constructive talents and qualities, potential for growth, and unclaimed gifts and finer qualities. Until leaders and members of organizations examine their inner lives and learn to observe themselves with detachment, the shadow will go unchecked and they will remain unaware of its impact on others. Failure to take responsibility for the shadow disrupts the health and wellbeing of leaders and organizations in different ways. The manner in which the shadow expresses itself differs within each of the seven stages of soul development.

When leaders do not honor the shadow and attend to the quality and health of their inner life, they go forth like a wave carried by powerful undercurrents.

When leaders do not honor the shadow and attend to the quality and health of their inner life, they go forth like a wave carried by powerful undercurrents. These undercurrents, manifesting as projection, denial, or neglect, represent unconscious shadow challenges to the quality of their inner lives and therefore to the quality of their leadership. The shadow can do significant harm and stifle new growth. For example, one leader may project her family patterns onto those in her organization, such as by imposing her will because she believes that she is responsible for everything. Another leader, having experienced extreme chaos in his family, might stymie creativity by establishing rigid rules and procedures. It is common for people to blame individuals for organizational problems rather than examining their own motivation and behavior. When leaders believe their personal identity depends on the power of their leadership, they can project their insecurity. The leader's lack of security and confidence negatively impact the identity and power of the organization's members. Fear of failure or loss can also prevent leaders from terminating a faltering project.

Shadow tendencies of individuals blend together to form a group or collective shadow. For example, groups can project their finer qualities outward, making other people into heroes with qualities they believe are superior to their own and unattainable. They may collectively project their authority issues onto the leader and challenge the leader's role and knowledge. They may view the leader as a parent figure who is superior, flawless, and unreachable. Or they may disown their potential for leadership, project the total burden of responsibility for the organization onto the leader, and not participate in the creation of a shared vision. If individual members of an organization have scarcity issues about money, they will form a collective shadow of scarcity and affect the financial viability of the organization.

The collective shadow of members of a group can overlap the leader's shadow. For example, when the leader feels powerless and insecure, group members can react in one of two ways. They can assume the leader's unworthiness and hesitate to acknowledge the leader's contribution

Leaders in the Aquarian Era progress toward wholeness when they accept the challenge of balancing the light and the dark.

to the organization's success. Or a person or persons in the group can exert power and attempt to take on the leader's role.

Leaders in the Aquarian Era progress toward wholeness when they accept the challenge of balancing the light and the dark. They experience balance by standing in the middle and honoring the truth of both sides. Their self-knowledge rises to the level of spiritual wisdom. They shift from being distant, judgmental, and self-involved to being gentle, humble, and open to their own and others' mistakes. The psychic energy once held in their disowned parts becomes available for evolution, creativity, and the wellbeing of the organization. Aquarian leaders can openly examine their hidden motives, asking whether they lead in order to satisfy their need for power, fame, affection, or validation. They witness their tendency to act as if they are superior to the rest of humanity. They acknowledge the many ways their personality distorts the spirit of their participation in the organization.

In Stage Five, leaders are willing to meet their shadow, allowing them to consciously make another choice. By meeting and owning the shadow, the pure light of the soul spontaneously pours through. Once this blending of energy occurs, the leader's soul and personality work together and the highest good is served. Stage Six leaders are those who have journeyed into their inner darkness and have reached the place of their hidden wholeness. They can lead others with integrity because they have been there and know the way.

Challenges in the Aquarian Era

Leaders and groups experience the shift of energy from the Piscean to the Aquarian Era as a force toward change. As discussed in Chapter Two, if the shift evokes reactions because of fear of change and polarized thinking and behavior, the difficulties experienced by leaders and groups will increase greatly. Other shifts requiring adjustment and acceptance are the transition from the emotionally-centered element of Water to the mentally-centered element of Air, the initiation of the true partnership of feminine and masculine energies, the influence of the Millennial Generation, and the paradox of technology. Resistance because of rigidity in styles of leadership and group life and the intolerance of individuality will create obstacles and feed chaos. Likewise, the disruption of human development and wisdom produced by the reliance on technology may distract leaders and groups from fulfilling their missions and serving the greater good. Further challenges will arise once this shift has passed and the Aquarian Era is firmly established.

The nature of these challenges differs for leaders and groups in each stage of soul development. For example, leaders and groups in the outer-directed stages will resist change and increase their fear and polarized thinking. Those in inner-directed stages may welcome change and a new way of being in the world, but experience challenges related to accepting the unknown and the daunting task of creating new and workable approaches to leadership, group life, and organizational design.

Anticipating changes in the Aquarian Era before they occur and resolving them with wisdom and competence is a challenge for leaders and groups. Openness to the unexpected and a willingness to remain in the strength of the present moment is essential.

Additions to the Curriculum for Inner-Directed Stages

In the fifth and sixth soul development stages, leaders have two additions to the curriculum in their soul classrooms—spiritual awakenings and tri-leadership. These additions reflect the readiness of these stages to consciously engage in the evolution of the Aquarian destiny; namely, to open to the soul through progressive expansion of human consciousness and to work together in leadership teams of three from an energetic perspective.

Spiritual Awakenings and the Soul Stages

The unfoldment of the soul through progressive expansions of consciousness is inherent in the seven stages of soul development. The individual soul—leader or otherwise—experiences an increasing awareness of its "spiritual eyes" through markers identified as spiritual awakenings or expansions of consciousness. The markers of spiritual awakenings are not discrete outer events. They are inner experiences of an expanded awareness of the Divine reflected in outer behavior and actions.

The outer-directed stages of soul development are preparatory to conscious spiritual awakening. Preparation for spiritual awakening in these stages takes several forms—expressing concern for others, living responsibly in the world, having ethical standards, and attempting unsuccessfully to find meaning in life in the outer world of work, causes, and relationships.

Persons in these stages may unconsciously step onto the spiritual path. They begin to feel inner discontent or question their long-held religious beliefs. Also, the process of personality integration can progress unconsciously. It is possible for those in outer-directed stages to develop an integrated personality and operate in the world without having opened up to the soul.

Typically, it is not until an existential crisis occurs between Stages Four and Five that a person steps consciously onto a spiritual path. This crisis, often triggered by a significant loss, reflects an intense yearning for meaning in life at the soul level. Every assumption, thought, belief, and premise upon which life has been built is now in question. Individuals recognize they must engage in emotional healing and bring the heart and the qualities of the higher mind into their life and work through meditation and service. The struggle that ensues during this crisis is between an intense desire to "find a better way" and a fierce attachment to material values and ambitions.

Contrary to popular hopes and wishes, spiritual awakenings are not attained by a sprinkle of magical stardust from a high being. Rather, awakenings happen through self-discipline, self-responsibility, and dedicated effort. Once the goal in any given awakening is attained, a Master Teacher—someone in physical form or from a higher realm—acknowledges success in a simple and straightforward manner. Individuals are then encouraged to continue their walk on a spiritual path that expands their consciousness.

According to Ageless Wisdom, the evolution of human consciousness during the Aquarian Era will encompass developing group consciousness, contacting the Divine, experiencing a growing awareness of Oneness, merging personality with soul, and welcoming the Light, Love, and Will of Divine Source as it pours forth into the world. These evolutionary attainments are mirrored in the soul development of Stages Five and Six. At these stages, especially in Stage Five, the Soul begins working through the individual to dissolve personality obstacles. The individual learns to let go of attachments and open to the Soul's presence.

The following spiritual awakenings of persons and leaders in Stages Five and Six are the shifts necessary for the evolution of human consciousness in the Aquarian Era. Each shift in consciousness provides a different view of the experience of spiritual awakening; therefore, spiritual awakening is holographic. Parallel spiritual awakenings occurring in group life are presented in Chapter Seven.

- *Awakening One: The true source of equanimity is within.*
  As individuals and leaders discover that the outer world of relationships, places, and material goods does not satisfy the inner need for peace of mind, they turn inward and begin to view their life from a spiritual perspective.
- *Awakening Two: The highest good for one includes the highest good for all.*
  This awakening moves individuals and leaders away from preoccupation with meeting their own needs to respecting the needs of all sentient beings.
- *Awakening Three: Work and service are the same.*
  As individuals and leaders evolve, they experience work and service as interchangeable, resulting in a state of harmony and joy.
- *Awakening Four: The world is interconnected and nondual.*
  As individuals and leaders become inclusive, they recognize the universality of human experience and the interdependence of all things.
- *Awakening Five: True Sight sees the deeper spiritual meaning beyond appearances.*
  Individuals and leaders perceive the same life event differently as they uncover truer and clearer levels of awareness and interpretation.
- *Awakening Six: Answers lie on the level of cause.*
  Individuals and leaders begin by searching for answers in the outcome, move through judgment and blame, and become self-responsible for their thoughts and actions.
- *Awakening Seven: Responses to life events are made from the Witness Self on the mental level.*

Individuals and leaders respond to people and situations from the Witness Self, that part of the psyche that can observe without judgment.

- *Awakening Eight: True Service expresses in the world at all levels of participation.*
  As their souls progress, individuals and leaders turn the energy of inward growth back out to flower in the external world.
- *Awakening Nine: True Service requires being service as well as being of service.*
  As they let go of judgments they hold against themselves and others, individuals and leaders free themselves to use all available energy to live in the present moment and *be* service.
- *Awakening Ten: Personal will aligns with Divine Will to allow the unfolding of the destiny of collective will.*
  As individuals and leaders evolve, they strengthen all aspects of the will—strong will, skillful will, good will, and alignment with Divine Will—until the will is in balance and its needed aspect can be called upon in any given situation. Collective will then unfolds.

As individuals and leaders evolve, they strengthen all aspects of the will—strong will, skillful will, good will, and alignment with Divine Will—until the will is in balance and its needed aspect can be called upon in any given situation.

Tri-Leadership: The Energy Triangle Model

In Stages Five and Six, leaders can implement the Energy Triangle Model of leadership. Triangles are a fundamental model for the circulation of energy. Scholar and spiritual teacher George Gurdjieff used the term "the Law of Three" to explain that all that exists results from an interaction of three. The power of three is represented in the teachings of many world religions, such as the Father, Son, and Holy Spirit in Christianity and Shiva, Vishnu, and Brahma in Hinduism. Another example is the fundamental Buddhist teaching that followers are to take refuge in the Three Jewels—Buddha, his Doctrine, and the Spiritual Community—in order to attain enlightenment for the sake of all sentient beings.

The law of three also occurs in modern physics. As Don Riso and Russ Hudson write in their book *The Wisdom of the Enneagram,* "On the subatomic scale, atoms are made of protons, electrons, and neutrons, and rather than there being four fundamental forces of nature as was once thought, physics has now discovered that there are really only three—the strong force, the weak force, and electromagnetism."

In his book *The Psychology of Cooperation and Group Consciousness*, Saraydarian posits that because cooperation has laws and effects, it is a science. In his view, cooperation requires representatives of three essential energies—light, love, and willpower. Light is "knowledge, skill, information, reason, and logic." Love encompasses intuition, the bonds of human interaction, and the heart. Willpower is the means to overcome the obstacles to cooperation and to open new avenues for working together. In an energy triangle, each person vibrationally embodies one of these elements. The people then form a triangle of linked focal points through which spiritual energy circulates, radiating waves of light and goodwill.

Tri-leadership using the Energy Triangle Model is one way to manifest the Aquarian values of cooperation and group consciousness. Three people can serve as leaders to fulfill leadership functions of a project or goal. This approach is currently in its infancy and has not been sufficiently implemented to determine its full potential and all of the variables involved.

Conclusion

In *The Clarion Call*, the proposed holographic template for leaders during the transition from the Piscean to the Aquarian Era draws upon the psychological and spiritual teachings of scholars and masters and the author's observations and personal experience. This template combines the strength and safety of structure with the flexibility to adapt to unexpected events and challenges. The relevance of this holographic template is the congruency of its elements: soul development, Soul-soul alignment, soul lessons, feminine and masculine energies, leadership and group shadow, Aquarian challenges, spiritual awakenings, and tri-leadership expressed through the Energy Triangle Model.

CHAPTER FIVE
SOUL-INSPIRED LEADERSHIP: OUTER-DIRECTED STAGES OF SOUL DEVELOPMENT

Introduction

The universal template of the evolutionary stages of soul development provides the foundation for leadership in the Aquarian Era. Understanding the stages provides leaders with a way to assess their self-development, the progress of their leadership, and the level of their group's soul development. Using the stages for assessment delineates next steps in terms of areas of study and avenues for action. The template therefore provides a steady measure of the creative tension between where leaders are and where they intend to go.

This chapter explores how leaders at each of the four outer-directed stages of soul-inspired leadership can meet the changes and challenges of the transition. Leaders in these stages primarily lead from the personality with limited awareness of their Inner Leaders. Each of the four outer-directed stages of leadership is discussed in terms of leadership style, the nature of group relationship, and the curriculum of that stage's classroom.

Stage One Leader: Awakening to Lead

Leadership Style and Nature of Group Relationship

Leaders in the awakening to lead stage have crossed the threshold and entered the spiral of the soul's evolution. They find the leadership role a challenging and painful one and typically do not want to accept it. If they do, they will be preoccupied with having their needs met and will see their leadership as a series of duties and obligations necessary for physical and emotional survival. They often cannot sustain their role as leader because they lack sufficient energy and leadership skills.

True to the Piscean values of idealism and appreciation of individual needs, these leaders are most comfortable leading groups and organizations that address helping people and animals with immediate physical needs of food and shelter. Simple acts of kindness are common among Stage One leaders. Emotional sensitivity, especially to the distress of others, is their major gift. They express a strong desire to have deep bonds with coworkers and are willing to work toward that end.

Because they value honesty, they often convey their leadership limitations in a forthright manner. They may embrace personal development, self-help, and psychological and spiritual knowledge to resolve their limitations.

Classroom Curriculum

Inner Leader

Before leaders in the first stage of soul evolution can be aware of their Inner Leader, they must first develop their personality and a sense of self-identity. Key questions for these individuals are "Who am I?" and "How are my values and beliefs the same or different from those of others?" The answers to these questions provide the foundation to a sense of self by enabling them to establish their personal physical and emotional space and develop their beliefs and attitudes.

Soul Lessons

Learning to formulate a vision is the bedrock underlying all soul lessons of leadership. The primary soul lesson for leaders in the awakening to lead stage is to form a **vision** for their life. Vision is a specific picture of the ultimate goal toward which to strive. The ability to determine a personal vision precedes the capacity to formulate a vision as a leader. A personal vision typically reveals itself over time and is often reflected in personal preferences. For example, leaders in this stage who relate well to nature may have visions of opening their hearts by organizing groups that care for abandoned pets in their communities.

Feminine and Masculine Energies

✦ WOUNDING

The wound for people in this stage is of an undeveloped inner self. As a result, they fail to generate and effectively use personal power in their leadership. They are vulnerable to the influence of the beliefs and behaviors of those whom they perceive as stronger than themselves, both male and female. If their parental models did not have a strong sense of self, both their feminine and masculine energies were wounded. They may have a life-long struggle to internalize a healthy model of feminine and masculine energies. With an undifferentiated sense of self, their emotions—the feminine—are diffuse, and their learning and job skills—the masculine—are undeveloped. This wounding is also evidenced in their tendency toward abusive and codependent relationships.

✦ HEALING AND SYNTHESIS

Leaders in this stage need specific and practical support. The search for identity requires them to address emotional wounds that have led them to abdicate personal power and to seek validation outside themselves. They begin to heal their hearts by learning healthy boundaries. A later developmental step entails learning how to recognize and utilize healthy feminine and masculine energies in their relationships. Although they have pervasive emotional needs, Stage One leaders are often motivated to understand spirituality and the nature of the psyche.

Shadow of Leadership and Organizations

The behavior of Stage One leaders reflects their shadow's unrealized potential and unconscious beliefs about emotional and physical survival. Their undeveloped leadership and organizational skills and their inability to grasp group needs often impede bringing ideas into reality. Stage One leaders approach abstract information in a slow and deliberate manner and have difficulty articulating their ideas.

Indecision, making decisions to please others, and responding to challenges to their decisions with defensive and passive-aggressive behaviors reflect the shadow of Stage One leaders' unmet emotional needs. For example, they may compensate for their lack of inner strength and sense of self by refusing to allow ineffectual programs or projects to close down. To accommodate insecurities about their competence, they attempt to gain rigid control of their outer world by avoiding chaos at all costs. Leaders who try to eliminate chaos stifle their organizations' creativity.

Organizations in this stage, like leaders, flounder when their members have undeveloped leadership and organizational skills. Without the safety net of clear structure and expectations, members of the organization become embittered and depressed. Inertia prevails in a system that lacks competence and organizational structure. Without a solid foundation, a Stage One organization typically fails and closes its doors.

Challenges in the Aquarian Era

Most leaders in Stage One feel more secure with Piscean values and will want to continue practicing them in their leadership. They may resist Aquarian values because they feel challenged by the new learning required and fear the change it demands. These leaders feel comfortable with clear boundaries of right/wrong. They rely on faith that things will work out and cannot grasp the Aquarian mindset that uses both spiritual inner knowing and scientific knowledge. Their tendency to respond emotionally anchors them in the worldview of the water element of the Piscean Era.

Those leaders in Stage One who are willing to consider Aquarian values have difficulty understanding and implementing them with ease. For example, their insecurities about their skills, difficulty in hearing and trusting their Inner Leader, and unclear personal boundaries cause them to subjugate themselves to others and depend on other leaders. As a result, they find the concepts of shared decision making and leader-as-partner difficult to grasp. Their focus remains self-centered and personal so that the idea of feminine and masculine energies eludes them. They do not see their part in the bigger picture of greater good.

Stage One leaders who are competent using the Aquarian value of technology may use e-mail and Internet social networks to avoid confronting conflicted relationships and face-to-face interactions in general. By retreating into the cocoon of technology, they limit opportunities to acquire communication skills and to learn the soul lesson of right relations.

Stage Two Leader: Work Ethic

Leadership Style and Nature of Group Relationship

As doers and wage earners of the world, leaders in the work ethic stage represent Piscean values. Their goal is to learn to live meaningfully by making things happen, transforming chaos into order, and fulfilling the duty of earning a living. With productivity as their major gift, work ethic leaders have a sense of duty to make the world "work," and they prepare themselves to do so through education, training, and experience. They often have a wide range of interests and make significant contributions to family, church, career, education, business, politics, economics, technology, and culture. They readily accept financial obligations to charities and participate in the care and development of their communities.

Leaders in the work ethic stage ignore their inner life and look for validation and security in the outer world of work.

Work ethic leaders demand immediate compliance and excellence and expect employees and staff to be self-directed. They manifest a need to be powerful and in control through competitiveness, increased productivity, and effective change. Staff relationships become strained when work ethic leaders impose their will by expecting personal sacrifice, including high performance and long hours. When their motivation includes openness, willingness, and flexibility, Stage Two leaders may refocus their leadership style and mobilize people toward a vision and effective teamwork. Work ethic organizations carry out their activities with concentration, persistence, and deliberation because the skilled aspect of their will is developed and strong. They are competent and readily create systems for meeting their goals.

Classroom Curriculum

Inner Leader

Leaders in the work ethic stage ignore their inner life and look for validation and security in the outer world of work. Seeking to solve the struggle concerning the pull between their inner world and the outer world, they increase their efforts to find security in people, circumstances, religions, and corporations. They become achievers, producers, and competitors. Their goal is to prove to themselves that they have "the right stuff" to succeed in the world.

Although they sense a quiet call to move deeper into the interior of themselves, they take only a few cautious steps in this direction. Life is not viewed as a classroom for psychological and spiritual growth. They have yet to experience the authority of inner wisdom gained from authentic spiritual experience. Although unrecognized, their Inner Leader works through their conscience to lead them through their life's classroom, enabling them to develop a skillful and good will and to master living in the world.

Soul Lessons

The journey of mastering some components of the leadership soul lessons of vision, right relations, and analysis begins in the work ethic stage. The importance of learning these initial lessons cannot be overestimated. Without attaining a strong, initial foundation for the development of these three soul lessons, a leader's progress in later stages will be thwarted.

Competency, efficiency, practicality, and problem solving are major work ethic values that comprise components of the soul lessons of **vision** and **analysis**. Work ethic leaders know how to formulate, sustain, and ground a vision. They work efficiently as leaders and team members to analyze and solve problems. Although they sense the importance of **right relations** with others, they are not ready to understand the nature of the human psyche and to do the necessary inner work to have healthy emotional boundaries in their personal and work relationships.

Feminine and Masculine Energies

✦ WOUNDING

The wound of self-worth drives this stage. Whether male or female, leaders in the work ethic stage tend to distort masculine energies and devalue the feminine. They pride themselves on mastering the outer world of form by emphasizing, developing, and implementing qualities of masculine energy—reasoning, problem solving, ordering, and engineering reality. Work ethic leaders want to achieve, prove, and win. They look without rather than within for wisdom, insight, and wellbeing. Because Stage Two centers on mastery of the outer world, men and women leaders at this stage are vulnerable to becoming addicted to work, power, competition, relationships, material goods, and/or sex.

To counter the message of the patriarchy, a woman must be firmly grounded in her feminine. From this place she can make skillful use of masculine characteristics.

Men who develop these traits to the extreme exert authority over all others with a distorted masculine energy known as the patriarchy. The patriarchy views itself as having power over women, children, and nature. The patriarchy determines what is best for those it considers beneath it and implements these values with force rather than true power. It controls the economy, business, the church, and the military. Adherents of patriarchal values do not attend to their inner life or embrace feminine energies. As a result, the patriarchy lacks subtlety and restricts the creative expressions of those it oppresses.

Women, as well as men, can adhere to the superiority of patriarchal beliefs. Programmed to blindly accept and internalize the subjugated role given to them, women unwittingly teach their sons and daughters to believe that devotion to work and power gives meaning and value to life. To counter the message of the patriarchy, a woman must be firmly grounded in her feminine. From this place she can make skillful use of masculine characteristics. Without grounding in the feminine, she loses herself while attempting to find fulfillment through imitating the masculine role in the patriarchy.

Richard Rohr identifies the "father wound" as the reason women and men fail to honor and integrate their masculine energy. This wound occurs when children do not receive the masculine energy of their fathers. Fathers mirror masculine energy through trust and belief in the children's uniqueness. Fathers acknowledge their children by spending time with them and participating with them in activities. Fathers teach children the practicalities of living in the world. When fathers trust their children's value, the children gain self-confidence and a connection to their inner authority.

Women and men leaders in the work ethic stage are not reflective and avoid psychological and spiritual growth; by focusing on the outer world, they devalue and deny the existence of an inner life. To journey inward, the energy of the feminine needs acknowledgment and nurturance. Only then can the feminine qualities of cooperation and relationship provide the support and safety that the leader requires for seeking the true fulfillment that lies within rather than without.

✦ HEALING AND SYNTHESIS

The initial step toward healing neglected, distorted, and unbalanced feminine and masculine energies in leadership commences towards the end of the work ethic stage. Because they do not readily recognize the oppression of the work ethic stage, men leaders find it more difficult than women leaders to begin this journey. Leaders must desire to be liberated before the process can begin.

The healing journey begins when leaders begin to doubt the value of devoting all their time and energy to working in the world and to leisure. They become concerned about their addictive behavior and its impact on their health, work, and relationships. Having tried everything imaginable to find peace and happiness in the world, they begin to realize that they have reached the limits of what the outer world has to offer in validating their existence. Their Inner Leader calls them to begin examining their psychological and spiritual values. Their response is often tentative and cautious. The awareness of a deeper self remains hidden. Yet they consider turning inward and reach out for support in understanding themselves and their relationships with family, friends, and colleagues. Because work ethic leaders are people of action, they benefit from practical approaches, such as cognitive psychotherapy. Many choose to face their addictions by participating in twelve-step programs.

When wholeness has not been reflected back to children by their parents—their first leaders—they often have to look outside their family circle for older women and men leaders who can serve as mentors or models for healthy feminine and masculine energies. A younger leader can receive feminine energy from an older woman who values and teaches the gifts of the feminine—human connectedness, nurturance, relatedness, warmth, and spontaneity. The gifts of masculine energy can be received from an older male leader who values, protects, and teaches a younger leader how to survive and succeed.

Shadow of Leadership and Organizations

Leaders in the work ethic stage use positions of authority to validate their self-worth in the eyes of the world. The consequence of ignoring and

Work ethic leaders and organizations strive to bring order out of chaos, not just in the workplace but also in the world.

denying their inner life includes addictions, misuse of power, and neglecting self-care.

Because the existence of a personal shadow is often denied, leaders may act out their need for power, which they believe gives them personal value or worth, by violating ethical principles, dominating others, telling white lies, and hungering for physical or material pleasures, such as sex, power, and money. One example is found when corporate executives take huge salaries and severance pay while workers' health care and retirement needs go unattended. When leaders feel insecure about their identities, they deprive their workers of their identity in an attempt to bolster their own. They focus the efforts of their organizations on productivity and competition at the expense of the personal wellbeing of their staff. Projection of blame, contempt for weakness, and accumulation of material goods are common.

Work ethic leaders and organizations strive to bring order out of chaos, not just in the workplace but also in the world. To reduce chaos, they form rigid rules and procedures. Flexibility to meet the unique needs of a work situation is not encouraged. When orderliness is controlled, its shadow of messiness will invariably express itself. A messy shadow in such a workplace might emerge in the form of a whistle-blower who challenges the rules, procedures, or ethics of the organization.

To project a favorable image to the public, work ethic leaders and their organizations can adopt a collective persona. Although community-minded, they do not see the impact of their work practices on humanity as a whole. For example, they may ignore or resist the consequences of technology or business on the planet's ecology while supporting their local anti-litter and

To incorporate an Aquarian leadership model demands major shifts in leadership style that most work ethic leaders interpret as a threat to all they have worked to achieve.

recycling campaigns. They overvalue achievement and sacrifice other aspects of life, such as family and interpersonal relationships.

Challenges in the Aquarian Era

Because work ethic leaders and their organizations created and perpetuated economic, social, and educational structures in the Piscean Era, Aquarian values challenge their personal sense of authority and power. To incorporate an Aquarian leadership model demands major shifts in leadership style that most work ethic leaders interpret as a threat to all they have worked to achieve.

One shift for work ethic leaders would be moving from requiring their employees to invest authority in them to honoring their employees' inner knowing and inviting their input as true partners. A second shift would entail changing from using teams as a way of getting the job done to emphasizing a spirit of cooperation that rewards individual creativity as well as team effort. The use of financial rewards, productivity, technology, the economy, and money to override global and environmental health is a Piscean value that demands a third shift. Leaders would have to change to the Aquarian value that embraces a win/win orientation to life and balances human needs with the care and consideration of nature. Another major shift required would be for work ethic leaders to move from a hierarchical dynamic of masculine-dominant and parent/child relationships to the practice of a true partnership of feminine and masculine. As the Millennial Generation matures, their demands for gender equality will force work ethic leaders to face this issue.

Stage Three Leader: Missionary Attitude

Leadership Style and Nature of Group Relationship

When they do not find personal fulfillment by laboring in the world, Stage Two leaders move into Stage Three. At this stage, leaders seek validation of their self-worth by engaging in social causes, institutions, or organized religion in order to save others from what they view as the wrong way. In this worldview, the world is one of absolute dualities of good/bad and right/wrong, and the purpose of Stage Three leaders is to crusade for what is good and right. They devote themselves and their organizations to defending the public by using political and social arenas to repair what they feel is damaged. With a strong and capable will, missionary attitude leaders can rebound quickly from seeming defeats.

Stage Three leaders and their organizations offer many gifts of social responsibility to the world through their participation in good works and social action. They become agents of change who are willing to take action to raise social awareness that results in the enactment of protective regulations that serve the common good. To work hard at doing what they define as "good" becomes as important now as it was to work hard at earning a living in Stage Two.

Missionary attitude leaders are action-oriented and demand immediate compliance from their staff. They expect excellence and self-direction. Although this style provides the power to initiate and sustain social causes, it results in great physical and emotional stress for both leaders and their staff. Breakdowns in health, communication, and relationships result when activists sacrifice themselves for the benefit of others and neglect their physical, emotional, and spiritual wellbeing. Exhausted and burned out, group members either rebel against the leader or leave missionary attitude organizations.

Classroom Curriculum

Inner Leader

Although outer-directed, missionary attitude leaders have moved a step closer to an awareness of their Inner Leader. Driven by an inner call to service, they take action that ensures all levels of society are served and protected. As activists, they are modern warriors with strong personalities. They are willing to sacrifice themselves for the benefit of others.

The push toward action-oriented leadership competes with a pull to look within. The rigidity of thought stemming from believing in a right versus wrong way leads to avoidance of examining their own thinking, behavior, and effect on others. They choose the outer call at the expense of exploring and developing their inner psychological and spiritual life and override their Inner Leader.

Soul Lessons

The opportunity for leaders to learn aspects of the soul lessons of vision, right relations, and analysis continues from the work ethic into the missionary attitude stage. Stage Three leaders bring forward the gifts of the work ethic stage, including the ability to realize their **vision** through organizations and productivity.

Stage Three leaders begin to learn the **analysis** soul lesson to determine the cause of a problem and its greatest point of leverage for change. Their tendency to polarize, however, inhibits their ability to truly perceive the whole. As they become willing to question their mental models, they are more able to see the whole and more skillfully apply analysis. Questioning mental models begins in this stage and flowers in Stage Five.

Having **right relations** is another important soul lesson in Stage Three. These leaders tend to fear contradiction of their reasoning and impose their will onto others, leaving no room for dialogue or differing opinions. These behaviors impact the effectiveness of relationships with group members who have joined their vision and with those they feel called to serve.

Feminine and Masculine Energies

✦ WOUNDING

Powerlessness, a major wound of the masculine and feminine energies, drives the motivations of leaders in the missionary attitude stage. They compensate for inner feelings of powerlessness by projecting outer power to convert others to their point of view.

Feelings of powerlessness derive from childhood experiences in which the basic needs to be loved and protected were threatened by abandonment. Abandonment, whether subtle or dramatic, represents helplessness, a loss of personal power. Without power, individuals cannot change their circumstance and move to a place of inner or outer safety. To be emotionally abandoned by the mother devastates a child and interferes with the development of the mother-bond. This bond is a spiritual one and represents a child's first clear image of the Divine. To be abandoned emotionally by the father, especially for a son, results in a deep emotional deprivation that can lead to the son's passivity and disconnection from his body and emotions.

Leaders become activists against an issue that they believe represents what caused their powerlessness, or they rebel against those people or ideas that they perceive as more powerful. They compensate for their inner powerlessness by becoming authoritative and forceful in order to prove to themselves that they are indeed powerful, or they are passive-aggressive in their leadership. Either way, they approach change through manipulation and imposing their will. They identify with their role and status because these give them the masculine power they did not receive from their fathers.

✦ HEALING AND SYNTHESIS

Healing progresses slowly when leaders in the third stage of soul development rigidly hold to their belief of right/wrong and good/bad. Such leaders do not easily move beyond a dualistic belief system. The only way they can experience a breakthrough is through humility, facing the truth of their rigid thought and the possibility that perhaps their worldview is not true after all. An experience of humility may come in the form of a personal crisis or a relationship with a trusted person who reflects true power to them. Once validated and secure, leaders no longer need to fight to secure their position of rightness or be manipulative. They are willing to participate in activist activities with compassion and without judgment.

Shadow of Leadership and Organizations

The shadow of Stage Three leaders is visible in the use of their positions of authority to convert others to their point of view. Because they and members of their organizations believe in duality, their desire to support one right way necessitates an equal desire to annihilate any opposing view. Leaders and members alike fear any contradiction of their reasoning and impose their will onto others, leaving no room for dialogue or differing opinions. This rigidity of thought leads to avoidance of examining their own thinking, behavior, and effect on others. They feel superior, resist acquiring new skills, and believe they do not make mistakes.

Leaders and organizations in this stage typically believe that they are responsible for demanding that others change.

Stage Three leaders and organizations compensate for inner feelings of powerlessness by projecting outer power; in other words, their psyche attempts to rebalance its energies through an opposite action. As such, they may punish or condemn anyone who acts out the behaviors they have forbidden in themselves, such as misuse of sex, power, and money. At the same time, they are vulnerable to acting out these "forbidden" activities themselves. They develop a strong persona at the expense of exploring and developing their inner psychological and spiritual life. This dichotomy results in severe stress on their psyche and health and a neglect of their family and relationships. They have strong tendencies toward martyrdom, suffering at the hands of those they serve in order to feel justified in their many sacrifices.

Leaders and organizations in this stage typically believe that they are responsible for demanding that others change. In the process of forcing change, they impose their will and disempower others. Because others will not bend to their will, leaders often become discouraged, depressed, and embittered. These prevailing negative emotions tend to cause the leader to swing between frenzied activity and exhaustion. Stage Three leaders and organizations believe they must focus on getting attention for their cause or change will not occur, rather than doing what they can do, doing it well, and trusting others to do the rest.

Challenges in the Aquarian Era

The Aquarian worldview of shared responsibility and cooperation will challenge the entrenched polarizing worldview of Piscean leaders and organizations in Stage Three. Having polarities questioned can destabilize the psyche and create a loss of certainty. A loss of certainty, for Stage Three, is equivalent to a loss of physical, psychological, and spiritual safety. Feeling exposed and unsafe, Stage Three leaders and organizations may be tempted to quickly find a means to return the world to their right/wrong worldview so that they feel secure once again.

Stage Four Leader: Wounded Healer

Leadership Style and Nature of Group Relationship

Although leaders in Stage Four have stepped closer to an awareness of their soul, they, like those in the previous three stages, continue to seek for wholeness in the outside world, this time in relationships. If only they had the perfect personal and work partner or the perfect family member or employee, they would be happy. Leaders in Stage Four sum up happiness by saying, "When I give to you, my needs are met. When I rescue you, I am rescued." The paradox of the leadership style of Stage Four leaders is that they look as if they are the givers, but often they are giving to get. They want to know they are worthy and that they are seen as helpful and kind. Although what they are seeking is self-serving, it is also an attempt to reach out and serve others.

Often serving as directors of self-help, human resource, social service, and spiritual groups, wounded healer leaders employ a style that prefers harmony, empathy, and communication in relationships. They are at ease with mobilizing people toward a vision and developing people for the future. Competence is important to Stage Four leaders and they become strong students of their craft. However, they can impose their will by expecting others to do what they have not applied to themselves.

Classroom Curriculum

Inner Leader

The inward call to the Soul becomes clearer in Stage Four. Inner Leaders call Stage Four leaders to become aware of their own needs and to care for them. In this way, leaders learn to give from a place of a full rather than empty vessel. Wounded healer leaders are ambivalent about receiving and ignore the call from their Inner Leader to receive through taking care of themselves. They help others by using their personal energy rather than the energy of the Soul. Eventually the overcare of others at the expense of their own wellbeing results in a depletion of energy and subsequent loss of motivation to help others. The Inner Leader's call to awaken to the Divine as the true source of energy often goes unheeded because leaders in this stage still believe they are the doers. They are unable to sustain a consistent spiritual practice because of their impatience and an unwillingness to look within.

Issues of self-care and interpersonal relationships grow to full expression by the end of the stage as an existential crisis.

Wounded healer leaders are typically impelled toward a fuller awakening by a personal crisis, the gift of which is to motivate them to look within for their true identity and stop seeking validation from others, work, and causes.

Soul Lessons

Right relations is the major soul lesson for leaders in the wounded healer stage. Having mastered many aspects of the **vision** and **analysis** soul lessons in the work ethic and missionary attitude stages, leaders bring forward into this stage their neglect of self-care of physical, emotional, and spiritual wellbeing and their lack of healthy boundaries with those they lead. Conflicted self-care and boundaries manifest behaviorally as fatigue, insecurity, isolation, discouragement, depression, and anger. The suppression and neglect of their inner life is often visible in behaviors that are controlling and impatient. These leaders often avoid addressing inappropriate behaviors in the workplace and foster ineffective interpersonal communications. Although these leaders may be dedicated people who genuinely want to help, unhealthy boundaries and lack of self-care taint their leadership and their service.

Issues of self-care and interpersonal relationships grow to full expression by the end of the stage as an existential crisis. Mental models begin to unravel and foretell the coming of another way to be in the world. Leaders face their demons and move into a readiness to learn how to be in proper relationship with themselves and with those they lead.

Feminine and Masculine Energies

✦ WOUNDING

Unhealthy boundaries define the major wounds of those in Stage Four. Whereas Stage Two is the stage in which the masculine wound fully manifests, Stage Four is the stage in which the wounds of the feminine are fully revealed. When the feminine is wounded, whether the leader is a woman or man, qualities of nurturing, mercy, forgiveness, and tenderness are degraded to overcare, high tolerance for inappropriate behavior, projection of blame, and imposition of will. These wounds manifest in leadership as a failure to see beyond appearances to how things truly are, a tendency to assume responsibility for another's happiness, and an inability to sort out what is one's own and what belongs to another.

Individuals carry their unresolved emotional issues from childhood into their leadership. A family history of rigid boundaries or no boundaries, or a childhood of emotional, verbal, physical, or sexual abuse, wounds the feminine. To survive, children adapt their behavior to an abusive adult and take actions that lessen the possibility of a dangerous confrontation. Children develop into people pleasers, focusing on the needs of others rather than themselves. They believe that doing this will protect them and others from harm. As leaders, they extend this protective behavior to their work relationships.

✦ HEALING AND SYNTHESIS

The transition from Stage Four to Stage Five heralds the beginning of the leader's healing of the feminine wound of Stage Four (unhealthy boundaries) and the masculine wound of Stage Two (self-worth). This transition typically occurs between the ages of thirty-five and fifty as a significant crisis of personal identity and life purpose. This crisis signals a psychological readiness to redirect outward-focused energies inward. Every belief about the meaning of life and the relationship between head (masculine) and heart (feminine) stands ready for review and challenge. An intense inner upheaval and disorientation accompanied by a sense of urgency characterizes this death and rebirthing process. Leaders begin an intense period of personal growth and healing. They now make a commitment to their wholeness, the integration of all parts of self—physical, mental, emotional, and spiritual—and to the synthesis of their feminine and masculine energies.

Leaders in this transition benefit from examining their mental models by questioning beliefs, identifying areas of unfinished business, and exploring codependency and boundary issues in personal and work relationships. This inventory assesses the self-deception they have engaged in using work, relationships, and addictions to meet their emotional needs. Transpersonal psychological approaches, including depth psychology and metaphysics, are useful during this transition and throughout Stage Five: Healing the Healer. Exploring a deeper spiritual dimension to life within both Eastern and Western traditions is also beneficial. For purposes of encouragement and sharing of information and experience, leaders profit from being in the company of others engaged in a similar transition.

Shadow of Leadership and Organizations

Shadow issues involving boundaries and codependency abound for Stage Four leaders. Their relationships are fraught with expectations and dependencies. They feel betrayed and abandoned when their emotional needs are not met and project blame onto others, including those they serve. They do not integrate intellectual knowledge and experiential wisdom into daily life, although they expect others to do so. For example, they refer others for therapy, but rarely ask for help for themselves, or recommend daily meditation, but do not have their own spiritual practice. They may also have rigid boundaries and compartmentalize their lives by walling off experiences from one another. They fear being totally known and so may have different friends for each separate role or interest. Their friends may not know one another or about other aspects of the leader's life. As a result, the life of the wounded healer leader tends to be sectioned into separate boxes of experiences, rather than a whole with a continuity of feelings and events.

Leaders may never question their action if it brings the result they want, even if it is neither wise nor honorable.

Because Stage Four leaders are unaware of their true feelings, they are unable to discern the highest good in a given situation. They unconsciously camouflage truth with manipulative words to get the result they want. Leaders may never question their action if it brings the result they want, even if it is neither wise nor honorable. For example, a wounded healer leader may say "yes" to a team's request in order to feel accepted and generous and to make the team members happy. Later, the leader may realize that the best answer for the team and the organization would have been to say "no." Politicians manipulate the truth to play the game to win and diplomats call such manipulation "tact." The business world calls it "good marketing." When this behavior is rewarded over time, it becomes ingrained and even addictive.

Stage Four leaders approach feelings of inadequacy by seeking answers in yet another training, book, or system of knowledge. Such leaders and their organizations resolve inner conflict by helping others. Unfortunately, leaders expect their members to follow their example of serving at the expense of inner work and of attending to their self-care.

Many helping professions and self-help, human resource, religious, spiritual, and "new-thought" groups are in this stage. These organizations have unhealthy boundaries and codependency issues and often defend against receiving help with an attitude of "other people need it and we do not." Because members believe they can bypass inner work and self-care on behalf of the needs of others, they experience a high incidence of mental and physical burnout.

Challenges in the Aquarian Era

Leaders and organizations in the wounded healer stage will be challenged during the transition of the heart-centered Piscean Era (water sign) to that of the mind-centered Aquarian (air sign). As strong adherents to a heart-centered style of leadership, they will devalue the Aquarian air sign, viewing it as lacking emotional depth and practicality. Only when wounded healers begin to view the Aquarian era as bringing values of the heart to values of the mind can they strengthen their leadership competencies and succeed in developing and materializing ideas that serve others.

Because they prize the Piscean emphasis on individual needs and self-discovery and fear the loss of their individuality, members of wounded healer organizations will resist the Aquarian focus on the greater good of the group. Their boundary issues will vacillate between depending on the leader's authority and assuming self-responsibility for their own choices and inner knowing.

Unless women heal their feminine and masculine wounds, they will continue to hold back from assuming leadership roles. Choosing to hold back impedes the transformation of the Piscean model of parent/child, masculine-dominant leadership and group life to a partnership dynamic of group consciousness and balanced masculine and feminine relationships. The viability of Aquarian leaders and organizations depends on women and men reclaiming the feminine energy of relatedness and synthesis.

Conclusion

As leaders move on in their soul development, they bring the skills and wisdom they have gained from one stage into the next. As they progress in leadership, they naturally integrate skills and styles learned at previous levels, becoming increasingly adept at choosing which is most effective in the present situation. Three factors determine whether leaders remain at one level of soul development or continue to deepen their soul's learning:

- Readiness to evolve
- Ability to use crisis experiences as opportunities to learn and make new choices
- Willingness to transcend rigid ego structures that inhibit growth

In each stage of leadership, the level of soul development shapes leaders' worldview and affects their manner and style of leadership.

CHAPTER SIX
SOUL-INSPIRED LEADERSHIP: INNER-DIRECTED STAGES OF SOUL DEVELOPMENT

Introduction

Intense crisis periods of healing and soul growth occur during transitions into each of the three inner-directed stages. One crisis begins as a leader moves from Stage Four: Wounded Healer to Stage Five: Healing the Healer. Another crisis occurs when the leader moves from Stage Five to Stage Six, and the third when the leader dies and moves into Stage Seven. At each transition, leaders' understanding of organizational structures shifts. In the latter part of Stage Five and in Stage Six leaders incorporate relevant elements of both the Piscean hierarchical organizational model and the Aquarian holographic model.

The early Aquarian Era needs the strengths of both models. Although primarily operating from the holographic model, Stage Five leaders know when a hierarchical approach is appropriate. For example, in early stages of development, certain members or programs benefit from a leader telling them what to do as a step toward self-responsibility.

Great service can be accomplished when both the leader and group are aligned with Divine Purpose. Functioning as a conduit of energy from the higher planes to the group, leaders in Stages Five and Six help group members emanate energy from their hearts. Once heart energy is distributed throughout the group, the group can more easily stay on purpose for the greater good of the whole. The group's consciousness is then aligned with a collective, group-centered way of being and living in the world.

Table 8: Comparison of Two Models of Organizations

Hierarchical (Piscean)	Holographic (Aquarian)
An organization in which the vision is determined by a top level of leadership, and members create programs and perform tasks without necessarily sharing the vision or having knowledge of the organization's overall philosophy	An organization in which the vision is shared by all members so that the philosophy of the whole is reflected in every program and task, from creative design to administration
Strategic plan that is product oriented with goals and objectives	Fluid organic process of seeing the desired whole and letting the process unfold
Rational approach	Intuitive approach
I have the answers and solutions	Learning comes from attitude of "don't know"
Wants advice and direction	Wants to be self-responsible and empowered
Predominately masculine	Both feminine and masculine
Rules and regulations	Creative and open-ended
Problem is person based	Problem is systems based
Immediate gratification	Delayed gratification
Unconscious projections	Projections are conscious

Together, leaders and groups create a magnetic impulse that reaches upwards to high beings who watch over humanity and extend Light into our struggling world.

Stage Five Leader: Healing the Healer

Leadership Style and Nature of Group Relationship

As leaders enter Stage Five, they make a commitment to wholeness, the integration of all parts of the self—physical, mental, emotional, and spiritual. They use the Universal Laws of Service on page 163 and apply the Universal Tributes and their tenets on pages 165 - 175 to their personal and work lives. Development in this stage is a long process because it involves undoing the mental models of the previous four stages while creating a new reality.

Aquarian values of cooperation and teamwork are visible in the leadership styles of Stage Five leaders. For example, Aquarian leadership supports the efforts of group members to own their inner authority, engage in shared decision making, and share responsibility for the growth and wellbeing of other members and the group. Aquarian leaders use flexible styles when their organization needs to adjust to the unexpected. When appropriate, they call upon styles preferred in earlier stages such as the authoritarian style of Stage Two required to ameliorate a crisis. Motivated to master self-awareness, self-management, social awareness, and social skill, leaders are able to set aside their personal agendas for a larger purpose than themselves. They lead with efficiency, organization, and vision and are the glue that holds teams and the organization together.

Aquarian teams recognize and accept the leader's role. Like the leader, Aquarian teams focus on a purpose greater than themselves. They, too, set aside their personal agendas so their personalities do not interfere with the vision and mission of the tasks. The leader and team members respect one another for the varied areas of expertise each exhibits. Teams engage in free-flowing relationships that allow problems to be solved with cooperation and creative ideas to emerge from anyone on the team or in the organization.

Stage Five leaders exist in any setting but are most often directors of personal growth, spiritual, humanitarian, and social service organizations, and, at times, work ethic and activist groups. If deemed appropriate, three Aquarian leaders in an organization can choose to join to form an energetic triangle of tri-leadership in order to share leadership and management responsibilities.

Classroom Curriculum

Inner Leader

Leaders in this stage make significant progress in self-transformation through service. They now have the willingness and maturity to enter the uncharted territory of their psychological and spiritual natures. Experience gleaned from previous stages has prepared them to cross the evolutionary threshold from being outer-directed to inner-directed. They begin to move out of dualistic thinking and behavior into nondualistic energy. No longer searching outside themselves for their right "to be," they turn inward and begin the journey of actualizing their soul's destiny. Their focus now is to become more sensitive to their Inner Leader. Alignment with Source generates the inspiration and energy necessary to express the uniqueness of their soul's destiny.

In the later phases of this stage, leaders sense a nondualistic or wholeness reality, known in depth psychology as *creative synthesis.* In the same way that they begin to view their personal healing and service as a single impulse, they begin to experience the energies of the masculine (mind) and feminine (heart) in partnership as one energy. They are on the cusp of achieving creative synthesis when they enter Stage Six: Selfless Action.

Soul Lessons

Leaders make remarkable progress in mastering the soul lessons of leadership throughout Stage Five. The fruits of commitment to their psychological and spiritual wellbeing become increasingly visible in each of the five soul lessons: vision, right relations, analysis, synthesis, and to stand alone.

Communicating the holographic nature of an organization is a central function of Stage Five leadership.

In this stage, leaders understand **vision** as a *hologram*—a three-dimensional image created by interacting light sources with each individual part containing the entire image within it, although each from a slightly different perspective. The holographic nature of vision supports systems thinking—the discipline of recognizing the interconnections between the parts of a system and synthesizing them into a unified view of the whole.

Communicating the holographic nature of an organization is a central function of Stage Five leadership. The hologram of an organization represents a synthesis of the totality of the organization—its purpose, shared vision, mission, and philosophy. Regardless of the roles they play, members of an organization have different perspectives of the hologram. These perspectives are honored when members contribute in the shared decision-making process. Leaders learn how to recognize the complexity that arises from these perspectives, knowing that members cannot see what they do not understand. Leaders learn that members can share the vision yet differ widely in their perspective of the vision. For example, some members experience the hologram of the organization through the eyes of management or the duties of a particular department, others from the aspect of a program participant or a workshop teacher. Regardless of the perspective a member has, he or she recognizes that it embodies the totality of the organization's purpose, vision, mission, and philosophy.

The hologram of an organization can also be viewed from the perspective of customers or clients. When clients attend a workshop, for example, they experience the hologram of the organization by how the workshop is designed and how it is taught.

The challenge of Stage Five leaders is to engage wisdom and intuition in order to maximize the talents of members with diverse levels of readiness and understanding. For example, leaders intuit which people are appropriate for what projects and who would work well together on a team.

Stage Five leaders practice the soul lesson of **right relations** by modeling healthy boundaries, self-responsibility, and self-care for members of their organizations. They consider every encounter in their leadership as a reflection of their inner state. To them, every interaction is an opportunity to look within to find both their obstacles and strengths for their psychological and spiritual growth. Although they may use different terminology to articulate this knowledge, Stage Five leaders understand:

- the nature of the human psyche
- the pervasive role the shadow plays in the organization
- the way the leader's shadow impacts others
- how the shadows of others impact the leader
- the true partnership between leaders and those they lead

Within each organizational system are interrelated structures. For example, a department of human services is a system having structures such as hiring policies and employee evaluation procedures. Progress in **analysis** is evidenced when a leader can establish and maintain structures and simultaneously engage systems thinking to evaluate a system's effectiveness. With greater consciousness, they move their leadership into creative synthesis. They develop sensitivity to energy and learn how to use *double vision*, the ability to see the reality of a situation while simultaneously seeing beyond it to its spiritual essence. They maintain a holographic organization, recognizing that each person, role, task, and activity reflects a **synthesis** of the whole.

By the end of Stage Five, leaders have made significant strides in learning **to stand alone** in their true identity regardless of the challenges they experience in their leadership. Only in Stage Six when they fully master the lessons of vision, right relations, analysis, and synthesis, are leaders able to stand alone with a soul-infused personality.

Feminine and Masculine Energies

✦ WOUNDING

The awareness of the depth and extent of feminine and masculine wounds is recognized, understood, and healed in Stage Five. Any unhealed wounds from previous stages rise to consciousness from the unconscious as leaders address their mental models and the behaviors those provoke. Not until the wounds are addressed can the feminine and masculine energies begin to relate to one another and synthesize in wholeness. When women or men find

The separation within the psyche of developing the mind and not the heart can cause leaders to build a wall around their hearts and be untouched by the pain and suffering of others.

wholeness in themselves, they no longer depend on external women or men to feel complete.

Whereas masculine energies relate to capacities of the mind, feminine energies relate to those of the heart. These energies are not gender related but reside within every human being, male and female. When these energies work in partnership, the human psyche is integrated.

Wounding of masculine and feminine energies occurs when individuals develop capacities of the mind and ignore those of the heart, or develop the heart and ignore the mind. In each instance the function of the mind or heart is over- or underdeveloped. Priority is given to the mind rather than the heart in Stages Two and Three, and to the heart rather than the mind in Stages One and Four.

According to Torkom Saraydarian, when people overdevelop the mind and dismiss the heart, they tend to equate having knowledge, position, and possessions with success and prosperity. Professions that foster this preference include scientists, technicians, physicians, economists, lawyers, business executives, politicians, legislators, and educators. The separation within the psyche of developing the mind and not the heart can cause leaders to build a wall around their hearts and be untouched by the pain and suffering of others. Leaders who close their hearts dismiss the higher, divine nature of life and manipulate and exploit others through domination and force of will. Psychologist and psychosynthesis founder Roberto Assagioli writes that the will-to-good, the heart, must accompany the will to be competent and develop skills. Leaving the heart out of the

Men grieve not having had a positive masculine energy mirrored to them by their father. They unconsciously know this is the root cause of their emptiness and subsequent lack of self-confidence in many areas of their life.

equation results in conflicts, wars, materialism, and crime.

When individuals overdevelop the heart and dismiss the mind, they lose their sense of individuality and self-esteem. Their emotions become diffuse and confusing because they fail to use the mind to clearly define their emotions. As leaders, they inadvertently make others dependent on them, develop pride in sacrificing themselves for others, or become all-agreeing. Giving from the heart without calling on the mind for discernment and discrimination engenders "blind love" that results in energy drain and unhealthy boundaries. The energy of love must be applied with intelligence. Just as the mind needs the heart to avoid harm, the heart needs the mind to question and analyze the situation and wisely choose the action. When leaders develop heart over mind, they also become vulnerable to being dominated by those with strong intellects and wills.

In American culture, knowledge, industry, science, and technology take precedence over the heart, resulting in masses of people being overly influenced and manipulated by the opinions and biases of developed minds. The combination of underdeveloped heart and overdeveloped mind inhibits the will-to-good. Likewise, heart-infused visionaries with underdeveloped minds are unable to actualize their visions.

According to Richard Rohr, a major wounding of the masculine results from the failure of fathers to transfer positive masculine energy to their sons. Over time, the absence of fathers modeling masculine energy for their sons creates an emptiness that men experience as loss of the ability to relate meaningfully in their personal relationships. They fail to intuitively read situations and people and to have confidence in their own judgments. They do not know how they feel, how to empathize, or how to cry. Although Rohr acknowledges that men often express their frustrations through anger, underneath the anger is unresolved grief. Men grieve not having had a positive masculine energy mirrored to them by their father. They unconsciously know this is the root cause of their emptiness and subsequent lack of self-confidence in many areas of their life.

A primary wound of the feminine is the message of inferiority that comes from an internalized patriarchy or negative masculine. The debasement of the feminine and elevation of the masculine reflects cultural values of the Piscean Era that have been absorbed by both women and men. The negative masculine and its impact on women has been explored and documented by many scholars, including Marion Woodman, Jean Bolen, Robert Johnson, and Sue Monk Kidd. Psychotherapist Anne Wilson Schaef speaks of this wound as "the original sin of being born female." In her book *Women's Reality: An Emerging Female System in a White Male Society*, she writes, "To be born female in this culture means that you are born 'tainted,' that there is something intrinsically wrong with you that you can never change, that your birthright is one of innate inferiority. I am not implying that this must remain so. I do believe that we must know this and understand it as a given before it can be worked through." The wound of women's innate inferiority lies buried so deep in the unconscious that the majority of both genders do not recognize it.

✦ HEALING AND SYNTHESIS

To arrive at creative synthesis, leaders in this stage address, reconcile, and heal the depth of masculine and feminine wounds. They recognize the wound and move beyond feeling victimized by naming the truth of the victimization, working with it, and moving into their true inner power. Willingness and patience are required of those who delve into self-examination, inner work, and the unknown that lies ahead.

Two riveting questions emerge and direct a leader's healing and evolutionary passage:

- How do I welcome and express the joining of practical, mind-centered capacities and heart-centered behaviors in my personal, work, and leadership life?

- What new ways of being and doing will emerge as I move into wholeness and into a synthesis of feminine and masculine energies?

Facing the truth of undercare of self and overcare of others begins the healing of the feminine (heart) in this stage, whereas confronting the addictions of work begin the healing of the masculine (mind). Higher aspects of heart cannot be developed without the development of the mind. Leaders should pay particular attention to a feeling that heart and mind are competing for power and influence in decision making or that the heart needs protection from attacks of reasoning and rationalization.

Leaders develop the heart through self-education about its psychological and energetic function and by:

- Courageous and fearless service to all sentient beings and the natural world to deepen and expand compassion
- Daily meditation, prayer, worship, and devotion to Divine Source done with and in the heart
- Appropriate boundaries and communication in relationships

Leaders develop the mind with:

- Education, study, and scientific thinking—particularly in the areas of physics, chemistry, mathematics, history, and politics
- Work ethic competencies, duties, responsibilities, and roles

To identify and acknowledge the existence of the feminine wound, women leaders at Stage Five recognize that their unconscious has been programmed by values, teachings, and practices in religion, media, work, school, and family. The unconscious mind is literal and accepts words in a concrete way. Repeated messages of closed opportunities, lowered expectations, reduced incomes, and minimal acknowledgment of the myriad contributions of women throughout history convey to females that they are unseen and "less than." Use of masculine pronouns to designate both genders impacts the self-esteem of women of all ages. To assume that women should know that they are included when only the male pronoun is used is a defense of the negative masculine against its fears of what will occur if the feminine is allowed to be an equal partner. Exclusive use of masculine pronouns for the Divine further wounds the feminine. Leaders in Stage Five know that God is neither masculine nor feminine. Use of names like Mother-Father God, Divine Source, Source, The Absolute, and All That Is alleviates the issue and advances understanding of the synthesis of feminine and masculine energies.

Shadow of Leadership and Organizations

Shadow issues of leaders typically match those of their organizations and vice versa. For this reason, leaders and members in Stage Five often share the primary shadow of this stage—spiritual pride. Both believe they have special powers, qualities, and talents to give, and they project weakness onto others. Often they are attached to outcome in order to prove their specialness. They can deny what remains unhealed in the shadow and become impatient for the rewards of their endurance and hard work.

Under stress, Stage Five leaders and their organizations tend to regress to previous stages. Unable to discern what is theirs to do or not to do, they revert to the unhealthy boundaries of Stage Four. These patterns include an inability to say no, taking things personally, and believing others have the power to take their peace away from them. Regression to Stage Three is evident in right/wrong polarization, pride, lapses of vigilance, and neglect of inner work and spiritual practice. Addiction to work, productivity, and competition characterize a regression to Stage Two.

Challenges in the Aquarian Era

The Aquarian Era invites leaders to shift their style, purpose, and form of leadership away from and into something different than that of the Piscean. Although leaders in Stage Five are open to Aquarian leadership, they can be overwhelmed by the extent of personal and professional growth needed to reinvent their leadership style to match Aquarian values. Merging with the new while letting go of the old is not an easy, fast, or comfortable transition.

During the transition, Stage Five leaders may experience polarities that destabilize the psyche and create a loss of certainty and safety. For example, receiving a negative projection that polarizes leadership into leader/no leader engenders feelings of isolation and abandonment.

The following feelings and experiences will also present challenges:

INCOMPETENCE

Experience: "I don't know how."

Feelings: confused, uncertain, unappreciated, unsupported

Triggered by the need to:

- Build a new holographic model of leadership and organizational design
- Implement, at a practical level, the shift from authority invested in leaders to individuals being led by their own inner knowing
- Transition from hierarchical decisions to shared decision making
- See the bigger picture in which equal care and consideration are given to humanity and nature, a win/win orientation to life
- Adapt to the rapidity of technological development and its impact on leadership and group relations
- Incorporate the positive legacy of Piscean leadership
- Adjust to the needs of the Millennial Generation
- Assess the effectiveness of unproven and untried approaches

LOSS OF CONTROL
Experience: "My authority is being challenged."
Feelings: overwhelmed, powerless, impatient, intolerant
Triggered by the need to:

- Shift away from being in power to allowing others to be empowered
- Cooperate rather than compete
- Temper the overemphasis on mental (air element) approaches and the negation of emotions (water element)
- Lead with the feminine and masculine energies in true partnership
- Increase tolerance for individuality

RESISTANCE
Experience: "I can't do it. Too much change is being asked of me."
Feelings: bereaved, isolated, disconnected, angry, self-absorbed
Triggered by the need to:

- Resolve grief and loss issues provoked by change
- Be loyal to the past and competent in the present
- Recognize the activation of spiritual pride and competition with other leaders
- Remain diligent with inner work and spiritual practice
- Believe that organizational structures are as important as they were in the Piscean

Spiritual Awakenings

Spiritual awakening is a way to describe Stage Five leaders' intense desire to wake up, rub their eyes, and stretch their limbs as they progress along their spiritual path. They are motivated to open to the influence of the Inner Leader in their life and in their leadership.

With self-effort, Stage Five leaders go beyond where they are presently to another level of expanded consciousness. They do this by undoing the belief system of the previous four stages. They engage in personal healing and are willing to look within and discover obstacles to the awareness of their true nature. They reclaim qualities that they have lost or disowned and begin to work with the concept of self-responsibility. Developing an awareness of the Witness Self, they observe without judgment and become proficient in self-inquiry. They know events and relationships mirror their inner reality and become increasingly aware of the power of thoughts, beliefs, and choices.

Service becomes a means of purification, providing opportunities to remove the obstacles to inner peace.

The undoing of the belief system that occurs in the first four stages leads to wholeness, also referred to as the integration of the personality. Conscious participation in personality integration begins when individuals become aware that their true identity is at the level of Soul—beyond the personality. As they move deeper into Stage Five, they consciously call forth and experience the presence of the Soul.

Stage Five leaders view service as an inherent part of the spiritual awakening process. Service becomes a means of purification, providing opportunities to remove the obstacles to inner peace. They choose to use each encounter as service and every service as a reflection of their inner state. Through this process, they understand that their state of mind is the foundation of their service and that service is a path to self-transformation.

Tri-Leadership: The Energy Triangle Model

Incorporating a three-person leadership model is one innovative way for Stage Five leaders to express the Aquarian values of cooperation, group consciousness, and shared decision making. A team of three—a triangle—can lead an organization, and leadership teams of three can lead departments, programs, and projects. Each person on the three-person leadership team can have two people assisting her or him, forming yet another triangle. Bonded in purpose, triangles branch off to form other triangles. For example, if each leader of the three-person triangle has two partners, there would be three additional triangles and six additional people, with a total of four triangles and nine people. Triangles can be replicated to meet the needs at all levels of an organization.

A three-leader team functions as an energetic unit, circulating three elements of Divine Energy—Light, Love, and Willpower—through the three linked focal points of the triangle. The Light element represents the knowledge, reason, skill, and problem-solving aspects of the masculine principle. The feminine qualities of intuition and cooperation are visible in the Love element. The Willpower element represents a synthesis of the masculine and feminine principles and serves as the needed driving force to overcome obstacles and pave new ways of cooperation. The spiritual energy of the triangle is dynamic, continuously moving throughout all activities and relationships, thereby increasing the energy circulating to the team and to the organization.

A successful triangle leadership is first possible at the level of soul development and personality integration of Stage Five. Leaders at this stage are able to use the leadership triangle as a classroom curriculum by setting aside personal interests on behalf of their service, promoting goodwill, building friendships that are a source of inspiration, and raising the level of group consciousness.

A leadership triangle in Stage Five performs all tasks in the spirit of service and maintains a holographic team and a holographic organization. All parts of the organization are in relationship with all other parts and

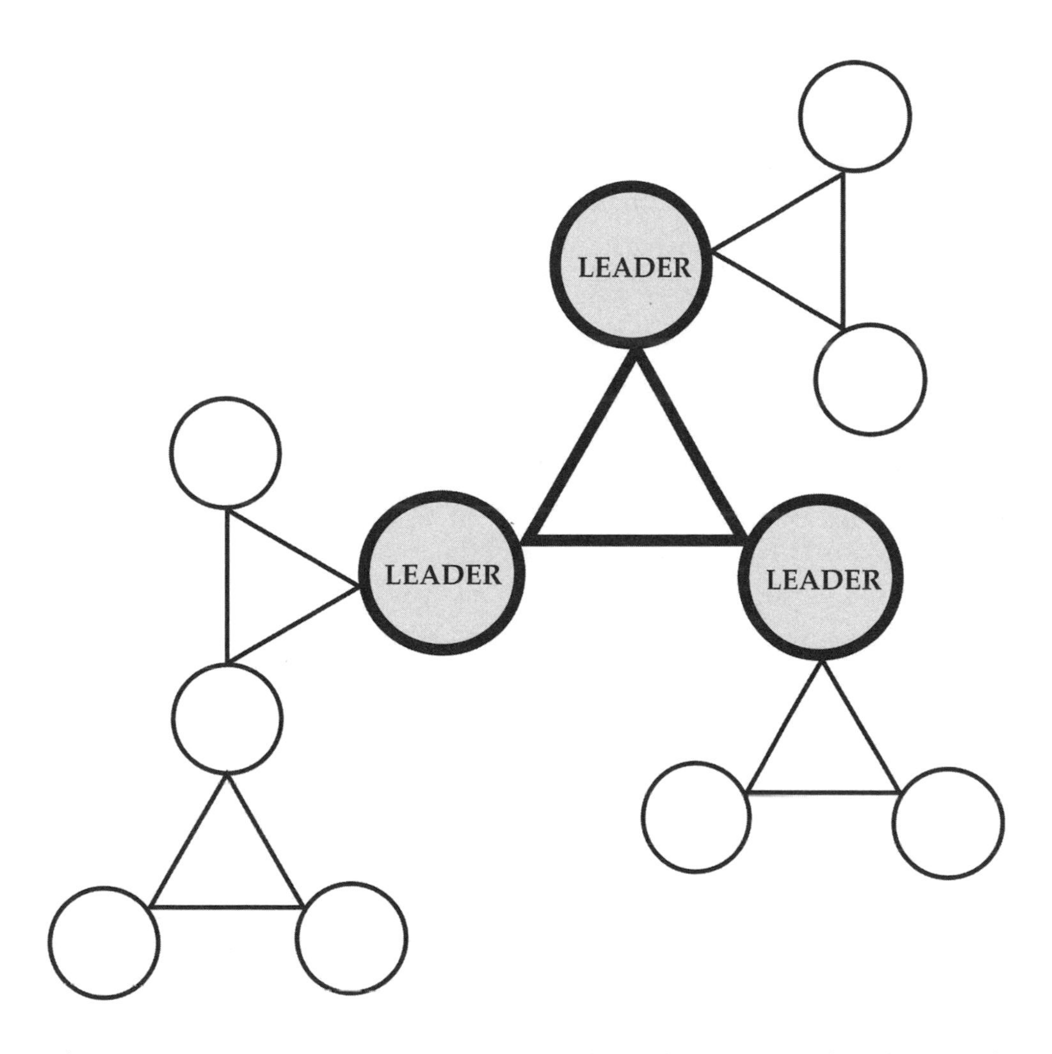

Figure 8: Tri-Leadership: The Energy Triangle Model *is formed when three people come together for a common purpose with the will-to-good. Interlinked triangles are formed when two additional people join one of the leaders. Exponentially, an infinite number of triangles can be created from the first triangle. The model shown is applied to tri-leadership, but it can apply to any purpose or task.* Drawing by Ginger Graziano

reflect the organization's vision, mission, and philosophy from different perspectives.

Transition to Stage Six

Only when leaders thoroughly live and practice the soul lessons of Stage Five are they prepared to move into Stage Six. Impetus to change reflects the soul's readiness to reveal more of its true destiny.

When and if it occurs, the onset of the transition to Stage Six begins between midlife and elder years as a crisis of liberation from attachments. This crisis is accompanied by a surrender of safe and defined opinions, accomplishments, careers, and living styles. The process of eliminating or detaching from outer and inner distractions challenges the stability of leaders' inner reality. Stripping away the unnecessary can feel like an extreme loss of identity and clarity. While searching for wholeness and intimacy with the Divine, leaders can fall into a "dark night of the soul." During a dark night, persons transform at the soul level and are liberated from attachments. They emerge from the darkness with a deep trust of their relationship with the Divine. Placing all matters in the care of Source, they obey their inner direction and the form it takes regardless of criticism or rejection from family, friends, and coworkers.

Stage Six life is completely centered in wholeness. The personality is now infused with the Inner Leader and all actions benefit the greater good. This union with the Divine releases an extraordinary creativity into the world.

Stage Six Leader: Selfless Action

Leadership Style and Nature of Group Relationship

Stage Six leaders, identified here as mystics, live a life of selfless action. With their spiritual eyes open, their single vision is to find their way back to the Oneness from which they came. The path to full realization of this stage is arduous, requiring years of sustaining a spiritual practice while undoing the obstacles to the presence of the Divine within.

In contrast to earlier stages, those in Stage Six no longer hold an ego-based, black/white view of the world or seek their identity in achievements, relationships, work, or causes. Their language and lifestyle are humble, offered from a place of being rather than doing. Because they value the ordinary, insignificance is what matters and not fantasies of power and fame.

Compared to those in previous stages whose service is oriented to benefiting individuals or groups, those in Stage Six are capable of loving all sentient beings and the natural world simultaneously. They experience Divine Love and are willing to extend that love unconditionally to others. They know that the more they love, the more they can love. As mystics, they see the Divine as nameless and neither masculine nor feminine.

Through a faculty of expanded perception, Stage Six leaders "see" others' obstacles to spiritual growth. They intuitively know the appropriate words to say and actions to take to assist group members with their next step in soul development. Mystics simultaneously see the cause, the effect of the cause, and the solution of a member's physical, emotional, mental, and spiritual condition.

Leaders in Stage Six rely on solitude, silence, and contemplation to unite with their Inner Leader and to give meaning to life and refine their inner growth.

The presence of Stage Six leaders is healing. They have arrived at or are attaining the status of what Buddhists call *bodhisattvas*, people who have extinguished desire and individual consciousness, yet choose to return to Earth to serve others until all beings have achieved enlightenment. Bodhisattvas vow that as long as sentient beings exist, they will return in order to serve.

Stage Six leaders are not readily visible. Their leadership style is to do their work quietly without fanfare even when their work involves being in the public arena as a teacher or an activist. Their humility is pure. They have no need to speak of their inner state as being one of selfless action. Leaders in this stage can effectively engage all leadership styles and have developed self-awareness, self-management, social awareness, and social skill. They support right action and shared decision making by living and leading with precision, respect, and presence. Every action in leadership is a service to the true essence within themselves and others, and an acknowledgment of love for humanity.

Stage Six leaders ceaselessly practice saying and doing the right thing at the right time for the right reason and in the right way to help raise the level of spiritual vibration of group members.

Classroom Curriculum

Inner Leader

Leaders in Stage Six rely on solitude, silence, and contemplation to unite with their Inner Leader and to give meaning to life and refine their inner growth. This ongoing spiritual process liberates them from attachments and compulsions that bind them to relationships, possessions, beliefs, and daily routines. The realization that they are not separate from Source allows them to recognize their own inner beauty and express creative and practical service. They surrender to the Eternal Dharma of right living and to their dharma or duty in the world. Because they are unattached to the fruits of action, the uniqueness of their personality becomes a conduit of the expression of Source. They lead selflessly on behalf of the spiritual wellbeing and growth of others, intuitively aware of what is and is not needed. In this way, their leadership is an act of devotion, characterized by effortlessness and synchronistic events.

Mystics live an impersonal life. Standing in Divine Light, they emanate a spontaneous and ceaseless vibration of joy and peace. David Hawkins writes in his book *Power vs. Force: The Hidden Determinants of Human Behavior* that "a capacity for enormous patience and the persistence of a positive attitude in the face of prolonged adversity" characterizes the energy field of mystics and advanced spiritual students and healers.

Self-effort and Divine Grace allow mystics to surrender into a state of complete safety and comfort in not knowing. This is the state of emptiness, that state of Oneness in which nothing material clings, that state in which only awareness exists. Guidance and protection from the higher realms support the safe transition into the finer vibrations of this stage.

Soul Lessons

Leaders in Stage Six master the soul lessons of vision, right relations, analysis, and synthesis and are prepared to live the lesson **to stand alone**. They glean wisdom from firsthand experiences of leadership and from attending to their inner lives. With focused attention, they seek to understand and integrate the meaning of their leadership experiences and to express the learning from those experiences in ways others can understand. Thcy honor and learn from the inner lives of those they lead and participate with attentiveness in team and group struggles.

Aligned with Source, Stage Six leaders recognize the different psychological and spiritual needs of those in their groups. With wisdom and intuition, they guide the spiritual development of others, knowing what to say or do to facilitate the growth of their group members in the context of the bigger picture of life. Stage Six leaders ceaselessly practice saying and doing the right thing at the right time for the right reason and in the right way to help raise the level of spiritual vibration of group members.

Mystic leaders see the truth of wholeness and cohesiveness beyond the dualities of life—truth that unifies the joys and the sorrows, the masculine and the feminine, work and play, sickness and health, success and failure, birth and death. They prefer to "work-play" above all else and have no need to use work to gain status or to engage in recreational activities to relax or feel good. They have a profound, passionate, and selfless feeling about their "work." They live life in the present moment, the Now that embodies the energy of Source. They engage in what author and researcher Duane Elgin calls "voluntary simplicity," a life that is inwardly rich and outwardly simple.

They live, serve, and lead with certainty of their divinity. Competent, flexible, precise, and joyful, they are leaders who are also poets, storytellers, artists, intuitives, creative thinkers, and inventors. Their inner spiritual vessel is continuously full and ever increasing in power and purity. Like an endless river of spiritual nectar, the more Divine Energy that flows out, the more flows in, and the more that flows in, the more flows out. They can control how much energy flows and where it flows as directed by Source. They have moved to full awareness of their true identity in Source and, divinely inspired, they experience union with Source and all creation.

Feminine and Masculine Energies

✦ WOUNDING

Entry into this stage necessitates having purified and relinquished any remaining wounds of the feminine and masculine energies. Throughout life to this point, serving others has functioned as a purifying agent for the ego's defensiveness. True Service is not tainted with ego needs.

✦ HEALING AND SYNTHESIS

Leaders who have assimilated the nutrients from multiple life experiences know who they are and stand firm in their authenticity. Their center is strong and their experience is an unobstructed and unending flow of Divine Energy. They act with inner authority and a new consciousness. Whether male or female, Stage Six leaders express the synthesis of masculine and feminine energies in which the mind and heart are equally developed.

Leaders who have developed both heart and mind view their leadership as combining knowledge with the application of that knowledge through experience. To accomplish this, they encourage education about and respect for healthy boundaries, support of continuous personal and professional development of members, and use of effective communication skills. The creative arts—painting, musical composition, writing, sculpting, and rhythmic movement and dance (especially sacred dance)—strengthen this integration.

Integration of mind and heart limits the degree to which leaders can be deceived, controlled, manipulated, and exploited. When their minds and hearts work together, leaders discern the larger picture and intuit the truth. A woman is whole when she has a true feminine center (heart) and an inner masculine partner (head). Conversely, when a man is integrated, he has a true masculine center (head) and an inner feminine partner (heart). Higher potentials of the mind and heart are evoked when they have parallel development, and the human soul enters the path of perfection, blooming day after day with light and beauty. The mind, heart, and Divine Presence work as a sacred trinity in the form of beauty, goodness, righteousness, will, love, and light. The wellbeing of the planet lies in the hands and with the voices of the minority of people with integrated hearts and minds.

Shadow of Leadership and Organizations

Although mystics have moved out of darkness, they do not forget or fail to recognize the nature and qualities of darkness. They understand that the more enlightened they become, the more vigilant they must be about their shadow side. They maintain this vigilance by acknowledging the nature of duality while standing in the place of creative synthesis. With this understanding, they become able guides and helpers to those who wish to move out of duality into full and complete awareness of Oneness.

Regression is also possible if mystics have not fully experienced and integrated all the lessons of their lives. If they have only partial understanding, they can believe themselves to be at a level of spiritual realization they have not yet attained. Denying weakness and priding themselves on spiritual attainments lead to relaxed vigilance and subsequent succumbing to the pull of sex, power, and money. A fall from grace or regression to a lower stage of spiritual development becomes possible if there is any failure to maintain vigilance or the spiritual disciplines upon which this level of spiritual vibration depends.

Stage Six organizations are rare in today's world. Such organizations would not speak of their inner state as being one of selfless action; their humility is pure. Similar to leaders in Stage Six, Stage Six organizations express their shadow when they relax their vigilance, neglecting their inner work and spiritual disciplines. Like leaders, organizations may succumb to shadow issues of sex, power, and money if they have not fully experienced and integrated all the soul lessons into their lives. They may deny weakness and be prideful of attainments.

Challenges in the Aquarian Era

Stage Six leaders face an unusual dilemma in the Aquarian Era if they become frustrated by not being able to communicate to others what is to

When Stage Six leaders remain authentic, they steadfastly live in a state of being that radiates their universal values.

them most sacred and real. Because their spiritual journey and its reality are misunderstood, they may appear to be inactive participants in the world.

Absorbed in their relationship with the Divine, their spiritual path and life activities are one and the same. As contemplatives, their work is "being life itself" rather than a specific career, job, or project. They live in Divine Presence, whether they are in solitude, engaging in daily activities, or relating to others. They reduce their involvement with the world of things and do not participate in obligatory and unsatisfying social activities.

When Stage Six leaders remain authentic, they steadfastly live in a state of being that radiates their universal values. The awakening of Aquarian values depends on their presence and the inspiration, strength, and will they exhibit in modeling the Golden Rule by allowing their deeds to flow from their being. Their choices illustrate their integrity.

Spiritual Awakenings

Stage Six leaders have easy access to their Soul for inspiration and guidance. The progressive unfoldment of their divine nature is clear. Stage Six leaders sense the true and special purpose of their lives and join the true path of service. Radiating love out into the world, they serve by showing humankind its divinity. They faithfully assist the masters on higher dimensions that oversee the evolution of humanity.

Tri-Leadership: The Energy Triangle Model

Stage Six leaders welcome participation in an Aquarian model of tri-leadership. Mystics find it easy and natural to join together to circulate Divine Energy of Love, Light, and Willpower for the benefit of a group, organization, project, or task. Because they live in Divine Presence at all times, their words and behavior reflect Oneness. In the company of other mystics, three people forming a leadership triangle move beyond duality to unity and exemplify true partnership with the feminine and masculine principles. They experience their work together as play.

Transition to Stage Seven

At death, people transition to Stage Seven: Beyond the Physical, regardless of their previous stage of soul development. During this shift, they must adapt to a reality on a dimension other than the physical. The need for healing from their life experiences and the vibration of their soul's light determines the nature of their transition and the reality in which the soul finds itself. Buddhist traditions refer to this passage as transiting the *bardos*, the vibrational levels of differing realities. The word "bardo" derives from the Tibetan words *bar* meaning "in between" and *do* meaning "marking point" or "island." As its healing progresses through the bardo states, the soul is energetically drawn to its soul group for continued learning and soul development.

Stage Seven: Beyond the Physical

The evolution of soul development and leadership continues after physical death. Leaders progress and move into higher vibrations and more expansive responsibilities. They are energetically attracted to soul groups that match their energies and interests, such as philosophy, peaceful coexistence, economics, education, health, the arts, family systems, or

High beings can more easily give energy, ideas, impressions, and direct communication if the human mind is free of distractions and sustains an attitude of surrender, trust, and self-forgetfulness.

practical application of spiritual principles.

The soul may choose to continue its development and eventually become a high being on the physical, metaphysical, or cosmic planes. High beings have different missions and are at various stages of awareness. Ageless Wisdom texts described high beings who serve humanity. Saraydarian writes that high beings give people thought impressions and transmit higher energies to those on Earth. High beings can more easily give energy, ideas, impressions, and direct communication if the human mind is free of distractions and sustains an attitude of surrender, trust, and self-forgetfulness.

As souls progress on Earth, they learn how to receive and serve directions from these higher planes. In the Aquarian Era, leaders and groups will advance to a level of consciousness that allows high beings to give them impressions and energy. It is possible to be in a physical body and to go to another dimension during sleep or a meditative state. At these vibratory levels, the soul can serve others on Earth or in another dimension or engage in study with its soul group. According to Saraydarian, "The more the world has such groups, the more contact the world will have with Higher Worlds and the more wisdom, knowledge, and blessings will pour into this world." Because permission from individual souls is required before the high beings can give thought impressions, humans maintain free will. Rather, they develop conscious cooperation with these beings. Souls become increasingly aligned with Divine Will. Divine Will or Will-to-Good then becomes their main motivation.

In-depth exploration of this topic is beyond the scope of this book but can be found in the writings of Edgar Cayce, Alice Bailey, Lucille Cedercrans, and Torkom Saraydarian.

Conclusion

Leaders in Stages Five, Six, and Seven stand strong in psychological and spiritual readiness to transition from a leadership style built on Piscean belief in the ascendancy of human life over nature, to a style built on the Aquarian belief in the interdependence of all things, sentient and insentient. With patience, leaders and groups engage in inner work to remove the obstacles to self-transformation through selfless service. They strive to rid their lives of rigid and imposed beliefs and to be guided by their inner knowing. In all life circumstances, they want to express their unique and best selves, that which is most sacred and good within them. Authenticity and wholeness, integrity and dignity, self-effort and grace, adaptability and intuitiveness serve as the nectar of their entire life. They desire to "be in the world, but not of it."

Guiding Principles for Aquarian Leadership and Group life

GUIDING PRINCIPLES FOR AQUARIAN LEADERSHIP AND GROUP LIFE

The Guiding Principles presented here are inherent in the evolutionary stages of service. This body of teachings contains universal truths received as inspired messages by the author while writing *The Soul and Service Trilogy*.

The **Universal Laws of Service** bring the soul's urge to serve into full expression. Practicing these laws supports the psychological and spiritual development of individuals and groups and brings learning, clarity, and greater ease to their life of service.

The **Universal Tributes and Tenets** guide those in Stage Five in actualizing the unity of inner work and service. They show how to shift thoughts, actions, and words in order to look within rather than without for wholeness, and they provide a road map for attaining self-transformation through service.

The **Universal Tributes of Mastery** delineate the shifts required during Stage Six as the individual or group moves from a dualistic choice of perception to one established in the absolute certainty of Oneness.

The **Universal Principles of Group Energy** specify the principles by which a group's vibration reveals how its members interrelate consciously and unconsciously. A group's stage of soul development conveys a unique energy, level of consciousness, and shadow.

The **Overarching Principles of Holographic Leadership and Group Life** represent the holographic nature of the philosophy and practices of the Aquarian values delineated in *The Soul and Service Trilogy*.

The **Spiritual Awakenings** delineate specific shifts in individual awareness and behavior required for the soul to move forward in its evolution through service. When a critical mass of individuals has made these shifts, the collective consciousness will evolve to the next evolutionary stage.

The Universal Laws of Service

1. **Law of Synchronicity**
   Through synchronicity, we are, seemingly "by accident" drawn to people who need us and/or whom we need. We thereby serve and are served by the universe with the right amount in the right way at the right time and in the right place. These "calls for help" are made at both conscious and unconscious levels. The more we align with this connectedness, the more often synchronistic events appear in our lives.
2. **Law of Dharma**
   How we serve and whom we serve are determined by our dharma; this law expresses the Divine's purpose, vision, and mission for us as individuals or as groups of individuals. A person has dharma, an organization has dharma, a country has dharma.
3. **Law of Omnipresence**
   Service pervades all of life; everything is service. At all times we are serving and being served. Who serves us is not necessarily whom we serve; how we serve is not necessarily how we are served.
4. **Law of Evolution**
   Service is a spiritual path with seven developmental stages. A person's developmental levels of service range from little or no inner awareness of the urge to serve to the mystic's inner state of selfless service.
5. **Law of Receiving**
   As vessels, we are full when we allow the Life Force to continuously flow through us. To give, we must first receive, accept, and integrate all that is given to us. We simultaneously receive and strengthen what we have given; we need to give to keep what we have received. Our ability to receive dies when we are not open to receiving.

6. **Law of Uniformity**
   Our service to another is simultaneously offered as a gift to the whole of humanity and the universe. This occurs because we share a collective unconscious.
7. **Law of Extension**
   We naturally become healers of that which we ourselves have been healed. The qualities of the healing energy we extend are specific to our own healing.
8. **Law of Agreement**
   This law suggests the possibility that prior to incarnation souls can choose to make commitments to serve by playing a particular role in another soul's life experience. Agreements may be between individual souls, between an individual and a group, or among groups of souls.
9. **Law of Transmutation**
   This law allows the energy of an initial negative experience or troubled state of mind to alchemically convert to the positive energy of learning and growth. This law also permits any experience, positive or negative, to stimulate the unfolding of new layers of understanding awareness.
10. **Law of Transcendence**
    We are served at a level of the soul that goes beyond human knowledge. An event can serve us at a conscious level as well as at an innermost and unconscious level. The soul experiences an event at a level separate from conscious awareness.

The Universal Tributes

TRIBUTE ONE: My life goal is to align my will with Divine Will and to increase the time I function in this state of Higher Knowing.

Tenets

1. Universal Will expresses Itself through my Transpersonal Will to my personal will; in this way, my life purpose and mission are manifestations of the Divine.
2. The clarity of the expression of Divine Will through my personal will is dependent upon my willingness to develop and strengthen my will through inner work.
3. Experiences of synchronicity and an increased sense of inner wellbeing provide feedback that Divine Will is expressing Itself through my personal will.
4. Because the energy and skill of the will are neutral and can be used for good or for harm, I am responsible for learning to use my will in a beneficent way.
5. The Witness Self and the will form the center of my consciousness; the Witness Self passively observes and the will actively selects, initiates, directs, or inhibits my thoughts, feelings, and actions.
6. Failure to develop and strengthen my will leads to a sense of meaninglessness and mental inertia and loss of the ability to make decisions and changes and to recognize and act upon intuition.
7. Continually developing and exercising the will throughout my lifetime leads to increased inner strength and greater certainty of my connection with the Divine when faced with challenges and responsibilities and when serving others.
8. A psychologically and spiritually healthy will selects, initiates, and carries out actions that serve the psychological and spiritual wellbeing of self and others.

TRIBUTE TWO: I know my chosen life's purpose is in alignment with a Higher Purpose for me when I am inspired and when I experience the joy, spontaneity, and gratitude of service.

Tenets

1. To live life fully, I ask myself in every moment: Why am I here? How am I to be? What am I to do? Who am I to do this with? Where am I to go?
2. I have been given a unique assignment by the Divine and, having accepted this function, I live my life with integrity, commitment, and gratitude.
3. When I am out of harmony with the Divine's purpose for me, I become attached to the material world and its tangible rewards.
4. To be inspired is to put the Divine first in my life, thereby aligning my will with Divine Will and fulfilling my assigned life purpose and mission.
5. To inspire is to be inspired.
6. The energy of the Divine is spontaneous because it is only in the moment that the highest good can be served.
7. It is not what I do in my life that matters but the love, joy, and gratitude with which I do it.
8. Experiences throughout my life, even when seemingly inconsequential, serve as stepping stones to the eventual fulfillment of my chosen life purpose.

TRIBUTE THREE: Divine Will works through me as me when I have no attachment to the form of the task and no expectations of outcome.

Tenets

1. The manner, style, and form of my service is unique to me because the Divine expresses Itself through the personality.
2. The "me" that the Divine works through reflects a soul engaged in a certain stage of spiritual unfoldment; this "me" has a unique psychological and spiritual history, both consciously and unconsciously lived.
3. I cannot decide for others what or how they use what is offered to them.
4. The level of my service is limited by identification with the suffering of others and by attachment to my beliefs and to the material world.
5. I am here solely to offer my service to others with the purest inner motivation possible.
6. When I offer service with no expectations of return or outcome, I simultaneously offer a psychological space in which the receiver can see and accept what is best for them in that moment.
7. No direct correlation exists between the form of service and the level of service; therefore, the highest level of service can be expressed in any action.
8. The quality of service offered is dependent upon the nature of the inner state of the one who serves; I need do nothing and yet perform the highest service.

TRIBUTE FOUR: By continually doing my inner work, I engender compassion for myself and others.

Tenets

1. Inner work is a moment-to-moment, day-after-day, year-after-year, lifelong commitment and process.
2. When I genuinely do my inner work, denied parts of myself reveal themselves for purposes of integration and purification.
3. While engaging in my inner work, I invite my higher consciousness to aid me in the purification of my lower consciousness.
4. The fruits of my inner work are reflected in the quality of my inner state and manifest in the world through selfless service.
5. Inner work is psychological and spiritual in nature; meditation, contemplation, and self-inquiry facilitate my process.
6. I cannot have compassion for another without first having compassion for myself; consciously striving to have compassion for others strengthens having compassion for myself.
7. To be compassionate means to observe, but not identify with, the suffering of myself and others.
8. Compassion and truth are two major spiritual gifts I offer to those I serve.

TRIBUTE FIVE: With honesty and kindness, I take responsibility for my own choices and allow others to do the same.

Tenets

1. The courage to heal, grow, and serve begins with being honest with myself about who I am and who I choose to become.
2. The wellbeing of myself and others depends on my ability to be honest without attack or condemnation.
3. Honesty asks that I speak the truth with compassion and self-responsibility.
4. I am free to choose my inner attitude regarding any given life circumstance; I can always choose again.
5. Once I choose again, I must do the inner work necessary to make that choice a reality.
6. I can only choose beliefs and attitudes for myself; I cannot choose them for another.
7. When I do not allow others to make their own choices or to take responsibility for themselves, I impose my will; by imposing my will, I disempower others, depriving them of the freedom of choice and the opportunity to discover their own uniqueness and their own inner strength.
8. I am responsible for the meaning and purpose I bring to my life and for choosing to learn and serve.

TRIBUTE SIX: I use each encounter as a reflection of either a remembrance of Divine Love or a grievance I continue to hold against myself or another.

Tenets

1. All individuals are students and teachers to each other; in this way, there is meaning and purpose in every encounter.
2. What I see in others is a reflection of what I see in myself; what I see in myself, I project onto others.
3. When I react instead of respond, I am experiencing a denied part of myself; my reactions serve to remind me to continue my inner work.
4. Reflections of Divine Love come to me in many forms and serve as witnesses for my true reality, reminding me that I am not alone.
5. The extent to which I recognize and use reflections of Love or grievances as part of my inner work is dependent upon my willingness to be self-responsible.
6. The energy of my psyche is restricted by grievances I hold against myself, thereby limiting my creativity and service.
7. I can hold the space for resolution of a grievance for someone else only when I have released that same grievance within myself. Therefore, I hold the space for healing in others of that which has been healed within me.
8. All encounters involve service at some level and therefore have the potential for bringing comfort or for being a catalyst for change.

TRIBUTE SEVEN: I acknowledge the reciprocal relationship between giving and receiving, understanding that both are essential for the wellbeing of myself and others.

Tenets

1. To receive and not to give results is an implosion of my energy, leading to narcissism and continued unmet needs.
2. To give while refusing to receive strengthens the arrogant belief that others are not worthy to give and that others, not I, need to receive.
3. I give to others by allowing myself to receive.
4. I am renewed and revitalized when I give selflessly; when I give, I am also being given to, I am receiving.
5. My experience of the outer world mirrors my inner beliefs concerning abundance and scarcity.
6. I am unconsciously giving and receiving all the time; the more conscious I am of the level on which I give and receive, the more helpful my giving and receiving is to the wellbeing of myself and others.
7. When I give, my energy moves outward and I manifest the fruits of my healing energy in the world.
8. Giving and receiving are human qualities that need nurturing and developing in early childhood and throughout life.

TRIBUTE EIGHT: I see the external reality of a situation as well as seeing beyond it to the personal lessons, inner strength, and spiritual essence of myself and others.

Tenets

1. Serving others requires double vision, simultaneously seeing the facts of a circumstance and its deeper spiritual meaning.
2. Double vision develops through meditation, prayer, contemplation, self-inquiry, and inner work.
3. Discernment is an essential aspect of double vision; I develop discernment as I integrate psychological and spiritual knowledge with wisdom gained from life experiences.
4. When responding to a situation, I honor the self-responsibility of the choices of those involved while ensuring their physical and emotional safety.
5. I do not deny a person's behavior; I strive to see the inner spiritual strength present in the person, although it may be temporarily inaccessible to them.
6. A spiritual essence is within all human beings; this essence is a manifestation of the spark of the Divine.
7. My responsibility in any situation is to remain focused on the condition of my inner state and my motivation for serving while simultaneously carrying out any action I am called to take.
8. My inner knowing determines how I respond in service in any situation.

TRIBUTE NINE: I support my healing process and that of others with patience, gentleness, and unconditional acceptance.

Tenets

1. Support is having a loving manner.
2. The healing process unfolds in five stages: choosing to heal, making the commitment to do inner work, exploring alternatives, letting the process unfold, and acknowledging growth and healing.
3. Patience provides a psychological and spiritual space for healing to occur with greater integrity and depth.
4. The degree to which I release expectations of outcome in any given situation is the degree to which I am unconditionally accepting.
5. Unconditional acceptance sees the spiritual essence beyond an individual's behavior.
6. Gentleness provides a psychological and spiritual space that allows old patterns and beliefs to be disentangled and released.
7. The presence of patience, gentleness, and unconditional acceptance lessens resistance to change and growth.
8. When I genuinely support and honor my own healing process, I simultaneously honor and support that of others.

TRIBUTE TEN: I accept the reality of the presence of Divine Love within my own mind and invite others to accept that same Love within themselves.

Tenets

1. Willingness to see differently results in recognizing that Divine Love resides in all minds.
2. Lack of self-love is the major obstacle to accepting the presence of Divine Love within myself.
3. Self-doubt keeps me from experiencing my true reality.
4. Accepting the presence of Divine Love within me is a prerequisite to accepting the presence of Divine Love in another.
5. Divine Love is reflected back to me from the loving mind of every person or living creature.
6. "To invite" is to provide a psychological and spiritual space in which persons feel emotionally safe to make new choices without fear of having my will imposed upon them.
7. In many ways and with different words, I practice inviting myself and others into the energy of Divine Love.
8. Naturally, with willingness and without effort, the energy expressed by my inner state extends to others my silent invitation to accept Divine Love. I have no expectations about when or if they will accept my offering.

The Universal Tributes for Mastery

TRIBUTE ONE: My will is an instrument of Divine Will.

TRIBUTE TWO: I serve with joy, spontaneity, and gratitude.

TRIBUTE THREE: I have no expectations or attachment to the form of my service or to the fruits of my actions.

TRIBUTE FOUR: I have compassion for all sentient beings.

TRIBUTE FIVE: I allow others to make choices using their will.

TRIBUTE SIX: I ceaselessly remember God's Love in all interactions.

TRIBUTE SEVEN: I experience giving and receiving as the same.

TRIBUTE EIGHT: I see beyond appearances to the Divine Love in others.

TRIBUTE NINE: I serve with patience, gentleness, and unconditionality.

TRIBUTE TEN: I am a reflection of God's Love.

The Universal Principles of Group Energy

PRINCIPLE ONE: Groups are living organisms whose nature is holographic.

PRINCIPLE TWO: The Group Soul oversees and guides the evolution of a group.

PRINCIPLE THREE: A disruption in the energy flow from the Group Soul to the group members causes group problems.

PRINCIPLE FOUR: Individuals are attracted to particular groups according to spiritual laws.

PRINCIPLE FIVE: To support the greater good of the group, members relinquish lower energy levels of consciousness for higher ones.

PRINCIPLE SIX: Individual groups form a collective consciousness that joins the collective consciousness of all of humanity and nature.

PRINCIPLE SEVEN: Groups fulfill their spiritual function when members master the skills and knowledge of cooperation.

PRINCIPLE EIGHT: The shared vision of a group is manifested through a synthesis of feminine and masculine energies.

PRINCIPLE NINE: Energy is the conveyor of the group's true message.

PRINCIPLE TEN: When one group member is healed, all are healed.

The Overarching Principles of Holographic Leadership and Group Life

PRINCIPLE ONE: Within the holographic field of an organization, a balance of giving and receiving provides opportunities for members and leaders to learn, grow, and serve.

PRINCIPLE TWO: As an organic and evolving system, the organization is made up of parts that are interconnected, interrelated, and interdependent.

PRINCIPLE THREE: Leaders and members generate visionary thinking, conscious intention, and right action through observation, listening, reflection, and inquiry.

PRINCIPLE FOUR: With inspiration and commitment, leaders and members join personal visions to form a shared vision.

PRINCIPLE FIVE: The organization evolves in stages that reveal the shared vision, its philosophy and application.

PRINCIPLE SIX: Willingly, the leader serves with integrity as a demonstration teacher and as steward of the vision.

PRINCIPLE SEVEN: Leaders and members cocreate a safe physical, emotional, and spiritual environment that supports the shared vision, its philosophy and application.

PRINCIPLE EIGHT: Members, regardless of role, view events, relationships, and reactions as learning opportunities for personal and spiritual growth.

PRINCIPLE NINE: Members coshare responsibility for the creation and well-being of the organization through participation, dialogue, shared decision making, and feedback with one another and with the leadership.

PRINCIPLE TEN: Persons in all roles endeavor to "walk their talk" by gleaning wisdom from experience and applying what they know.

The Spiritual Awakenings

AWAKENING ONE: The true source of equanimity is within.

AWAKENING TWO: The highest good for one includes the highest good for all.

AWAKENING THREE: Work and service are the same.

AWAKENING FOUR: The world is interconnected and nondual.

AWAKENING FIVE: True Sight sees the deeper spiritual meaning beyond appearances.

AWAKENING SIX: Answers lie on the level of cause.

AWAKENING SEVEN: Responses to life events are made from the Witness Self on the mental level.

AWAKENING EIGHT: True Service expresses in the world at all levels of participation.

AWAKENING NINE: True Service requires *being* service as well as being *of* service.

AWAKENING TEN: Personal will aligns with Divine Will to allow the unfolding of the destiny of collective will.

Part Three

Soul-Inspired Group Life

True Groups consist of members
who practice the Universal Principles
of Group Energy and whose consciousness
blends to form One Mind.

Susan S. Trout

CHAPTER SEVEN
FOUNDATIONS OF AQUARIAN GROUP LIFE

Introduction

The same stages of soul development exist for individuals, leaders, groups, organizations, and countries. An overarching group is called an organization. Within an organization, there are internal groups. There are also groups that are not within an organization. Soul levels exist for each organization and each group within an organization. An organization can move from stage to stage as a group. As the organization develops, individuals will join or leave depending on their vibrational alignment with the group. At minimum, members need to be attuned to the vision of the organization; they need not be at the same stage of soul development as the organization or its more advanced members.

As with leaders, groups evolve in a natural progression from little or no conscious awareness of their shared divinity to abiding in the Divine as a unified instrument of Divine Will. Readers are invited to review the stages of soul development in Chapter Four. Group members in the outer-directed Stages One through Four focus on meeting their individual personality needs and seeking value from something or someone in the group or outside in the world. Groups in Stages Five and Six are inner-directed. In Stage Five, group members strive to purify their obstacles to the awareness of Divine Presence and join together to practice service as self-transformation. Embodying a high vibration of the purest form, inner-directed Stage Six group members are committed to being instruments of Divine Will and devote their group life to selfless service. Groups in Stages Five and Six are called True Groups. True Groups consist of members who practice the Universal Principles of Group Energy and whose consciousness blends to form One Mind.

Group Life as a Classroom of the Soul: An Aquarian Curriculum

Advancement in understanding and evolving group consciousness has been seeded by Aquarian energies. Whereas the Piscean Era focused on authority invested in a leader, the Aquarian Era shifts its focus to the group, embracing the authority or inner knowing of the individual members through group cooperation and discovery.

Aquarian group life serves as a classroom of the soul for one purpose—to learn how to be in a group as an expression of higher consciousness rather than as an expression of the individual personality.

In the 1980s, astronomers and astrologers began writing about the convergence of the Piscean and Aquarian eras. Inspired by this information, futurists focused on exploring group consciousness and cooperation, the hallmarks of the Aquarian Era. As the forward-moving energy underlying the transition of the Piscean Era to the Aquarian intensified during the 1990s, an urgency arose to address group needs and challenges. A thorough study of history, religion, sociology, and spirituality, as well as a gathering of empirical data and research, revealed that with the exception of certain metaphysical writings, relatively little is known about the unique spiritual nature and struggles of group life during the transition or during the early years of the Aquarian Era.

Aquarian group life serves as a classroom of the soul for one purpose—to learn how to be in a group as an expression of higher consciousness rather than as an expression of the individual personality. When groups decide to engage wholeheartedly in the evolutionary process, they enroll in the unique curriculum of the soul classroom of group life. From a soul perspective, this curriculum includes: the stages of soul development, the Group Soul, the Universal Principles of Group Energy, group soul lessons, and challenges of the Aquarian Era. Groups in Stages Five and Six have two additions to the curriculum: the Energy Triangle Model and spiritual awakenings.

Group Soul

The Group Soul is the magnetic impulse that holds a group together in much the same way as the sun holds the planets in orbit. It guides, teaches, and protects each group just as an individual's Inner Leader guides, teaches, and protects each person. The ability of group members to receive and recognize impressions from the Group Soul is dependent upon the group's stage of soul development and its awareness of the Universal Principles of Group Energy.

The nature of the Group Soul's relationship to groups in the outer-directed stages of soul development differs from that of the inner-directed stages. Because outer-directed groups have yet to confront and heal their wounds, they are unaware of a Group Soul. They cannot set aside their personal agendas for the greater good of a group and are often unwilling to be self-responsible for their thoughts and behavior. They have yet to feel secure in their true spiritual identity.

The level of soul development of inner-directed groups enables members to experience the relationships among their personalities, their souls, and the Group Soul. If they have faced their psychological wounding, members are able to practice cooperation and engage in healing and spiri-

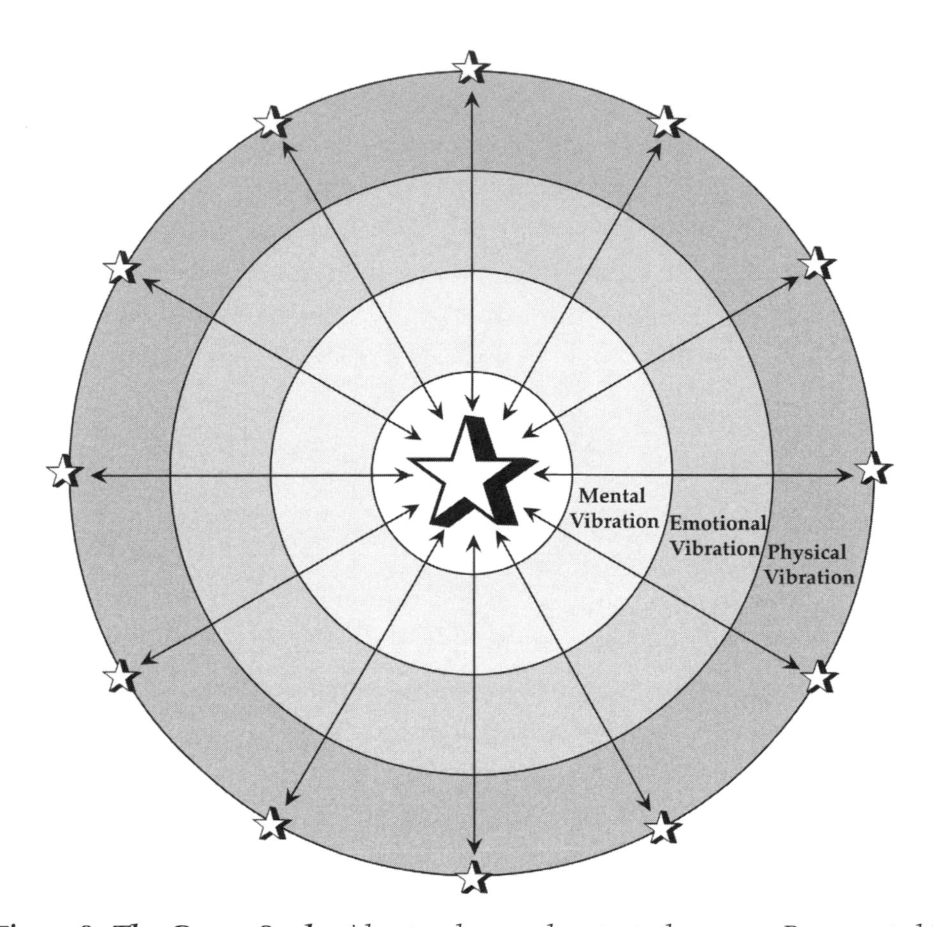

Figure 9. The Group Soul *guides, teaches, and protects the group. Represented in the drawing by the central star, It is aligned with Divine Source. The Group Soul communicates through the group personality, comprised of the collective physical, emotional, and mental vibrational bodies of the members. In turn, members, represented in the drawing by the small stars on the circumference, communicate with the Group Soul through their hearts (souls) and Souls. The lines of communication strengthen through intention and practice. The stronger they grow, the more conscious the group becomes. Healing, vision, and love increase within the group, which in turn allows the group to radiate these qualities outward in service. The power to manifest for the group good deepens and expands.* Drawing by Ginger Graziano

tual practices. Group members resonate with the Group Soul when they do their inner work and let go of ego-driven motivations and behaviors. The Group Soul can then express Itself through the group personality, which is comprised of the physical, emotional, and mental bodies of the members.

The spiritual goal of groups, like individuals, is to attain a soul-infused personality. A soul-infused personality allows members to more easily access the intuition received from the Group Soul on behalf of the greater good of the group. The Group Soul helps group members remember their true identity and move into group consciousness. Because the intent of the energy of conscious groups is to see beyond duality to unity, members sense an atmosphere that encourages growth, support, and healing.

Universal Principles of Group Energy

The vibration of any group reflects a synthesis of the Universal Principles of Group Energy. How members interrelate consciously and unconsciously with these principles reveals the nature and quality of a group's vibration. Each stage of soul development conveys a unique energy. A stage's level of consciousness, energy, and shadow determines the quality and nature of what a group believes and how it feels and acts.

Nearly every aspect of human life takes place at a group level, yet more information exists about the interactions within groups of animals, insects, and plants than about how human beings interact within their groups and with other groups. People spend most of their days in some sort of group setting at home, in school, or at work. In these varying settings, they experience different group energies. Even solitary tasks such as walking, shopping, or driving exist within a group context in which the energy is diffuse and focused mainly on individuals moving about within a group of people doing the same activity. Groups can be energetically joined regardless of where they are geographically, even though they may have different interests and motivations. For example, citizens of a country form a group made up of numerous and diverse racial, cultural, political, economic, and intellectual subgroups. Humanity is a collective group of global citizens residing in various nations. Human beings, animals, birds, and insects form a group identified as sentient beings.

Although the aforementioned groups have common purposes, metaphysicians do not consider them True Groups. True Groups, according to Saraydarian, consist of members whose collective consciousness forms One Mind. Members no longer see themselves as separate from other sentient beings or from nature. By learning the science and art of cooperation, they experience a connection to all existence, from individuals to the cosmos.

The Universal Principles of Group Energy, based on a synthesis of the author's work with groups and the writings of Roberto Assagioli, Alice Bailey, Lucille Cedercrans, Torkom Saraydarian, and Ludger Scholl, assist groups in identifying the nature of their energetic makeup, the quality of energetic flow, and the possible energetic obstacles and shadow.

⁂ *Principle One: Groups are living organisms whose nature is holographic.*

As living organisms, groups are in constant development. The creative tension between their current reality and what they are growing toward provides the needed energy to actualize their potential. Creative tension occurs when there is a gap between the desired goal of a group and the reality of where it presently stands in achieving this goal.

Groups are holographic in that they consist of a complex structure of interacting energies. Their interdependent and subordinate elements reflect the whole from different perspectives. Lucille Cedercrans, a teacher of Ageless Wisdom, uses the human body as an analogy to describe groups as living organisms. Each individual in a group represents an organ that is sep-

Just as a breakdown in the function of any one organ would affect the entire physical system of the body, the failure of individuals in a group to fulfill their functions disrupts the vitality needed to fulfill the group's purpose, vision, and mission.

arate in function yet mutually dependent on the function and wellbeing of the entire body. Cedercrans writes that the group leader represents the head and provides the will energy that enables a group to accomplish its purpose, vision, and mission. Some group members represent the heart. They bring love and wisdom into the group by balancing the will energies of the leader, fostering peace during conflict, and holding the group together. Other group members act as the throat of the group. They serve through public relations, bringing the group's work to the attention of the outer world. They foster right relations between the group and those outside the group. The leader as head and a few members who represent the heart and throat view the group from their perspectives and ensure that head, heart, and throat work together to bring the vision into manifestation.

Like any living organism, a group must face obstacles to its growth in a constructive and positive manner in order to survive and thrive. Working through challenges offers the gift of attaining a higher level of awareness. Just as a breakdown in the function of any one organ would affect the entire physical system of the body, the failure of individuals in a group to fulfill their functions disrupts the vitality needed to fulfill the group's purpose, vision, and mission. Groups, like bodies, sustain health when they learn which energies to use and which ones to reject or diffuse.

Just as all parts of the body are affected when the flow of energy is blocked in any one of its parts, an energetic block within one member impacts all members of a group. For example, when a group member is consistently late to meetings, trust is eroded, impeding the synergy of the group.

Each member brings previously acquired mental models, experiences, behaviors, skills, and knowledge into a group. These variables interrelate, interact with, and influence the group energy.

Prevalent variables regarding individuals in a group are:

- Mental models from individuals' First Group, their families of origin
- Attainment of inner work practices
- Knowledge and practice of healthy boundaries
- Commitment to regular spiritual practices
- Awareness of Group Soul
- Nature of previous experience with groups
- Knowledge about group life
- Stages of soul development

In the group context, these individual variables influence and are influenced by group variables, such as:

- Number of members
- Distribution of generations
- Distribution of ages
- Distribution of gender
- Distribution of preferred natural elements (Air, Water, Fire, and Earth)
- Distribution of feminine (heart) and masculine (head) energies
- Level of awareness of group soul lessons
- Level of awareness of group energies
- Level of awareness of group structures like an agenda, time limits, and communication guidelines

Groups thrive when their members thrive. The health of the group organism depends on the nature and interrelationship of the diverse variables and their energetic contributions. When members understand groups as living organisms, they are better able to serve and be served by the greater good of their group. The steadier the flow of energy maintained by group members, the more wisely the group works as a unit. A group functions as a system with its own life and is more than the sum of its members. Like its individual members, groups are born, grow, learn, envision, hope, decay, and die.

☼ *Principle Two: The Group Soul oversees and guides the evolution of a group.*

The Group Soul prompts groups to question what they need to master and what they need to give up. When a group knows what it needs to grow, it knows its next step and welcomes actions that will raise the group energy and move the group closer to attaining its purpose, vision, and mission.

The Group Soul guides the meaning and purpose of the group through inspiration and intuition, acknowledging that group members need meaningful and challenging experiences to grow and evolve. The Group Soul is only interested in the growth of consciousness within members. It cares about personality matters only to the extent that doing so serves the group's spiritual development. The ultimate spiritual goal or healing of a group is to fuse the group personality with the Group Soul. This fusion is achieved through meditation. Individual and communal meditation and a spiritual practice are essential if group members wish to receive intuition from the Universal Mind and join with the Group Soul to serve the greater good of the group.

Because groups are entities with lives of their own, they, like individuals, experience dark nights of the soul in which they are liberated from attachments and empowered to transition into deep trust of their relationship with the Divine. A communal dark night of the soul can occur when the group feels powerless and its work seems uninspired. Things are not as they once were and members feel adrift as they lose contact with the group's purpose,

One could describe the current transition of the Piscean Era into that of the Aquarian as a dark night of the world's Soul. The old is falling away.

vision, and mission. Group members may feel confused and unable to grasp what is happening and fail to uncover and correct the problem.

Psychiatrist Gerald May believed that a dark night of the soul can manifest in a group if its members come together longing for compassion and simplicity and want to awaken to their union with the Divine and all creation. In his view, the dark night signals a positive movement, although the experience feels problematic. Through the dark night, the Group Soul leads the group where it would not nor could not go on its own—to a place of greater freedom and love in which the group can be liberated from attachments that have kept it restrained.

One could describe the current transition of the Piscean Era into that of the Aquarian as a dark night of the world's Soul. The old is falling away. Many feel powerless and confused. Yet with the emergence of global awareness, group consciousness, and the joining of diverse groups, something is also going right. Led by its Soul, the world is going to a place it could not go on its own.

⁂ *Principle Three: A disruption in the energy flow from the Group Soul to the group members causes group problems.*

Being in a group confronts members' attachment to their individuality and their belief that they are separate from others and separate from Source. Projection, unhealthy boundaries, and failure to fulfill their function stem from this disruption of energy flow from the Group Soul. Like the unseen portion of an iceberg which exists under water, 90 percent of energies within a group operate at an unconscious level. These energies emanate from the shadows of the individuals and combine to form a group shadow. To develop full commitment to a group, members must focus on the deep layers of the iceberg and remove the energetic blockages. Personal inner work, therefore, is paramount to group work. By removing personality blockages and working with shadow issues, the Group Soul's energy can move into the group and bring about group consciousness.

The deepest layer of any group's unconscious shadow rests in the shadow of the members' First Group. Individual members are often unaware that they bring their experiences, unresolved issues, and attitudes about early relationships with parents, siblings, and other relatives into current groups. For example, individuals who experienced unhealthy boundaries in their family of origin will tend to develop codependent relationships within the current group. Additionally, members who have resisted healing their family wounds will resist removing personal blockages that interfere with meeting a group goal.

As in First Groups, personal problems can be projected onto individual members. In one instance, a member may react negatively to the behavior of another member because that person reminds him of a family member with whom he experienced conflict. If this projection becomes generalized, the person can become a scapegoat of the group. Sometimes, what appears as scapegoating is, in reality, a mismatch between an individual and the vision of the group. Discriminating between a mismatch and scapegoating is essential to healthy group functioning.

The individuals' shadows, arising from their First Groups, combine with their experience in subsequent groups and form a group shadow. The end result of combined shadows can be seen, for example, in a group that functions on a mental level and suppresses the emotional or physical. Such a group accumulates knowledge and philosophizes, rather than tending to their personal inner work.

❊ *Principle Four: Individuals are attracted to particular groups according to spiritual laws.*

People join, form, leave, and dissolve groups in a certain way at a certain time for a certain reason. Individuals may believe these choices and actions are conscious and logical. Viewed from a spiritual perspective, they make these choices at an unconscious level and are guided by their Souls to learn more about group consciousness. For example, a Soul might prompt a person to take a class for the single purpose of being introduced to the beginning concepts of spiritual growth or metaphysical teachings. This individual is meant to take a brief look at what may be coming into his or her life at a later time or even in another lifetime.

A group begins its formation first on an unconscious energetic level, which Ludger Scholl calls the group pregnancy. Those who are meant to join a certain group will be led by conscious and unconscious motivations and affected by a magnetic pull to join the group. He notes that most groups form out of a low vibrational magnetic pull, often from a motivation of fear. For example, a group may form out of a fear of not having their personal needs met. Members look to the group to reduce this fear by meeting their needs for friends or for an intimate partner. Scholl writes that, whereas most groups are presently born out of fear, the birth of spiritually inspired groups will increase, especially as the world moves more deeply into the Aquarian Era.

Principle Four operates in three ways. First, because of the energetic law that "like attracts like," individuals tend to join groups that match the resonance of their unconscious energy. Often this decision is from a level of intuition. Individuals may also be attracted at the personality or emotional level. The attraction may range from survival, as in twelve-step programs, to making friends or engaging in activism. As a group forms, the personalities of individual group members unite energetically to form a group personality.

A second way this principle manifests is when individuals seek a group with a higher resonance than their own. Their Souls may guide them to such a group for learning and development. Whereas initially their resonance is lower than the group's, over time their energy begins to match that of the group. Conversely, if individuals join a group for which they are mismatched—not energetically prepared—they may react by rejecting new ideas or attempt to destroy the group. The group often energetically rejects these individuals. Although this may appear to be a negative action from a spiritual perspective, the action protects the soul development of these individuals as well as that of the group.

At an entirely different level, groups of souls choose to incarnate at the same time in order to come together to fulfill a shared purpose.

The third way this principle functions is through a magnetic impulse that brings individuals into the group and sustains their participation. Their Souls attract those circumstances, people, and events that support their growth. Groups can be attracted to other groups in the same way. Diverse groups can also be brought together through a magnetic impulse.

At an entirely different level, groups of souls choose to incarnate at the same time in order to come together to fulfill a shared purpose. The soul bond of this group is so strong that members will be drawn together against what seem like great odds. A soul group of this nature is so deeply bonded by purpose that they transcend personality challenges and stay together until they accomplish their goal with cooperation, love, and understanding.

⁂ *Principle Five: To support the greater good of the group, members relinquish lower vibrational levels of consciousness for higher ones.*

The vitality or level of consciousness of any group is determined by the collective thoughts and feelings of group members. Because this energy is not static, it can develop into higher vibrational levels. The nearer their consciousness is to wholeness, the higher the group's vibration. If group members choose to grow and evolve and to reframe chaos into learning opportunities, the consciousness of the group progresses to purer vibrational levels.

Upon becoming a group member, individuality is relinquished to some degree, while talents, competencies, and creative capacities remain in place. Group members willingly assume different roles and responsibilities, such as taking minutes, sending reminders, networking, and attending to group alignment. Because individuals within a group have different levels of consciousness, they differ in what personal needs they need to relinquish. The lower the level of group consciousness, the more difficult it is for individuals to relinquish their personal needs for approval and achievement. As group members move into soul-personality integration, they give up these ego needs and focus on working together for the greater good of the group. Eventually, group members relinquish personal needs to fulfill the group's purpose.

When a group member dreams about a group or about the organization, the dream can alert the group to an unacknowledged obstacle or it can be a prophetic dream about the nature of future work.

Often, members experience intuitive awareness and dreams about the group's development. When a group member dreams about a group or about the organization, the dream can alert the group to an unacknowledged obstacle or it can be a prophetic dream about the nature of future work.

☼ *Principle Six: Individual groups form a collective consciousness that joins the collective consciousness of all of humanity and nature.*

Individual and group consciousness are part of Divine Mind. If the group has attained Stage Five or Stage Six of soul development, it can tap into Divine Mind and connect with the collective consciousness of humanity, with other species, and with nature. Such a group can emanate the vibrations of its energy field into the community, country, and world. Because more than one person or one group can receive the same transmission from Divine Mind, a new creative idea or development can arise spontaneously and simultaneously from individuals and groups in more than one city or country. Groups can communicate with other groups, including those of the animal and plant kingdom. Vibrational communication of this nature brings about true partnership and a win/win approach to solving problems.

One responsibility of individuals within the group is to ensure that a group's collective consciousness serves the greater good. The motivations underlying choices made and actions taken by individuals in a group enhance or disturb the group's collective consciousness. In other words, a group is more than the sum of its parts, its individual members. The group is a collective of individual members who create the spirit, or fire, of the group and the spark that ignites it.

The collective consciousness of groups can emanate a vibration that is received by groups with a similar vibration. The more powerful the signal and the more groups that attune to that signal, the greater the number of groups that feel connected. In this way, groups serve the greater good.

⁂ *Principle Seven: Groups fulfill their spiritual function when members master the skills and knowledge of cooperation.*

When groups practice cooperation, they work in concert. As partners, they collaborate, pull together, and stand shoulder to shoulder. Their intent is to use their varied talents and competencies to act together for mutual benefit. Humanistic and transpersonal values are openly discussed, reinforced, and practiced within the group. All systems work together to ensure success—physical bodies cooperate with emotional and mental bodies, hearts cooperate with minds, personalities cooperate with Soul, and human beings cooperate with the creative forces of nature. When personal systems are in an active state of cooperation, it is easier for individuals to cooperate in a group and practice shared decision making.

⁂ *Principle Eight: The shared vision of a group is manifested through a synthesis of feminine and masculine energies.*

Two complementary functions, the feminine and masculine principles, coexist in a group psyche. Like two sides of a coin, the partnership of the feminine (heart) and masculine (mind) energies ensures that a shared vision is manifested. In a group, the feminine is receptive, reflective, relational, and collaborative. The masculine is active and provides words, analysis, and protection.

When groups focus only on the feminine functions of reflecting and relating, they experience inertia and fail to act in the world. Their emotions guide their view of the world, as though they speak only from the heart and negate the values of the head. When a group focuses only on the masculine functions of analyzing, deciding, and doing, they become task-centered and avoid the value of cooperation and relationship.

Regardless of gender, group members personally manifest the vision of their group when they synthesize feminine (heart) and masculine (mind) principles. Idealism combines with practicality, intuition joins with intelligence, synthesis develops with analysis, sensitivity and creativity work together, and feelings and ideas are verbally explained.

☼ *Principle Nine: Energy is the conveyor of the group's true message.*

The nonverbal, invisible energy of what is conveyed—and not conveyed—in a group carries the truth of the moment. Underlying this premise is the recognition that unspoken intentions have a vibration that permeates the group's atmosphere. Words have power only if they match the nonverbal energy—the true message—of the group.

Members' vibrations convey the level of spiritual development they have attained individually and as a group. The aura that a group radiates is a collective of the energies of its members. If there is a designated leader or teacher, the radiation of that person has a dominating influence. When members act as a group, they radiate as a group. The integrity of a group is its radiation.

The strongest resonances in the group create and determine a focus of the group energy. Gradually, the energies calm down and a basic frequency appears. Once this frequency is stabilized, it can be difficult to change without full participation of the members.

☼ *Principle Ten: When one group member is healed, all are healed.*

Despite appearing to be individuals acting independently of one another, group members are energetically connected and evolve together. Because groups function as one system in a living organism, all benefit from the healing of any one person in the group. To heal is to make whole. Wholeness is integration of the physical, emotional, mental, and spiritual selves.

As the energy of the Group Soul flows more freely through the group members, the group opens to higher learning. This principle, often stated as "giving and receiving are the same," operates in groups when individual members experience a breakthrough in their understanding. In a heart-centered, authentic manner, they share this epiphany with the group, either through words or action. A healing vibration emanates from the heart of the person that embraces the energy field of all the members. As members give, they receive. They give to themselves that which they give to others. As they receive, they give. In this way, the entire group can receive the healing of one member.

Soul Lessons

The group life curriculum consists of five soul lessons. The first four lessons are shared vision, greater good, right relations, and service. Once a group has mastered these four, it can attain the ultimate soul lesson—to stand strong in group consciousness. Each soul lesson has challenges and integrates experience with knowledge unique to each stage of soul development.

Shared Vision

The **shared vision** soul lesson serves as the underpinning that supports all other soul lessons of group life. A group successfully creates and manifests a shared vision when they learn how to translate personal vision into shared vision; to develop, ground, and sustain a shared vision; and to evolve a shared holographic philosophical framework.

✦ TRANSLATING PERSONAL VISION INTO SHARED VISION

Individuals have personal visions; groups have shared visions. A vision is a picture of a goal, dream, passion, or desired future that the group wants to materialize in the world. This picture and its manifestation expand and reveal themselves over time. The identity of a group is determined by the shared vision and understood by all group members.

Individuals in a group are responsible for defining their personal vision and monitoring its alignment with the shared vision. Individuals are in alignment with the shared vision only when they share both the vision and the actions taken to ground the vision. When personal visions of group members do not overlap with the group vision, conflict emerges and the group becomes unfocused and loses energy. When this happens, people leave the group, the group ends, or it is reborn with a new vision.

✦ DEVELOPING, GROUNDING, AND SUSTAINING A SHARED VISION

According to Peter Senge, shared vision develops in five levels that move from dependence on the leader to interdependence between the leader and the group. Piscean values are evident in the first three levels. In the first level, leaders play a major role in determining the vision and how it will express in action. Leaders initially identify the vision and the group members follow it. In the second level, leaders identify the vision and seek to have the group "buy in" before proceeding with the vision. Leaders at the third level test their ideas about the vision by gathering the group's reaction before proceeding. Levels four and five express Aquarian values. At the fourth level, leaders ask for creative ideas about the group vision before proceeding. At the fifth level, leaders and group members build a shared vision through a process of cooperation. Cooperation is successful when members understand that a vision must be appropriate for current reality and based on core values.

At the fourth level, leaders ask for creative ideas about the group vision before proceeding. At the fifth level, leaders and group members build a shared vision through a process of cooperation.

The group grounds its vision by holding the vision's energy all the way from conception to realization. A grounded vision is one that manifests in the real world. The mechanism of creative tension ensures that the vision will expand and reveal itself over time by telling the group where it is in relationship to attaining the vision and where it has yet to go. Creative tension forms once the vision is articulated and an assessment is made of the current reality of the group's development. Tension between current reality and the vision creates a force of creative energy for the group. This energy brings creativity because its tension seeks innovative ways for resolution. A group intentionally using creative tension attempts to realize its vision in a realistic manner.

The vision of a group cannot be sustained unless members of the group share core values and understand that a vision is manifested through action. Group members who have engaged in their personal development and have team learning skills can successfully develop and implement vision.

Competency determines whether the group's shared vision can be successfully attained. Members must discern whether they have the appropriate competencies to perform a certain task and to relate effectively and creatively on a team. The group makes progress towards its vision and its application when members correctly assess their values and abilities. Neither individuals nor the group progress when members do not possess needed practical skills. One of the responsibilities of a leader is to discern the readiness of individual group members to perform a specific task or participate on a given team.

Personality development impacts relationships within the group. The potential for unresolved conflict lessens when group members assume self-responsibility for their inner work. Group members negatively triggered by certain behaviors of other members can set their personal issues aside and hold to the inspired vision of the group. Interpersonal conflicts affect the energy field of the group and disrupt the energy flow between the Group Soul and the group members.

The vision of a group cannot be sustained unless members of the group share core values and understand that a vision is manifested through action. Group members who have engaged in their personal development and have team learning skills can successfully develop and implement vision. A group is inclusive when it consists of members who share both the vision and how the vision will be actualized. Shared vision is created when group members make every effort to do their part in bringing the vision closer to realization. The vision is more easily attained when groups meditate together regularly.

✦ EVOLVING A SHARED HOLOGRAPHIC PHILOSOPHICAL FRAMEWORK

Another aspect of the shared vision group soul lesson is learning to develop a holographic philosophical framework or container. A group is holographic when its philosophy permeates all activities and structures and when the manner of each member reflects the group's philosophy. As a container, the philosophical framework supports members to stay on purpose while carrying out the group's mission. Components of the group philosophical framework include purpose, vision, and mission statements; philosophical foundations; policies and standards; and communication guidelines. Developing a philosophical framework requires preparation, education, reflection, cooperation, and humility.

Greater Good

To understand and apply the concept of a group's **greater good** is a complex and profound group soul lesson. It depends on emotional, mental, and spiritual maturity, the development of intuition and will, and the practice of synthesis.

Greater good is an ideal of the group mind. Greater good means more good for everyone, the entire group, including the individual. No lesser or greater good exists for either the individual or the group. The greater good for the individual is the greater good of the group and vice versa. Greater good means GREATER good—more individual good, more inclusive good, and good or greater quality for the group and all individuals in a group. Practicing greater good in a group is an Aquarian value.

✦ SEEKING EMOTIONAL, MENTAL, AND SPIRITUAL MATURITY

A major obstacle to practicing the greater good soul lesson arises out of dualistic thinking. Dualistic minds find the contrast between greater good and individual rights unsettling. Such a mind feels a constant inner pull, believing that individuals must be sacrificed for the group, or that the group must be sacrificed for the individuals. The development of the roots of this belief begins in childhood, the First Group experience. When emotional needs are not met, children feel unsafe and become preoccupied with having their needs met. Insecure children become insecure adults who cannot address the good of a group without feeling they are sacrificing their own needs and wellbeing. They cannot put their personal agenda aside for the good of a group because they have not developed mental clarity, emotional stability, and an ability to observe others without fearing the loss of self. Concern about the loss of self in a group is a Piscean characteristic. This concern can stem from years of religious, cultural, and political suppression and loss of individual rights. Similarly, people can be so attached to a familiar group like their family, church, or tribal community that they fear losing their self-identity in a new group.

✦ DEVELOPING INTUITION AND WILL

Intuition is the mechanism for creating greater good in a group. Without intuition, greater good is impossible. Through intuition, group members are aware of the presence of the Group Soul. They connect with the Group Soul and learn how to practice greater good in a group. Rational thinking and conventional wisdom are insufficient means of analyzing complex group problems and identifying the next best step in the group's evolution. It is impossible to know the full complexity of the group without integrating reason and intuition, qualities of the head and the heart. Group members begin to rely on their hunches, their heart's felt sense, a body-sense awareness that provides answers aside from mental reasoning. Relying on the felt sense of the heart, members look for analogies and recognize parallels that exist in seemingly disparate situations.

Intuition is the combined truth of mind and heart, the result of the ever-flowing energy of Source. Intuition occurs with an open heart and a sense of heart connection and appreciation of others. Intuition arises when group members ask their hearts for help. In a state of peace and balance, intuition comes through images, feelings, or thoughts. Sometimes intuitive knowing arises like whispers, quiet feelings barely noticed. The heart answers what the mind cannot. Heart intelligence reveals the cause of a problem and the path to take to resolution. When the heart manages the emotions, group members access their intuition and wisdom. Many spiritual traditions have long acknowledged the subtle workings of the heart. Today, science confirms the neurological connection between the heart and brain and verifies that head/heart coherence enhances powers of creativity, intuition, and wisdom.

The Piscean Era in the West gave precedence to the head and the intellect over the heart and intuition. Discounting the knowing of the intuitive heart, it denied the voice of wisdom. When group members deny the voice of wisdom, they disown their inner authority. When they dwell on their own needs and disappointments, they close their hearts and therefore negate their intuition. Discounting the heart reinforces the belief in separation from others and the Divine and creates psychological isolation.

When group members seek help from intuition, they use the will to state an intention that the right form of help will come to them at the right time for the good of their soul and for the souls with whom they work. Metaphysical levels of insight come from spiritual masters, spirit guides, dreams, and the voice of the Inner Leader. Authentic beings from the unseen realms offer, but do not impose, support and protection. They help by giving impressions of thoughts and ideas. They make it clear, however, that these thoughts and ideas are to be checked using intuition and reason to determine their usefulness. Intuition is nurtured by developing a spiritual practice of meditation and quiet contemplation. Solutions, ideas, and next steps begin to synchronistically appear.

Through meditation, prayer, contemplation, and right use of will, members are responsible for their behavior, reactions, and inner work and align themselves with the unchanging and eternal qualities of Source.

Through meditation, prayer, contemplation, and right use of will, members are responsible for their behavior, reactions, and inner work and align themselves with the unchanging and eternal qualities of Source. This alignment fills their spiritual vessels and supports their ability to be in a group with equipoise in all that they think, do, and say. A steady mind and balanced energy field help protect them from personal attacks. When they react to circumstances, their energy field becomes unbalanced and chaotic. Members lose their alignment with Source and thus their connection to intuition. Making accurate observations and wise decisions in this state is nearly impossible.

The voice of the Soul communicates through the heart as the seat of wisdom, intuition, and emotional experience. If asked, the heart conveys the cause of a problem and the path to overcome it. "Let me think about it" becomes "Let me take this matter to my heart."

✦ PRACTICING SYNTHESIS

Synthesis is the practice of nondual thinking, i.e., seeing connections and similarities that support integration of what might at first seem to be disparate information. Rather than seeing feminine and masculine energies as opposite attributes, group members view these energies working in partnership for the greater good of the group. The ability to perceive partnership instead of polarities extends to other energies and disciplines like science and spirituality or business and service. The nondual stance within a group supports the concept of a win/win approach to differences.

Right Relations

The **right relations** group soul lesson determines the physical, emotional, and spiritual health of the group and fosters cooperation and group consciousness among group members. The right relations soul lesson for groups includes three values: healthy boundaries, friendship, and integrity. All three values are spiritual principles that create cooperation and group consciousness among group members.

✦ HEALTHY BOUNDARIES

Healthy boundaries support the development of a strong sense of self-identity, which enables members to maintain a neutral space between others and themselves. Boundaries protect the authentic self so members can feel free and safe to be who they are in the group context. When a group has healthy boundaries, its members are not threatened by thoughts, views, and needs that differ from their own. Group members treat one another with respect and extend their respect to those they serve. Members do not have a need to correct or change the point of view of others to agree with their own. They are self-responsible for personal reactions and do not project them onto the group. They check out their assumptions and understandings of one another's point of view. They establish written guidelines for handling group conflict in advance, assuring that all group members understand the policies and procedures.

Unhealthy group boundaries typically reflect childhoods that taught members that they are incomplete and need to search outside themselves for what is missing. Unhealthy boundaries create relationships fraught with expectations and dependencies that result in anger, resentment, and judgments when needs go unmet. Members project onto others what they believe to be missing within themselves. They intrude on the boundaries of others by giving away responsibility for their feelings and emotions. In this way, they abdicate self-responsibility and misuse their personal power. Typical unhealthy boundaries in groups include discounting, critiquing, or negating what another member has shared and making assumptions about a member's verbal communication or behavior.

Dual relationships—relationships in which group members have more than one kind of relationship such as being neighbors, spouses, or siblings—can cause boundaries to be ignored, disrupting group cohesiveness. Groups may tolerate inappropriate behavior of members and avoid seeking a solution. Often communication guidelines for appropriate boundaries are not written, reviewed, and accepted at the first meeting of a group. Because the cause of a problem often resides below the surface in the unconscious, things are not as they appear to be. A group with healthy boundaries is willing to resolve conflict and practice a synthesis of a diversity of views.

Groups have integrity when they value and respect communication and boundary guidelines, accountability, time, partnership, and all forms of life.

✦ FRIENDSHIP

Friendship in groups requires commitment, vision, and willingness to help another be healthy, happy, and prosperous. Friends support one another's growth, transformation, self-knowledge, and creativity. Friendship is a context in which to do shadow work, learn self-acceptance, and practice forgiveness. Envy, anger, and betrayal are common shadows of friendship. Most of all, friends honor one another's authentic specialness at the level of soul, seeing both the divinity and the idiosyncrasies. When this view of friendship is learned in a group, members are able to apply it at home and at work, eventually becoming friends with other nations, nature, and the world. An enlightened master was asked, "Who is the most advanced human being?" He answered, "The most advanced human being is one who is the friend of all."

✦ INTEGRITY

Group members have integrity or wholeness when the qualities and motivations they convey on the outside match the qualities and motivations they possess on the inside. To achieve integrity, Aquarian groups intentionally seek personality integration. Integration of the individual personalities within the group engenders integration of the group personality. Groups have integrity when they value and respect communication and boundary guidelines, accountability, time, partnership, and all forms of life. When a group has integrity, its members understand and practice all the soul lessons—shared vision, greater good, right relations, service, and, ultimately, group cooperation and consciousness.

Service

The group soul lesson of **service** is unique in that it integrates the previous soul lessons of shared vision, greater good, and right relations. This integration occurs when groups learn to see the bigger picture and practice True Service.

✦ SEEING THE BIGGER PICTURE

Through the practice of the soul lesson of service, members learn to see the bigger picture or destiny of their group. They recognize that every person, idea, task, program, or event serves to create their shared vision and mission and helps to extend their vision and mission into their communities, country, and world. No member is separate from the whole of the group or from the group's destiny of service. Members with differing talents and duties join to move the group forward toward a common goal and with greater good. They strive to see the bigger picture of a nondual world and live life from a perspective of universal truths and principles.

✦ PRACTICING TRUE SERVICE

The level of the group's soul development determines the quality of their service. Groups in the first four stages of soul development tend to serve in order to meet their needs, looking outside to work, causes, and relationships. These stages also express Piscean values, including dedication to public service, innovation and invention through technology, appreciation of beauty through the arts, and charitable giving.

True Service begins in Stages Five and Six of soul development. Group members are responsible for their motivations for service and engage fully in their psychological and spiritual wellbeing. They undo the belief system of earlier soul development stages while, with awareness and intentionality, creating a new reality. They view their service as a classroom for spiritual development and self-transformation, using every encounter and event to monitor their inner state and to reveal areas for inner work. In this way, their service becomes a means of purification, removing obstacles to the awareness of their true nature. They serve the greater good of humanity and nature.

To Stand Strong in Group Consciousness

To attain the Aquarian values of partnership, cooperation, and **to stand strong in group consciousness**, groups must first master the four group soul lessons of shared vision, greater good, right relations, and service. At this point, all the pieces have been assimilated, and the group is open to and embraces the fusion of group personality with the Group Soul.

✦ FUSING GROUP SOUL AND GROUP PERSONALITY

When a group is ready to stand strong in group consciousness, they are open to fusing their group personality with the Group Soul. This fusion emerges from within the group, expressing the group's inner resources and relationship with Source.

Connection to the organizing principle of the Group Soul anchors the group members. They practice shared decision making, which supports them in doing the right thing in the right way at the right time and for the right reason. Through action and state of being, they express their group's purpose, shared vision, mission, and philosophy. Groups welcome the oversight of the Group Soul as with steady wisdom it guides them in learning Aquarian values of cooperation and consciousness.

✦ STANDING STRONG IN THE FACE OF ADVERSITY

As they learn to stand strong, group members face their ambivalence about being in a conscious group. Ambivalence makes members vulnerable to judgments. When members take things personally, their alignment with the Soul wavers, and they become vulnerable to the negative energies and beliefs of others. They weather conflicts that arise within the group, with other groups, and when the general public projects negative thoughts and opinions onto them. They know that reactions of others are not their responsibility, and they do not shoulder responsibilities that are not theirs. They accept that they may be blamed for failures not of their making. They stand with deep compassion beside those who are suffering and bewildered. They help others learn needed lessons.

When the heart and mind are joined, members respect Aquarian values of partnership, cooperation, and group consciousness with joy, skill, and steady wisdom.

Regardless of group challenges and dangers, members know that they can stand strong only if they love unconditionally and enough. To love others no matter what they do or say is a matter for the heart. An inclusive concept, heart links all human beings and life forms in the world. When the heart and mind are joined, members respect Aquarian values of partnership, cooperation, and group consciousness with joy, skill, and steady wisdom.

Challenges in the Aquarian Era

Groups, like leaders, will react to the shift of energy from the Piscean Era to the Aquarian. Reactions from fear of change, polarized thinking and behavior, and the paradox of technology are already evident among people and governments. Further reactions can also be expected in response to the transition from the water element to the air element, the initiation of true partnership of feminine and masculine energies, and the influence of the Millennial Generation.

Potential group challenges during the transition include:

- Lack of preparation
- Rigidity of styles of group life
- Intolerance of individuality
- Disruption of human development and wisdom produced by the reliance on technology
- Fear of the unknown
- Use of unproven and untried approaches without testing their effectiveness

The shadow of the early Aquarian Era is already in evidence. Some groups interpret the Aquarian value of honoring the inner authority of individual members as meaning that groups should have neither leaders nor structures. To discard outer authority for inner authority is a value of Piscean duality. When members use their inner authority, guidance flows as inner knowing through their Inner Leader. Inner authority does not mean that there is no outer Aquarian leader to keep the group on purpose and in alignment with its vision. A group's decision to discard group structures, such as having a working agenda or communication guidelines, assumes direction can magically appear without the safety net of group boundaries. Without healthy boundaries, a group communicates on a personality level without skill and respect.

The nature of these challenges differs for groups in each stage of soul development. Groups in the outer-directed stages will resist change and experience an increase of fear and polarized thinking. Inner-directed stages may welcome change and a new way of being in the world as a group, yet experience insecurity when the task of creating new and workable approaches to group life proves a daunting one.

Additions to the Curriculum for Inner-Directed Stages

Groups in Stages Five and Six of soul development have two additions to the curriculum in their soul classrooms— the Energy Triangle Model and spiritual awakenings. These additions reflect the readiness of groups to consciously engage in the evolution of the Aquarian destiny; namely, to open to the soul through energy triangle teams and expanded group consciousness.

The Energy Triangle Model

The Energy Triangle Model is part of the additional curriculum for groups in Stage Five and Six. Groups or teams in these stages can choose to use triangles as a meaningful way to express Aquarian values of cooperation and group consciousness. The Energy Triangle Model can be used as a committee to plan and execute tasks, projects, and programs and as groups for support, study, meditation, and prayer. An infinite number of interlinked triangles can be created.

An energy triangle creates a structure through which energies flow and circulate in a specific way. As discussed in Chapter Four, three members come together with a common purpose to form a network of energy to invoke the will-to-good. Three elements of spiritual energies flow through the linked focal points of the triangle—Light, Love, and Willpower. Light is intelligence motivated by Love and implemented by Will. These energies resonate in harmony when the three members learn how to cooperate as they relate and work together and when they join in meditation or contemplation.

All three members in an energy triangle must be extremely efficient and flexible in their ability to hold the group field and become a vortex of Light, Love, and Will. This energy is dynamic and increases the energy circulating in the group as a whole. If all three individuals are at a level of soul development where understanding and communication are integrated, they can channel the circulating energy as it moves through the triangle. Like dancers, they can move in and out of different roles as they lead, teach, plan, and implement tasks. Sometimes they plan with deliberation, at other times they intuitively respond to the needs of the group.

Effective energy triangle work depends on all members of the trio attending to their inner work and integrating group tools.

Disharmony among the three people can block the circulation of energy causing them to be out of phase with one another. Effective energy triangle work depends on all members of the trio attending to their inner work and integrating group tools. Examples of behaviors that cause disharmony include:

- Inability to set aside personal agendas on behalf of the greater good
- Inability to listen at both the word and heart level
- A lapse of honesty or trust
- Withholding energy from the cocreative process
- Ignorance of the nature of the human psyche
- Resistance to implementing healthy boundaries
- Failure to appreciate one another's talents and acknowledge shadow tendencies

Spiritual Awakenings and the Soul Stages

The purpose of groups in Stages Five and Six, like leaders, is to expand group consciousness, to attain personality integration and fuse this personality with Soul, to recognize Oneness, and to experience Light, Love, and the Will of Divine Source as it descends into the world. Groups, like leaders, express the Divine through their service.

As with individuals and leaders, groups prepare for spiritual awakenings during the outer-directed soul development stages of group life. These stages represent unsuccessful attempts to find meaning in life in the outer world of work, causes, and relationships. They are also preparatory because they focus on concern for others, living responsibly in the world, and maintaining ethical standards.

Although groups in the outer-directed stages are engaged in an unconscious process of spiritual awakening, it is not until Stage Five that this process becomes conscious.

When groups experience a dark night of the soul between Stages Four and Five, their the spiritual path becomes conscious. Considerable group self-effort is necessary during the dark night. The group searches for the meaning and purpose of the group at a soul level and begins to question its assumptions and beliefs. Group members recognize that they must bring heart and higher qualities of mind into their group through meditation and service.

Although groups in the outer-directed stages are engaged in an unconscious process of spiritual awakening, it is not until Stage Five that this process becomes conscious. The mind opens to a broader framework by seeing beyond appearances. Gradually group consciousness develops. As the Aquarian Era progresses, groups will experience spiritual awakenings together as a group event, but during the transition this will seldom occur. When the Aquarian energy becomes fully present, group spiritual awakenings will supplant those of individuals.

In Stages Five and Six of group life, collective consciousness evolves through ten specific shifts. When a critical mass of individuals makes these shifts, collective consciousness emerges and people move more fully into values of the Aquarian Era.

- *Awakening One: The true source of equanimity is within.*
  As group members achieve equanimity and share their inner peace, collective consciousness increases. Service evolves to a new level at which groups no longer view service as separate from their natures.
- *Awakening Two: The highest good for one includes the highest good for all.*
  Collectively, service evolves into a global and universal concept in which the group values the good of the whole above the immediate needs of the parts.
- *Awakening Three: Work and service are the same.*
  As consciousness expands on collective levels, work and service provide daily opportunities for insight and growth. Groups serve continuously on community, national, international, and global levels. Served and server meld into partnership.
- *Awakening Four: The world is interconnected and nondual.*
  This awakening occurs as groups practice service holographically, recognizing the interconnectedness of all aspects of life—economic, political, social, environmental, and spiritual.
- *Awakening Five: True Sight sees the deeper spiritual meaning beyond appearances.*
  Groups embody their purpose and mission collectively. They feel increasingly connected to the spiritual essence of all humanity.
- *Awakening Six: Answers lie on the level of cause.*
  Collectively, groups ask the question, "What are the conditions that brought this situation about?" The groups then take responsibility for their own part in the matter.

- *Awakening Seven: Responses to life events are made from the Witness Self on the mental level.*
  Collectively, groups move towards objective observations of group dynamics by engaging the Witness Self, the part of the mind that observes without judgment. From this perspective of the bigger picture, interactions are seen as learning opportunities and as service.
- *Awakening Eight: True Service expresses in the world at all levels of participation.*
  As groups progress collectively in consciousness, they extend the energy of inward growth outward in service to affect change on all levels of life.
- *Awakening Nine: True Service requires* being *service as well as being* of *service.*
  The fruit of collective group effort is the bringing of virtues into consciousness for others to acquire and use. In this way, groups are not only being *of* service, but *being* service.
- *Awakening Ten: Personal will aligns with Divine Will to allow the unfolding of the destiny of collective will.*
  The energy of collective will radiates and raises group consciousness. The collective will paves the path to the destiny of each group, large or small.

Conclusion

The Aquarian Era introduces a significant change in group life that depends on the evolution of group consciousness. During the next twenty-five years, groups will be required to depend on the inner knowing of their individual members through group cooperation and discovery. To make this shift, groups must develop alignment with their Group Soul and focus on the greater good.

The foundational philosophy of group soul development presented in Chapters Eight and Nine permeates a spiritually based holographic template that groups can use to develop group consciousness and True Service.

CHAPTER EIGHT
SOUL-INSPIRED GROUP LIFE: OUTER-DIRECTED STAGES OF SOUL DEVELOPMENT

Introduction

Group life moves through seven stages of soul development. In the first four stages, groups are at the beginning of their spiritual journey and tend to reflect Piscean rather than Aquarian values. They look outside of themselves to work, causes, and relationships for validation of their purpose and value.

Outer-directed groups provide many valuable services to their communities and to their members. In these groups, members learn skills related to communication, organization, and service. They learn to put their own needs aside to meet a common goal. These groups provide the soil in which the seeds of more conscious groups take root.

The soul classroom for these stages includes acknowledging the Group Soul, the Universal Principles of Group Energy, the soul lessons, and the challenges in the Aquarian Era.

Stage One: Awakening to Group Life

Stage One groups focus on the Piscean value of individualism and seek to find an answer to the question, "Who are we as a group?" They look for answers in ways that meet their own needs. These needs usually concern immediate physical needs of food and shelter and basic emotional support. As a result, the group will offer these services to others. Because they are self-absorbed, awakening to group life groups have difficulty discerning how they differ from other groups with similar identities. For example, because of their open hearts and desire to help, groups in Stage One may choose to feed the homeless. Groups may be unaware of the necessity to be specific in their mission or they may not have the skills to define their group in a way that differentiates it from similar organizations.

Awakening to group life groups attract members who are unaware of what they feel, believe, and value; they depend on others for validation of their decisions and actions.

Awakening to group life groups attract members who are unaware of what they feel, believe, and value; they depend on others for validation of their decisions and actions. Left on their own, Stage One groups flounder due to undeveloped skills and an inability to grasp the group's need for clear structure, protection, and right/wrong beliefs. Because they function informally without focus or rules and they lack sufficient energy or skilled will, they often cannot sustain group membership. Bonding in a group may be limited to relationships among individuals without ever expanding to the group coalescing as a whole. If members join who have experienced more advanced group skills in other groups, the Stage One group has the opportunity to grow and see itself as a united group instead of as a collection of individual members.

Group Soul

A Group Soul gently and quietly guides Stage One group members in the birthing or early developmental steps of group life. Although individuals may not be aware of the support of the Group Soul, it is present nonetheless. A Group Soul's method of teaching through opportunity and practical experience is especially appropriate for groups in Stage One who are actively seeking to discover their identity as a group. For example, the Group Soul may connect with the Souls of individual members and prompt them with suggestions that would develop a sense of group safety.

Universal Principles of Group Energy

As is true for all outer-directed stages, Awakening groups have a distinct energetic makeup. Individuals come into a group in different states of mind, depending on what they have experienced that day, how they feel in the moment, and past experiences with groups and with their First Group. Stage One individuals and groups have little curiosity about the role of feminine and masculine energies. Their hearts are open, yet their emotions are not clearly differentiated.

What is distinctive for a Stage One group is its inability to shift its mental state during the group experience. For example, Stage One groups may be passive or may act out in an oppositional manner, especially when unfamiliar ideas are introduced because members have not yet developed strategies for how to be in a group. Members either try to process their feelings in the group, or they withdraw in silence. They also may agree with the majority without questioning. The concept that a group functions as a dynamic whole and creates energy is foreign to them. Stage One groups reflect the influence of past group experiences and/or the absence of common motivations for being in the group. These characteristics cause them to fluctuate between being stagnant and static and being chaotic and disharmonious.

Because stability anchors Stage One groups and they fear the loss of

Group members in this stage are often unaware of their hidden potential and subsequently do not recognize their inner resources. To them, success and achievement in the world seem beyond their reach.

physical safety, members resist the unstable edge required to move forward. They are content with static energy that does not demand mental or spiritual growth. The group does not know its inner purpose and therefore cannot manifest its mission in the outer world. Situations that demand active expression of their mission feel risky and cause the group to collapse in indecision.

Group members in this stage are often unaware of their hidden potential and subsequently do not recognize their inner resources. To them, success and achievement in the world seem beyond their reach. Because they do not feel connected to their potential, they become preoccupied with their limitations, conveying pessimism about their value as group members.

Soul Lessons

Those groups awakening to group life take the initial steps of three soul lessons—shared vision, right relations, and service. Because members lack a sense of personal purpose and mission and do not have the strong and skillful will to bring ideas into reality, they find articulating a vision difficult and do not have the skills and knowledge to develop a **shared vision**. Their purpose is personal and not group oriented. Because their dominant struggles are learning self-identity and self-responsibility, their primary duty is to themselves and not to a group.

Stage One groups focus most of their learning on the soul lesson of **right relations**, especially learning healthy boundaries. Because they are preoccupied with their own survival, these groups tend to project their sense of helplessness and victimization on others in the group. They project their fear of rejection and abandonment. The energy fields of members become enmeshed with one another and with those served. The inner reality of groups in this stage is one of sentiment, which results in emotions coloring both thought and behavior.

Out of a sense of powerlessness, groups in this stage tend to use passive resistance as an attempt to acquire power. Passive resistance is a way to control the emotions and decisions of others in order to meet the group's needs. For example, out of a need to please, a group might agree to do something for the community but not follow through with the action. The community and those who were to be served feel victimized and betrayed by passive-resistant behavior and often respond by withdrawing support. In turn, the withdrawal results in the passive-resistant group feeling rejected and victimized. Passive resistance arises from a constant need to prove the group's power by giving its responsibility to others. In the process, the group gives its power away.

Pride in this stage conceals or disguises itself as specialness. Groups express an exaggerated opinion of themselves where there is no evidence to validate this. They can even be prideful about their unsuccessful struggles. Such groups may also be vain, expressing an excessive desire to be admired by others for either positive or negative achievements.

Stage One groups are awakening to **service** and often attend to the physical and supportive needs of others with compassion. They feel inspired to extend a helping hand to neighbors, to become involved with projects focused on cleaning up the environment, and to join other groups that provide food and clothing to those suffering from natural disasters.

Challenges in the Aquarian Era

The major challenge of awakening to group life groups in the early Aquarian Era is adapting to change. Outer stability and a structured life assure them that their needs will be met. Group members fear the unknown and the unexpected when they experience a loss of safety and protection. They fear for their physical and psychological survival when they discover that what was once true is no longer so. Because fear exacerbates the instability of the psyche, Stage One groups lose their footing and fall into patterns of pessimism and victimhood. Not yet anchored in the functions of heart and head, they are unable to call on the resources of feminine and masculine energies, precursors to using the will to bring thought into action.

Technology will not be a challenge for Stage One groups who are members of Generation X or the Millennial Generation. Rather, it will provide them with opportunities to feel competent and to connect meaningfully with others.

Stage Two: Work Ethic Group Life

During the latter part of the awakening stage, members sense that groups can come together to accomplish a task, not merely to have emotional needs met. When this realization occurs, members shift their attendance to groups in the work ethic stage.

As in the Piscean Era, work ethic groups in the early Aquarian continue to be doers and wage earners who are able to be innovative and adjust to change. Their groups dominate business, government, and civic organizations, both as the central administration and in associated projects. Work ethic groups incorporate cooperation and support teamwork, not because these are Aquarian values, but because they are effective methods to create order out of chaos and to increase productivity. They contribute to society by searching for and implementing creative ways to solve economic, ecological, and technological problems. They also subsidize educational and cultural programs.

Work ethic groups collectively use their strong and skillful will to carry out activities with concentration and persistence. Although their contributions serve their communities and nation, the group focus on financial gain often obscures any concerns members may hold for human and ecological health.

Group Soul

The Group Soul gently guides Stage Two groups in early developmental steps of group life even though members are unaware of the support of Its existence. The Group Soul teaches through thought impressions that support personality development of work ethic group members. For example, because members focus on the material world at the expense of ecological, emotional, and spiritual realities, the Group Soul may impress upon them activities and approaches that will connect their work with the heart. Such opportunities can shift their limited perspective to a broader view that relates to the greater global whole. In the last decades of the twentieth century, many work ethic groups began to welcome the word "soul" into the workplace. Although used as a vernacular term and not within the context of the stages of soul evolution, usage of the word "soul" suggests a growing acceptance within the work ethic worldview of the spiritual and emotional dimensions of human life.

Universal Principles of Group Energy

Dominance of head and mental energy and the suppression of the energy of the heart and emotions pervade work ethic groups. Groups primarily controlled by mental energy reflect the masculine principle. These groups give precedence to action, production, achievement, and competition, and dismiss or even ignore the attributes of the feminine principles of relatedness, synthesis, cooperation, and nurturance. With head energy dominant over heart energy, the group makes decisions, takes action with little reflection, and remains task oriented. They do not call on intuition or consider the wide-range or long-term impact of their actions. As a result, their decisions reflect solutions that address the effects of a problem rather than the underlying cause or causes.

Mentally oriented groups do not feel safe in emotionally oriented groups and will avoid them. Likewise, emotionally oriented groups avoid mental groups.

Members who focus primarily on mental functions dominate work ethic groups. Often these adults were children who had to protect themselves by using reasoning to think or talk themselves out of distressing or even dangerous situations. The educational system's emphasis on left-brain functions of analysis of information, rational thought, and academic achievement compounded this tendency in terms of their adaptation. Reflecting their members' needs, work ethic groups engage in mental activity to feel energetically safe. Otherwise, their members become agitated, anxious, irritable, and impulsive. Mentally oriented groups do not feel safe in emotionally oriented groups and will avoid them. Likewise, emotionally oriented groups avoid mental groups. As a consequence, the mentally oriented groups label emotional groups as being "touchy-feely" and having shallow and inferior minds. In turn, the emotionally oriented label the mental groups as hard-hearted, arrogant, and unconscious of the true needs of humanity and the natural world.

The energy of Stage Two groups feels inflexible and exclusionary. Although comfortable with change they understand and can manage, they grow fearful when they cannot make sense of or control their experience. Fear of the unknown causes work ethic groups to become insular and return to old patterns even though they were not effective.

Soul Lessons

Work ethic group soul lessons are shared vision, right relations, and service. With a developed sense of purpose and mission, Stage Two groups articulate a **shared vision** and bring the vision into reality with their strong and skillful will. They are willing to work together in teams towards common goals. They validate their reason for existence in outer proof like productivity levels and profit margins. As a result, they often overlook the elements of the **right relations** soul lesson—building relationships, clarifying boundaries, and developing healthy communication skills. Stage Two groups engage in **service** activities that bring forth Piscean ideas and products, such as technology and medical services that benefit a specific targeted group. They rarely assess their service in terms of its applicability to the greater global good.

Challenges in the Aquarian Era

Piscean work ethic groups have achieved stellar advances in economics, industry, housing, health, and technology. As Piscean institutions, structures, and models fail, work ethic individuals and groups panic. Their mental problem-solving abilities cannot find answers for society's need for emotional and spiritual sustenance. Their identity is so dependent on the success of their work that they attempt to work harder in the old way. Eventually, the rewards of money and material goods fail to meet their emotional needs and they must face their fear of the unknown. They then may deliberately merge their work ethic gifts with Aquarian consciousness.

The Millennial Generation's sense of entitlement, need for acknowledgment, and demand for personal freedom and entertainment in the work place seriously challenge the Generation Xers and Boomers in work ethic organizations. While these organizations desperately need the Millennials' technological skills and their willingness to work hard, they correctly perceive that the Millennials threaten their long-revered hierarchical relationships and structures. They also fear that Millennials seek to replace human relationships with technology and human wisdom with data. Dealing with the challenges presented by the Millennials will force work ethic groups to become more responsive to the needs of all their members. Eventually, these changes may broaden to impact those they serve on a global level. The challenge for work ethic groups is to use their skills in innovation and productivity to build new models to solve economic, ecological, and technological problems for the global good.

Stage Three: Missionary Attitude Group Life

Individuals who fail to find self-fulfillment in work ethic groups eventually decide to shift the focus from productivity to saving what they see as a broken world. Their personal wounds direct their choice of arena for their work. Those wounded by religion select religious or spiritual groups with beliefs ranging from metaphysics to fundamentalism. Those with wounds caused by their sexual orientation join groups that support their point of view. Those wounded by having a power figure impose his or

The personality of missionary attitude groups expresses its certainty about "right" cultural values, justice, and religious beliefs.

her will on them join groups that advocate for the powerless or that expose corporate or government misconduct, and so on. Missionary attitude individuals and groups are defined not by the arena in which they work, but by their absolute belief that one right way exists to solve the problem at hand. Such groups exist in alternative and allopathic medicine, in industry and agriculture, in academia, and in psychology, sports, and environmental activism. They place tremendous focus and energy on doing whatever they feel is necessary to get the "right" results.

Usually, missionary attitude groups expect similar groups to adhere to their point of view. Because total agreement among groups rarely exists, they find themselves isolated. Their isolation then becomes a matter of pride and righteous indignation. Members are expected to adhere to the group's beliefs and may be asked to sacrifice their personal lives in order to focus energy and resources on the group's cause.

Intense emotions fuel groups in this stage. No matter what the arena of their work, they inspire participation by keeping the memories of their adversaries' wrongdoings alive. In their passion to defend their point of view, they may actually harm others. An extreme example of this is found in groups that advocate bombing abortion clinics and claim "supporting life" as a justification for killing and maiming employees and patients.

Group Soul

The Group Soul plays a guiding role in missionary attitude groups similar to that for groups in Stages One and Two. As outer-directed activists, Stage Three groups spend little time in reflection and contemplation. They do not see the role of reflection and contemplation in connecting to their wisdom and intuition. The personality of missionary attitude groups expresses its certainty about "right" cultural values, justice, and religious beliefs. These groups focus on defending their point of view through the eyes of a world of duality with absolutes of right/wrong, good/bad, and proper/improper.

The Group Soul works to soften the rigidity and certainty of group members in two ways. Knowing that the group must be emotionally confronted in order to change, the Group Soul provides opportunities for groups to question their stance by using a crisis of loss like the sudden death of a revered leader or a legal defeat. It also gently offers thought impressions that lead to broader ways of thinking about solutions. The Group Soul knows that a shift in mindset will occur for these groups only when, with humility, they become open to recognizing that they live in an uncertain world.

Universal Principles of Group Energy

The group energy of missionary attitude groups is charged with negative emotions and is intense and passionate. The founders of these groups usually carry deep wounds related to the arena of their group's work. Thus, the parents of an abducted child start a group related to protecting children from sexual predators, and the nurse who perceives standard medical practices as uncaring opens a wholistic wellness center. Each missionary attitude group draws members with similar wounds.

Individual and group wills are one-pointed and forced, and their emotions are caring and overstimulated. Because they are attempting to right the wrong that wounded them, they must stay alert to any threat to their survival, both as individuals and as a group. Members feel buoyed by being part of a group that is energized and united with a purpose dedicated to the common good. Joining in purpose bonds the group, and makes their work both intentional and meaningful.

Although the group is bonded by purpose, its passion to correct wrong arouses chronic and intense negative emotions of anger, resentment, anxiety, guilt, and fear. Taking a right/wrong, us/them stance fosters intense victim/victimizer attitudes. The more serious the issue being addressed, the stronger the threat to survival experienced by members. Deeply identified with their cause, members may adopt a martyr role, suffering physically and emotionally on behalf of those they serve. Attached to their victim status, missionary attitude groups must continually seek victimizers, whether identified as donors who withhold funding, other organizations perceived as antagonistic, or their own members rebelling against the rules.

Stress results from highly charged emotions, positive or negative, and a forcing of will energy, both of which overstimulate the heart and adversely affect heart rate and rhythm. Repeated threats, real or imagined, trigger stress that elevates levels of cortisol, the stress hormone in individuals. Members of missionary attitude groups are prone to physical health impairments resulting from chronic elevations of cortisol and low levels of the hormone DHEA (dehydroepiandrosterone). These hormone imbalances reduce immune function and bone and muscle mass, increase risk of heart disease, and destroy brain cells, the latter affecting memory and learning.

The intense emotional atmosphere common to the missionary attitude stage impacts the group's nature and quality of heart energy. Although their desire to do good arises from the heart-centered feminine, the urgent need for action—an attribute of the practical and skilled masculine—takes precedence. Unable to manage their emotions with the heart and access its intuition and wisdom, groups may feel discouraged and isolated. When the mind has no answer and group members cannot enter the heart, they experience anger and frustration. If they recognize that the heart holds the answer, the negative emotion will transform. For example, anger turns to compassion and frustration to understanding.

In Stage Three groups, as in Stages One and Two, fear of loss of safety drains energy. Stage One fears the loss of physical safety, Stage Two the loss of the known, and Stage Three the loss of certainty. Fear has a low vibration and limits personality growth.

Soul Lessons

Missionary attitude groups deepen the soul lessons of shared vision, right relations, and service learned in the first two stages, and they begin learning the soul lesson of greater good.

Like those in Stage Two, missionary attitude groups have a developed sense of purpose and mission and can articulate a **shared vision.** However, they confront practical in-the-world obstacles in bringing their vision into reality because they experience legitimate obstacles from those who oppose their point of view.

They use their skillful will to develop successful strategies for implementing their vision and their strong will to realize it. They are prone to forcing their will on those they wish to convert to their position. When people feel coerced, they respond with anger and resentment, contributing to the group's victim attitude and interfering with right relations.

Whenever individuals or groups relate through their wounds, they neglect **right relations**. Their either/or thinking necessitates right/wrong choices, and they will consistently choose adherence to their belief system over their relationships. People in the missionary attitude stage often resent the population they serve when the recipients do not appreciate their efforts or fail to follow their recommendations for change. Because they feel superior, they resist acquiring new skills, seeking professional help, and admitting mistakes. Group members develop strong personas at the expense of exploring and developing their inner psychological and spiritual life.

Missionary attitude groups offer gifts of **service** to the world through their participation in good works and social action. They feed the hungry, operate medical clinics, provide educational support in inner city and rural communities, and advocate for the benefit of humans, animals, and the planet. Aware of the harm that comes from neglect and ignorance, their intent is to be active participants working for and impacting the **greater good**. Stage Three groups are agents of change who ensure that society at all levels is served and protected. While their service impacts the greater good, their motivation to be right remains.

Challenges in the Aquarian Era

Piscean missionary attitude groups feel compelled to attack Aquarian values that encourage cooperation among groups that have opposing purposes. Ensconced in a moralistic Piscean worldview, their certainty in being right prevents others from questioning their view. Curiosity represents a threat. Expanded or opposing views or a need for change will intensify the threat. Their greatest fear is to have their certainty, and therefore their safety, threatened.

Because the water element nurtures and sustains their passion to bring about social change, Stage Three groups are hesitant to embrace the mental qualities of the air element of Aquarius. Action directed by passion rather than by the observing mind enervates their life and work.

The extent to which missionary attitude groups are challenged by Aquarian values relates directly to their readiness and willingness to engage in their psychological and spiritual growth and consider points of view other than their own.

Stage Four: Wounded Healer Group Life

When Stage Three groups begin to doubt that they will find meaning in causes, they search for wholeness through relationships and move into Stage Four. Wounded healer groups esteem values, ethics, and standards and willingly set themselves aside for the good of others and their communities. They look to relationships to find what is missing within themselves. Although they appear to be helpers, especially for the emotionally wounded, Stage Four groups desire to be rescued rather than to rescue. The addictive quality of their relationships often extends to work, clothes, food, sports, and other aspects of life. The central issues for these groups and their members involve developing healthy boundaries and correcting addictive behaviors.

Stage Four groups support the misuse of personal power with those they serve by overidentifying with their clients' needs, intruding on their boundaries by projecting their fears and emotions, and by believing they know what is best for others.

Wounded healer groups react to their prior missionary attitude experience by taking the opposite stance. An "anything goes" approach replaces rigid boundaries and right/wrong thinking. This freedom from restraint reveals itself as unhealthy boundaries exhibited in the relationships among group members, between members and those served, and between groups.

Stage Four groups support the misuse of personal power with those they serve by overidentifying with their clients' needs, intruding on their boundaries by projecting their fears and emotions, and by believing they know what is best for others. In their effort to be all things to all people, they fail to establish a group identity. Instead, they develop a group persona that matches social expectations. Although they themselves want to be healed, wounded healer groups ignore their own self-care and inner work.

Group Soul

The Group Soul works with three imbedded personality obstacles in the soul development of Stage Four groups—pride, unhealthy boundaries, and neglect of inner work. The Group Soul guides members to recognize the consequence of these obstacles so they can be dissolved. For example, the Group Soul may provide opportunities for group members to receive rejection and negative feedback that reflects the impact they have when they project their own fears onto others or attempt to solve others' problems. Because Stage Four members and groups seek to meet their own emotional needs for acknowledgment, acceptance, and praise, negative reactions can cause them to reconsider their motivations and the quality of their service.

Universal Principles of Group Energy

The energy of wounded healer groups swirls with contradictions. While the heart energy of the group can be expansive and generous as members extend it in loving care and service, it can also be overextended, sentimental, and willful as it projects into the energy fields of others. Projections are disowned energy directed at another person or group. Imposing the will on another, excusing inappropriate behavior, and offering advice exemplify forms of projection. What affects one in a group affects all. Interference with another person's process devalues the individual's self-knowledge and sets up the expectation that the group will change to meet members' needs.

Stage Four groups express the following symptoms and behaviors resulting from unhealthy boundaries that impact group energy:

- Tolerating inappropriate behavior
- Failing to set limits by saying no
- Failing to see events and people as they are and not as they appear to be
- Lacking of discernment about who is responsible for the problem
- Confusing their needs with the needs of others
- Imposing their will on others
- Taking things personally
- Failing to recognize the complexity of dual relationships
- Assuming responsibility for another's happiness

Although unresolved shadow issues from First Groups impact the energy field in all outer-directed groups, they come fully to the surface in Stage Four. When members experience situations in the group that remind them of unconscious and unresolved childhood events, they feel as unsafe as they did when the event occurred. The situation triggers their emotions and releases confused and turbulent energy. Because those in Stage Four have unhealthy boundaries, this uncontained energy triggers other members, until the colliding energies create a chaotic wobble. For example, when an individual feels energetically unsafe in a group meeting, she unconsciously directs her remarks to the person she identifies as a safe parental figure rather than to the whole group. This interaction shifts the group energy because other members feel excluded from the communication or presume a special relationship exists between the two.

Wounded healer groups develop a group persona of selfless service in order to gain wholeness in relationships by giving to get.

Any special relationship between two or more members creates a subgroup of the larger group. Instead of having one group united in purpose, subgroups separate themselves, united by purposes unique to their shared identity. Subgroups disrupt focused energy and create dissonance by siphoning off energy. Common examples of subgroups are close friends, family members, or those with similar experiences and perceptions. Dual relationships are also a form of subgroup. Members have dual relationships when they have more than one kind of relationship with another group member. People may be group members as well as colleagues, friends, relatives, spouses, or intimate partners.

Stages Three and Four are steeped in the belief that emotions define their reality. In Stage Three, missionary attitude groups protect their wounds by expressing negative emotions and demanding corrective action. Negative emotion and overuse of strong will damage the heart. In Stage Four, wounded healer groups open their hearts and move to embrace feminine energies; however, they confuse emotion with the intelligence of the heart. Because their emotions misuse their heart energy, they also damage their hearts. They overcare for others and ignore self-care. They eventually experience burnout in the form of mental and physical exhaustion. They resist calling upon the masculine quality of discernment to sort, label, and control the tumult. Wounded healer groups ultimately find themselves awash in a sea of chaotic energy. The fear of drowning and the pain of being lost to themselves compel them to swim ashore where they begin the long process of learning to set and maintain healthy boundaries.

Soul Lessons

Soul lessons in the wounded healer stage include shared vision, right relations, and service. Unique to this particular outer-directed stage, however, is the intimate relationship between group energy and soul lessons and the degree to which the individual soul lessons impact one another.

Stage Four groups bring forward a clear understanding of **shared vision** from Stage Three. Because they are rebelling against the restrictions of the missionary attitude stage and those of their First Groups, they overcorrect and the vision becomes tainted by **right relations** issues related to boundaries. Stage Four groups become overly inclusive, not understanding that being inclusive means to include those in alignment with the vision and mission, not just anyone. Confused by this right relations issue, they have difficulty defining their vision, which interferes with fulfillment of their mission.

Wounded healer groups also endeavor to throw out hierarchical group structures, believing that cooperation means groups can function without rules, organizational structures, or a leader. They create "floating boundaries" by avoiding implementation of policies, procedures, and standards that provide explicit structural support for the wellbeing of any group. Once a floating boundary for decision making is tolerated, Stage Four group members accommodate inappropriate behavior and often cannot reach an agreement that will move them forward into action. Multiple individual views within the group become polarized. Indecisiveness undermines the wellbeing of the group by creating conflict and resentment and impacts the ability to manifest shared vision. Without structure, members intrude on one another's physical, mental, emotional, and spiritual boundaries.

Wounded healer groups develop a group persona of selfless service in order to gain wholeness in relationships by giving to get. Because they give nurturance and support to meet their own needs, their **service** is disconnected from the greater good.

Challenges in the Aquarian Era

As they make the Piscean-Aquarian transition, Stage Four groups' difficulties in maintaining healthy boundaries will be magnified. The Aquarian values of cooperation and teamwork will challenge them to learn the importance of organizational structures. Because they take great pride in their service, they will be challenged to accept the great amount of learning they still have to do. They identify with their emotions and will resist transitioning from the emotionally based water element to the mentally based air element. They will have difficulty setting aside their personal needs in order to truly join in the greater good.

Conclusion

During the first four outer-directed stages, groups build a worldview aligned with certain outside standards. In the first stage, the world is unsafe and in need of protection. In the second stage, the world is chaotic and in need of ordering. Then, in Stage Three, the world is ignorant and in need of correction. Finally in Stage Four, the world is helpless and in need of saving. With these standards defining their worldview, groups relate through action and through wanting a world that is better for others than it has been for them. By the end of Stage Four, groups discover that the world they have seen so far has not filled their emptiness or fulfilled their need for meaning. Although still seeing a polarized world of we/they and right/wrong, groups begin to question their belief that other people have answers they do not have and that they can get what these people have through relationship with them. Eventually, groups fall into an existential crisis—a dark night of the group's soul—questioning their purpose as a group. To move out of the wounded healer stage, they must allow the preconceived structure of their group to collapse. Their worldview is no longer compatible with their group's emotional and spiritual evolution.

Rather than look to the world to give them security, confidence, and equanimity, they begin to look within. Every belief about the meaning of group life stands ready for review and challenge. All hidden motivations for service are examined and corrected. Groups that pass through the dark night between the outer-directed Stage Four and inner-directed Stage Five are ready to begin an intense period of group growth and healing. Rather than remain joined at the level of woundedness, group members commit to their wholeness, the integrating of all parts of the self—physical, mental, emotional, and spiritual.

CHAPTER NINE
SOUL-INSPIRED GROUP LIFE: INNER-DIRECTED STAGES OF SOUL DEVELOPMENT

Introduction

In Stage Five, healing the healer groups embark upon the long and often arduous journey toward embodying Aquarian group consciousness. In Stage Six, selfless action groups have attained sufficient inner strength and self-governance to set aside their personal agendas so that they can embrace an expansive understanding of soul development. Group consciousness becomes fully integrated into practice in Stage Six. Individuals enter Stage Seven: Beyond the Physical from whatever stage they are in when they physically die. Their stage of development and their vibration determine their group life on the other side.

Like leaders, groups experience dark nights of the soul–intense crisis periods of healing and soul growth. These crises occur during the transitions from Stage Four to Five and from Five to Six. Each transition is propelled by a specific commitment. To shift from Stage Four: Wounded Healer to Stage Five: Healing the Healer, the group commits to being self-responsible for healing on the personality level and to surrendering to the Group Soul for direction. To shift from Stage Five to Stage Six: Selfless Action, the group commits to releasing all attachments and to serving from Oneness with the Group Soul.

As groups transition, a slow dissolution process begins. We can image this as a person extending both hands, palms up and open. An empty cup

Groups create a magnetic impulse that reaches upwards to the Group Soul and to high beings who watch over humanity and bring Divine Light into our struggling world.

sits in the left palm. The right palm is empty. The cup in the left palm dissolves atom by atom. As an atom disappears on the left palm, one appears on the right palm. This dissolution and reemergence occurs simultaneously and continues until the cup on the left is gone and a radiant and sparkling new cup exists on the right. The cup in the left hand represents the group as a container. This container dissolves as the group undoes the mental models of the previous stages on the level of the personality. Each healing contributes to building a new consciousness container. Over many years, this new container, sparkling with radiance, reveals itself as one in consciousness with the Group Soul.

Aligned with Divine Purpose, groups in Stage Five and Six provide service on energetic as well as practical levels. Their members emanate energy from their hearts, functioning as conduits of energy from higher planes. With the distributed heart energy, the group supports members in claiming their inner authority and sharing responsibility for the group's growth and wellbeing. The group more easily stays on purpose for the greater good of the whole, aligning itself with a collective way of being and living in the world. Groups create a magnetic impulse that reaches upwards to the Group Soul and to high beings who watch over humanity and bring Divine Light into our struggling world.

The soul-inspired curriculum designed to help Stage Five and Stage Six groups meet the challenges and changes of the Piscean-Aquarian transition includes Group Soul, soul development, soul lessons, Universal Principles of Group Energy, and challenges in the Aquarian Era. Additions to the curriculum in these stages include the Energy Triangle Model and spiritual awakenings. Aspects of group life in Stage Seven are also discussed.

Stage Five: Healing the Healer Group Life

Stage Five groups engage in self-examination through inner work and self-transformation through service. Grounding themselves in the Universal Laws of Service, they develop their potential to function as True Groups. True Groups are those that practice the Universal Principles of Group Energy and whose consciousness blends to form One Mind. No longer believing in separation, they join together in cooperation on behalf of all group members.

Committed to growing in awareness, healing the healer groups strengthen the understanding that their inner reality—thoughts, beliefs, and choices—has the power to shape events and relationships. These groups use the Universal Tributes and their tenets as a roadmap to guide them through the uncharted territory of their group's psychological and spiritual nature. As part of this process, they become aware of the Witness Self—the capacity to observe themselves without judgment—and develop proficiency in self-inquiry. As they move deeper into this stage, they gradually become self-accountable without guilt or shame. A commitment to integrating the Universal Tributes into daily life requires self-effort, discipline, and practice until the group completes the transition into Stage Six and adopts the Universal Tributes of Mastery. Evolving group consciousness may take years, decades, or even lifetimes to manifest.

Group Soul

As members in Stage Five groups assume responsibility for their thoughts and actions by continually engaging in their inner work, they more easily receive and recognize intuitive impressions from the Group Soul. When members recognize guidance from the Group Soul, the group becomes conscious and aligns with its purpose, vision, mission, and destiny. Such alignment generates the inspiration and energy necessary to express the group's spiritual assignment as a joyful, spontaneous, and grateful instrument of the Divine. Conscious alignment with the Group Soul occurs when individual members have integrated personalities so that individual souls can connect and communicate with the Group Soul.

Group members set aside personal agendas while the group cooperates and practices shared decision making, collectively creating the means to attain the group purpose, shared vision, and mission.

The resulting soul-infused group personality, achieved through meditation and other spiritual practices, is more sensitive to receiving intuition from the Group Soul on behalf of the greater good of the group. Group members set aside personal agendas while the group cooperates and practices shared decision making, collectively creating the means to attain the group purpose, shared vision, and mission. The group philosophy emanates from all aspects of the organization.

Stage Five groups understand that the Group Soul radiates a magnetic pulse that holds the group together and, through impressions, prompts them to question what they need to master and what they need to give up. Members maintain vigilance until they approach Stage Six, at which time they attain mastery of the personal will and surrender to Divine Will.

Universal Principles of Group Energy

Groups in Stage Five relate to unpredictable and often chaotic energies of the Piscean-Aquarian transition in a manner unlike those in the first four stages. Rather than seeking to control or ignore disruptions, Stage Five groups reach inward for wisdom and strength. They view outside events as opportunities to practice the Universal Principles of Group Energy. Members develop sensitivity to energy and comprehend their group as a living organism, ever developing and actualizing its potential. Groups in Stage Five recognize that a group is a system of interacting, interrelated, and interdependent elements that form a holographic whole. They strive to function as one system in a living organism, knowing that all members benefit from the healing of any one person in the group.

Creative tension provides the fuel for striving toward the group vision. Obstacles and attainments are viewed systemically, as arising from a complex interrelationship among conscious and unconscious variables. Use of systems thinking enables groups to be flexible while maintaining necessary structures. Groups strive to be positive and uplifting, welcoming actions that raise their energy and move them closer to their purpose, vision, and mission.

Members recognize the presence of multiple group variables in the group's energy field, noting whether the group as a whole is affected by a blocked or incoherent flow of energy. They observe when personal shadow issues combine to form a group shadow. For example, individual pride in spiritual achievement can easily become group pride, a particular susceptibility in Stage Five. Vigilant to group energy, the group can acknowledge increasing ambivalence, resistance, or disruption of group process that often heralds a dark night. Stage Five groups willingly relinquish lower levels of consciousness for higher ones by reframing the purpose and experience of lower energies. Rather than viewing certain energies as unnecessary dissonance, for example, they respond to the energies as reflecting an ever-changing world and presenting a learning or healing opportunity. They use double vision to see the reality of a situation while simultaneously seeing beyond it to its spiritual essence.

The more deeply groups move into Stage Five, the more their members connect to collective consciousness. A group aura radiates the collective energies of its members. Groups that act as conscious groups emanate high vibrations into the community, country, and world. They can receive impressions from the Group Soul, illustrated by a creative idea developing simultaneously in several groups. This synchronistic communication instigates true partnership among groups with similar vibrations and ensures service to the greater good of many.

Stage Five groups create coherent energy through mastery of communication skills and practice of cooperation and team learning. All systems in the groups work together—physical, emotional, mental, and spiritual. The feminine (heart) and masculine (mind) energies work in partnership on behalf of the group vision and for the greater good.

Soul Lessons

Members of healing the healer groups make further progress in mastering the first four soul lessons of shared vision, right relations, greater good, and service, and achieve the early steps of the fifth soul lesson—to stand strong in group consciousness. They initiate the integration of Aquarian values into their groups. Members understand the relationship between their inner state and the quality of their service, and use the Universal Tributes and their tenets as a roadmap for self-responsibility and self-transformation through service.

Members of Stage Five groups vary greatly within this stage of soul development. They express a broad range of abilities to manifest the group's vision in a meaningful and practical way. For example, all members recognize the Aquarian value of cooperation, yet they do not all function at the same level of understanding or practice this value. Not all will fully grasp group consciousness, be fully self-responsible for their beliefs and behaviors, or breathe in inspiration and breathe out application of that inspiration through action.

Despite these variations, all members must hold an inner certainty that they share the group's vision, agree on how the vision will be manifested, and understand how decisions will be made. When a group of individuals come together to share a vision for the group, they energetically create a hologram in which each person brings his or her unique perspective of the whole. Each shares responsibility for the whole, as well as accountability for his or her individual piece. The component pieces are therefore not identical; each piece represents the whole picture from a different point of view. Joining the **shared vision** enables them to steadily progress in soul development, bringing them closer to the energetic vibration of the group. The group achieves their shared vision through creative tension—the tension between current reality and the shared vision that seeks to resolve itself through innovation. Members strive, individually and as a team, to bring the shared vision closer to realization.

Using inquiry, friends bear witness to one another's growth and avoid competition and comparison.

Group members in Stage Five define their personal vision and monitor its alignment with the shared vision. They understand that, as is true of any hologram, if a single beam of light (representing one member's energetic presence) is withdrawn, it diminishes the vitality of the whole image. If several rays are withdrawn, the hologram collapses. Members take responsibility for monitoring the alignment of their personal vision with that of the group and for leaving the group if they cease to feel aligned.

Stage Five groups strive to master the **right relations** soul lesson by using the group as a classroom with unlimited opportunities to heal and be healed. They see an ever-changing world, and with thoughtfulness, respond to healing opportunities. Should they react rather than respond to someone's words or behavior, they accept this as an alert to search for the unconscious parts of themselves and ask, "What do I need to heal?" They view every interaction as an opportunity to look within to find both obstacles and strengths for spiritual evolution. Individuals maintain healthy boundaries and refuse to become engulfed by the swirling chaos of other people's dramas. Their inner work and spiritual practices bestow upon them an inner calm and sense of order. They maintain their energy reserves, caring wisely for themselves physically and emotionally.

Friendship provides the foundation for learning and practicing right relations in this stage. Friendship nourishes the growth of group cooperation and group consciousness in an atmosphere of love and respect. As true partners, friends acknowledge the beauty of one another's souls. They support each other's soul development by using inquiry questions to open the door to their differences rather than by labeling and interpreting the other's behavior. The spirit of inquiry builds trust by avoiding assumptions and allowing friends to clarify their perspectives and examine their behavior. Using inquiry, friends bear witness to one another's growth and avoid competition and comparison. In Stage Five friendships, individuals:

- Hold a mutual vision for the friendship
- Sincerely desire for the other to be healthy, happy, successful, and prosperous
- Create clear boundaries that allow support without the imposition of will
- Model a refinement and beauty in thought, speech, and manner in their inner life and outer appearance that inspire growth in the other

- Maintain a calm manner, self-assurance, and sense of self
- Practice right relations and service
- Use humor that uplifts one another and provides space to see the absurdities of life

The progress in emotional, mental, and spiritual maturity coupled with the spirit and skill of shared vision enables groups to practice the **greater good** soul lesson, a predominant value of the Aquarian Era. Through intuition, groups connect with the Group Soul. By combining the truth of head and heart, they identify the cause of a problem and the path to its resolution. Stage Five group members put aside their personal agendas, apply cooperation, and discriminate between choices for the group's good and those that serve self-interest.

To serve the greater good, groups practice continuous inner work centered on the purification and integration of the shadow. In this way, their service becomes a means of purification, removing obstacles to the awareness of their true nature.

One way in which groups in Stage Five practice the soul lesson of greater good is by incorporating the Aquarian values of cooperation and consciousness through ongoing education, steady spiritual practices, vigilance, and willingness to learn from missteps. Three parameters guide the learning of these values—creating a safe emotional environment, honoring the process, and staying on purpose. These parameters provide the necessary structure for members to feel emotionally safe, to trust that their group process will unfold according to a higher plan, and to develop stable energy that comes from staying on purpose with the group's shared vision.

To serve the greater good, groups practice continuous inner work centered on the purification and integration of the shadow. In this way, their **service** becomes a means of purification, removing obstacles to the awareness of their true nature. They use every encounter and event to monitor their inner state and to reveal areas for inner work. The fruit of their unceasing inner work matures into deepened compassion for others, nature, and the planet. Their service depends less on the arena in which they serve and more on the state of mind with which they serve. With this understanding, groups become conscious of how they serve and are served. They experience the helping relationship as a dynamic and equal partnership between server and served. They apply double vision by acknowledging the true reality of Divine Love as they support the process of human life and nature.

The Aquarian Era requires a foundation of sound psychological and spiritual values to shift entrenched Piscean structures and attitudes. Groups may serve from a Stage Five perspective when engaging in activities commonly associated with work ethic, activist, or helping profession groups. For example, activism is associated with groups in Stage Three; however, Stage Five groups can fulfill activist missions by consciously combining inner work with service.

The soul lesson of **to stand strong in group consciousness** begins to manifest in groups during the latter half of Stage Five. With an integrated group personality and at one with the Group Soul, a conscious group practices shared decision making, doing the right thing in the right way for the right reason and at the right time.

To stand strong in group consciousness, groups must first master the four lessons of shared vision, right relations, greater good, and service. When groups stand strong, they hold steady to their ideals of cooperation and group consciousness regardless of internal and external challenges. They avoid becoming discouraged when blamed for failures not of their making or when others question their value. Aware that negative projections can enter the energy field of the group, they learn and practice methods of protection. They are alert to becoming ambivalent, knowing that this vulnerability reflects a lapse in remaining true to their vision and staying connected with the Group Soul and intuition.

As Stage Five groups develop self-responsibility for their inner state and actions, they begin to live their life in ways that support the to-stand-strong-in-group-consciousness soul lesson. They undertake the following actions:

- Practice the teachings contained in the section of *The Clarion Call* entitled "Guiding Principles for Aquarian Leadership and Group Life"
- Experience the self-transformational nature of service
- Resolve duality thinking and move toward creative synthesis of pairs of opposites
- Bring thought into action
- Develop a spiritual practice
- Live a life founded on spiritual, rather than ego-based, principles
- Bring the sacred into business, activism, and service activities
- Practice cooperation, group consciousness, accountability, and shared decision making
- Merge energies of head and heart, masculine and feminine

Challenges in the Aquarian Era

Although groups in Stage Five welcome the Aquarian Era and are aware of being in the world with Aquarian potential, the task of creating approaches to conscious and cooperative group life can feel overwhelming. While they practice inner work, integrate soul lessons, work with group energies, and apply Aquarian values, Stage Five groups are challenged to:

- Recognize their own arrogance when they believe that they are conscious while other groups are not and that they feel they know the answers and other do not
- Remain grounded in both/and thinking
- Stay on purpose with their inner work and spiritual practice
- Carry forward the positive legacy of the Piscean, including the legacy of the importance of group structures
- Support and value the vital role of leaders
- Support and value individuality
- Be alert to Aquarian styles of group life becoming as rigid and inflexible as Piscean styles
- Test new approaches without prejudging their effectiveness
- Consider mental (air element) and emotional (water element) approaches as having equal value
- Learn how to be, think, and act within true partnerships of feminine and masculine energies
- Adjust their leadership to the needs of the Millennials and future generations
- Practice discretion in using technology, not allowing it to replace wisdom, face-to-face human relationships, and partnership with nature

The Energy Triangle Model

Stage Five groups can incorporate the Energy Triangle Model into their group life. This model manifests the Aquarian values of cooperation and consciousness. The interaction of the three people at the focal points forming the triangle increases the flow of energy available for tasks, projects, leadership, and energetic support through prayer. The Energy Triangle Model succeeds only when each member of the triangle engages in inner work, uses appropriate communication skills, practices healthy boundaries, and views group life as a soul classroom.

Spiritual Awakenings

Groups in Stage Five are highly motivated to progress on the spiritual path collectively. With group commitment and effort, they endeavor to shift their awareness and to expand their consciousness. They strive to integrate the ten specific shifts for developing collective consciousness. These shifts are summarized here and detailed in Chapter Seven on pages 215-218.

- *Awakening One: The true source of equanimity is within.*
- *Awakening Two: The highest good for one includes the highest good for all.*
- *Awakening Three: Work and service are the same.*
- *Awakening Four: The world is interconnected and nondual.*
- *Awakening Five: True Sight sees the deeper spiritual meaning beyond appearances.*
- *Awakening Six: Answers lie on the level of cause.*
- *Awakening Seven: Responses to life events are made from the Witness Self on the mental level.*
- *Awakening Eight: True Service expresses in the world at all levels of participation.*
- *Awakening Nine: True Service requires* being *service as well as* being of *service.*
- *Awakening Ten: Personal will aligns with Divine Will to allow the unfolding of the destiny of collective will.*

With self-responsibility, Stage Five groups look within and discover obstacles to the awareness of the group's true nature. They develop the skill of

Commonly, groups find themselves beset by group discontent, ambivalence, resistance, and failed attempts to realize the shared vision. The resulting crisis is accompanied by a surrender of safe and defined opinions, accomplishments, and relationship styles.

using inquiry in the group to unearth mental models—beliefs and assumptions that impede the group's progress—and to resolve their differences. Group work becomes a means of purification when members view reactions as projections and as motivators for doing inner work. Through this process, they understand that the quality of the group's inner state determines the quality of their group energy and the quality of their service.

Like individuals and leaders, groups integrate the group personality through awareness of their true identity as expressions of the Divine. This recognition allows greater sensitivity to hearing the voice of the Group Soul. As the group moves deeper into Stage Five, it is able to consciously call forth and experience the presence of the Group Soul.

Transition to the Next Stage

Only when groups thoroughly live and practice the soul lessons of Stage Five are they prepared to move into Stage Six. The onset of this transition begins as a dark night of the soul, a crisis of liberation from attachments. Commonly, groups find themselves beset by group discontent, ambivalence, resistance, and failed attempts to realize the shared vision. The resulting crisis is accompanied by a surrender of safe and defined opinions, accomplishments, and relationship styles. The process of eliminating or detaching from outer and inner distractions challenges the stability of a group's inner reality.

Stage Six: Selfless Action Group Life

To bridge from the final steps in Stage Five into Stage Six, groups must have an intense passion and profound willingness to extend selfless service to humanity. To achieve this purpose, they must be fully anchored in the spiritual disciplines of meditation, prayer, contemplation, and self-inquiry, and be under the direction of an inner or outer spiritual teacher. Stage Six groups use the Universal Tributes of Mastery as a guide to help them acquire the quiet mind necessary to experience the purity of motivation and action that defines selfless action.

Group Soul

Stage Six groups are prepared to experience an intimate relationship with the Group Soul. Self-effort and Divine Grace have allowed them to surrender into the awareness of the Unknowable Absolute, into a state of complete safety and comfort in not knowing. They maintain humility by valuing the ordinary. "Insignificance" is what matters and not fantasies of power and fame.

Abiding in a state of emptiness—the state of Oneness in which nothing material clings and in which only consciousness exists—selfless action groups receive regular unobstructed impressions from the Group Soul. They recognize that maintaining alignment with the Group Soul depends on maintaining vigilance of personal will and its alignment with Divine Will. They know that a force greater than themselves is the true doer. Groups engage in selfless action and affect changes in others because they work in partnership with the Group Soul as spontaneous emanations of Divine Light living in the world.

Universal Principles of Group Energy

Members of selfless action groups emanate wisdom and love inherent in the Universal Principles of Group Energy. They know groups are living organisms that are guided in their evolution by a Group Soul and that this guidance can be disrupted by personality blockages. They grasp spiritual laws that determine who is attracted to particular groups and for what reason. Members support the greater good by relinquishing lower energy levels of consciousness for higher ones. As a group, they master cooperation and synthesize feminine and masculine energies as the means to manifest their shared vision. An awareness of collective consciousness of all humanity and nature pervades their work in the world.

Having integrated these universal principles, group members no longer defend against the energy of Divine Love. Their inner spiritual vessels are continuously full and ever increasing in power and purity. Stage Six groups have the unique ability to control how much energy flows and where it flows. Aligned with the intuition and the Group Soul, Divine Energy emanates through them in a manner that serves the highest good of others. Selfless action group members accurately perceive and read the energy fields of others, seeing what obstacles to spiritual progress reside in the subtle body. They can instantaneously become aware of what is needed to remove the obstacles and the chaotic energies these obstacles produce. They intuitively know what the person is able to learn to make spiritual progress.

Soul Lessons

Stage Six groups work with the soul lessons of group life at an advanced level. Having mastered the first four lessons and in the process of achieving the fifth, Stage Six groups function in an integrated and holographic manner. Shared vision, greater good, right relations, and service are totally integrated one with another. The gift of this integration is standing strong in group consciousness.

Selfless action groups express their **shared vision** by totally and consciously surrendering to the Eternal Dharma of right living and to their dharma or duty in the world. Members live the soul lessons of **greater good**, **right relations**, and **service,** and they serve with respect, presence, and right action. Unattached to the fruits of action, the uniqueness of the personality becomes a conduit for radiating Divine Light to convey a presence that is healing. As individuals, they bring wisdom into the world and ground it in the practical tasks of daily life. They focus attention in the present moment, trusting that Divine Light permeates all action and being. They work with precision, knowing that the Divine is in the details.

Because those in Stage Six have evolved to a state of selfless action, they exemplify the highest levels of service as duty, charity, purification, and devotion.

Because group members have developed and integrated all conscious and unconscious aspects of the human psyche, their personal will and its energy, skill, and goodness are a reflection of Divine Will. The personal self no longer feels separated from the True Self. They have assimilated the nutrients from the learning of multiple life experiences and allowed the outer shell that has been hiding and defending their true identity to fall away.

Groups in this stage have moved out of darkness, yet do not forget or fail to recognize the nature and qualities of darkness. They understand that the more enlightened they become, the more vigilant they must be about their shadow side. The temptation to return to duality is ever present, yet is counterbalanced by the strength of Divine Source. A fall from grace or regression to a lower stage of spiritual development becomes possible if there is any failure to practice vigilance or to maintain the spiritual discipline upon which their level of spiritual vibration depends.

They practice vigilance by acknowledging the nature of duality while standing in the place of creative synthesis. With this understanding, they become able guides and helpers to those who wish to move out of duality into a full and complete awareness of the Divine. In whatever ways they are called to serve, Stage Six groups combine the sacred with the practical. They relinquish any remaining selfish and hidden motivations and practice shared decision making in order to meet the needs of their service in the moment.

Because those in Stage Six have evolved to a state of selfless action, they exemplify the highest levels of service as duty, charity, purification, and devotion. They live selflessly on behalf of the spiritual wellbeing and growth of others and the health and care of the planet. To sustain an inner state that expresses selfless action and **to stand strong in group consciousness**, members must learn how to live and care for their human life in such a way that they can:

- Move into the effect to discover the cause
- Bring spirit into matter and consciousness into form
- Harmonize the frequencies of the body to the frequency of the Soul
- Maintain self as a vessel for Divine Energy
- Maintain an uncompromised discipline of spiritual practice
- Focus on personal dharma and on Eternal Dharma
- Practice the Universal Tributes of Mastery

Challenges in the Aquarian Era

Selfless action groups embrace the values of the Aquarian Era and teach these values through the example of group life. Still, they are challenged to maintain inner strength and steadiness during the chaos of the Piscean-Aquarian transition when stressed by the extreme demands to respond to calls for help. Stage Six groups bring the sacred into service while maintaining the bigger picture of evolution.

While participating in the Piscean-Aquarian transition, selfless action groups are challenged to:

- Maintain care of self, inner work, and spiritual practice during chaotic times in order to prevent physical, emotional, and mental fatigue
- Set boundaries that prevent being overwhelmed by demands for help
- Stay centered in Divine Light, vigilant to the pull of the world and negative forces
- Maintain a high frequency of vibration regardless of the situation
- Sustain patience with self and those served
- Persevere and persist despite appearances of "success" or "failure"
- Sustain a single focus on the ultimate attainment of a new level of consciousness
- Merge viable Piscean values with new Aquarian values
- Remain unattached to the outcome of their service

The Energy Triangle Model

Stage Six groups make extensive use of the Energy Triangle Model. They form triangles to circulate energy for the purpose of selfless service in all forms—tasks, leadership, activities, prayer, and guidance. Having attained skills in communication, access to intuition, and healthy boundaries, they work in teams of three with wisdom and love.

With cooperation and selfless service, the triangles increase the flow of light and goodwill. These service groups aid the Divine Plan by encouraging right relationships and goodwill worldwide. Manifestation of cooperation and group consciousness in the Aquarian Era depends on the prevalent use of the Energy Triangle Model.

Spiritual Awakenings

The expanded consciousness of Stage Six groups, like Stage Six leaders, is seen in the ease with which they connect to the Group Soul for wisdom and guidance. The group's divine nature continues to unfold. When the belief in separation dissolves, Stage Six groups combine pure love, will-to-good, and intelligence with their service. They view service to humanity as their purpose. Their pure love radiates without effort or thought to others and to the world. They serve unseen masters that oversee the evolution of humanity.

The soul's vibration at the time of death propels the individual soul through its transition and determines the nature of its journey and its destination on the other side.

Transition to Stage Seven

At death, people transition to Stage Seven: Beyond the Physical no matter what stage of soul development they have attained. In the Buddhist tradition, bardo states occur throughout life and after death whenever there is a juncture of endings and beginnings. In Stage Seven, the bardo states demarcate the soul's journey through planes of different realities between death and the afterlife. The soul's vibration at the time of death propels the individual soul through its transition and determines the nature of its journey and its destination on the other side. Helpers on Earth at the time of death and in other realities assist individuals in making a safe and peaceful transition. The practice of spiritual disciplines such as chanting, meditation, and prayer also serve to ameliorate the transition and ensure a swift and easy passage. The words spoken and the thoughts held at the moment of death impact this journey. Many traditions teach adherents to chant their name for the Divine to raise their vibration and ensure arrival in a place with the highest vibrational level possible. More detailed information about the bardos and practices for the dying can be found in Sogyal Rinpoche's book, *The Tibetan Book of Living and Dying*.

Stage Seven: Beyond the Physical

After physical death, individuals travel to other planes of existence where they continue to move through stages of soul development and participate in group life and group consciousness. A soul may first need to heal from life experiences. As its healing progresses, the soul is energetically drawn to a soul group that matches its aspirations, vibration, and capabilities through the Law of Attraction.

Every soul belongs to a soul group. Initially a soul's vibration may not match the advanced members of the soul group to which it belongs so it may not recognize its group or the group's members. A soul is able to rejoin its soul group when its vibratory level enables it to join in the group purpose. This change in vibration is evidence that the soul has shed the ego's mask that hid its true identity, and the quality of its vibration—the Light—radiates visibly to soul group members. Helen Greaves writes in *Testimony of Light: An Extraordinary Message of Life After Death*, "Seek for your own place. Ask that Light may open your mind to that which is for you; that your vibratory rate may be increased to respond to the vibration of your group; that you may become aware of them, for they are close beside you..."

A soul within a soul group progresses in its awareness of group consciousness and wisdom in developmental stages, eventually attaining advanced standards. Groups have purposes that differentiate them from other groups. For example, groups may focus on the studies of science and scientific development, medicine and healing techniques, mysticism, evolutionary patterns of the animal and mineral kingdoms, or the application of universal systems of thought and wisdom to human life. Very possibly, the embodied soul will be in a soul group that studies the same topic on the earth plane. For example, if the soul, when embodied on Earth, belonged to a group that focused on designing governance styles, it may find itself in a soul group studying that topic on the other side. Similarly, while embodied on Earth, soul group members with similar vibrations are often attracted to each other by specific life work or mutual interests.

Conclusion

The Divine Love that resides within groups invites members to use their life experiences for the purpose of awakening the innate knowledge of their souls. When members intentionally use group life experiences as opportunities for spiritual learning, their thoughts and motivations are purified and their souls' knowledge emerges. Sometimes, Divine Love penetrates their beings so deeply that It purifies deep and unconscious tendencies that have impeded their spiritual growth, perhaps for lifetimes.

Part Four

Practices for Living an Aquarian Way

Together, leaders and groups will
create a collective reality that simultaneously
honors each member, leader, and the entire
group. This collective reality is holographic,
with each person sharing responsibility
for the integrity of the whole from his
or her unique perspective.

Susan S. Trout

INTRODUCTION

The intent of Part Four is to support the integrity of groups and leaders during the Piscean–Aquarian transition between 2008 and 2025. Together, leaders and groups will create a collective reality that simultaneously honors each member, leader, and the entire group. This collective reality is holographic, with each person sharing responsibility for the integrity of the whole from his or her unique perspective.

Implementing Aquarian values in a new organization requires thoughtful reflection and necessitates writing a philosophical framework.

The task of founding a new organization with Aquarian leadership and group life values or implementing Aquarian values in an established organization can appear overwhelming. New organizations must tend to legal requirements, such as becoming incorporated, writing bylaws, and obtaining business licenses. They must also engage in vision planning, set up management structures, attend to staff needs, and determine program goals and activities. Organizations founded with Aquarian values have additional tasks involving specific practices and applications for leadership and group life.

Implementing Aquarian values in a new organization requires thoughtful reflection and necessitates writing a philosophical framework. Although this task initially delays the opening of the business, taking the required time to ground the vision, mission, and philosophy of the organization saves time in the long run. Being "born well" ensures longevity and a stable future.

Top leadership and management of some established organizations will be open to implementing Aquarian values in their organizations. Others will avoid the changes, viewing them as unnecessary and time consuming. Because instilling a missing philosophical framework or implementing change can be challenging, members become discouraged. Leaders may find it necessary to begin with small steps in a specific department with a few staff members who welcome the change.

While there is no specific roadmap for implementing change that meets the needs of all organizations, leaders can identify entry points—places where they can introduce a new concept or procedure that will meet the needs of the organization while also introducing Aquarian values.

Any one of the following can be an entry point for a leader, group, or organization:

- Establish communication guidelines
- Develop a philosophical container
- Determine ways leadership can partner with group members
- Assist members to integrate personal visions into the shared vision
- Assess the organization's current capacity and ability
- Strengthen team learning
- Implement systems analysis to address chronic problems

Structure

Chapter Ten focuses on Aquarian leadership. As leaders, you are the sculptors of your life and your leadership. Your responsibility is to explore your readiness for Aquarian leadership, engage in practices that prepare you for the role, and acquire tools, approaches, and applications that enliven your leadership and your relationship with the group.

In Chapter Ten, the following topics are addressed:

- Exploring Readiness for Aquarian Leadership
- Preparing for Aquarian Leadership: Practices
- Living Aquarian Leadership: Applications

Chapter Eleven focuses on Aquarian group life. As members of groups, you shape your relationships with fellow group members and with the leader. Together and individually, you explore your readiness for Aquarian group life, engage in practices that prepare you for the role of group member, and acquire tools, approaches, and applications that enliven your relationship with the group and with the leader.

In Chapter Eleven, the following topics are addressed:

- Exploring Readiness for Aquarian Group Life
- Preparing for Aquarian Group Life: Practices
- Living Aquarian Group Life: Applications

Any leader, organization, or department within an organization will find the materials related to groups instructive. Leaders often serve as a bridge to help their departments or organizations incorporate and practice the principles in *The Soul and Service Trilogy*. Among those who have adapted these principles to their settings are governmental agencies, university departments, banks, businesses, law firms, consulting firms, schools, and a range of nonprofit organizations. Corporate organizations also use Peter Senge's model of learning organizations and poet David Whyte's mediums of poetry and story to inspire creativity and soulfulness in the corporate environment.

Process of Study

Some exercises in Part Four are repeated, appearing in both Chapters Ten and Eleven. As a result the following recommendation is made:

- Leaders should work with the material in Chapter Ten, setting Chapter Eleven aside for a later time.
- Group members should go directly to Chapter Eleven to begin their work.

Through each exercise in Part Four engage your Witness Self. Refer to the witnessing practice on page 279 if needed. By learning to observe your process rather than react to it, you support your learning and your ability to see the bigger picture of your organization or group and the role you play in it.

Follow these steps prior to proceeding with your individual or group study:

1. Return to each of the evolutionary stages of the soul for leaders and for groups. Contemplate which stage best describes your leadership and/or your group.
2. Select the personal intention you would like to develop and express in your leadership or in your group. Contemplate the level of your commitment to this intention.
3. Select a point of entry from page 268 for implementing change in your

organization. Contemplate the level of your commitment to this point of entry.

4. Read through the material to gain an overview of its contents and return to it when ready to do deeper work.
5. Focus on removing the obstacles to leadership and group life by working with the exercises to prepare for Aquarian leadership and/or group life.
6. Along with or separate from doing the exercises, make a long-term commitment to studying the Universal Tributes and their tenets, the Universal Laws of Service, the Universal Principles of Group Energy, and the Overarching Principles of Holographic Leadership and Group Life. Choose one tribute, law, or principle per day or per week for contemplation and study. When studying the tributes, laws, or principles, read one in the morning and again in the evening. Recall the tribute, law, or principle several times during the day. After your evening reading, contemplate any insights that have arisen during the day and write them in a journal. Once you have completed all of the tributes, laws, or principles, begin again.

You may want to keep a log of your insights and awarenesses, adding various drawings, affirmations, sayings, or pictures that reinforce your learning process about service.

Writing in a journal will assist you in observing the process and progress of your leadership and group life. You may want to keep a log of your insights and awarenesses, adding various drawings, affirmations, sayings, or pictures that reinforce your learning process about service.

Joining with a partner or study group can be particularly useful and supportive. Small groups of three people can especially facilitate and support each person's process. Partners can share their responses to the self-inquiry questions and their experiences with the various exercises. Study group members might take turns facilitating a given chapter, topic, or stage.

Be sensitive to your emotional state as you work with the exercises and suggestions. Transitioning from a Piscean to an Aquarian worldview is a natural process and takes time. If at any time you feel overwhelmed or confused, set the material aside. Immediately tend to your psychological wellbeing by doing one or more of the following:

- Read uplifting or inspiring books or articles
- Listen to soothing music
- Contemplate uplifting qualities
- Meditate
- Go for a walk in nature

CHAPTER TEN
LIVING AQUARIAN LEADERSHIP

Introduction

To shift from Piscean to Aquarian leadership, leaders create innovative approaches aligned with Aquarian values while simultaneously bringing forward relevant Piscean skills. The Aquarian values and skills required of leaders emphasize inner knowing, cooperation, group consciousness, and shared decision making. With these values and skills in place, leaders dedicate themselves to the practice of conscious leadership in order to guide their group to a place the members would not go on their own.

The following suggestions are designed to support those who have heard the clarion call to learn and practice an Aquarian style of leadership and who have accepted the vast responsibility this call requires.

Exploring Readiness for Aquarian Leadership

A. Identifying Piscean and Aquarian Values

Objective: To assess your willingness as a leader to bring forth relevant Piscean values and skills into a leadership style based on Aquarian values

Directions: Engage your Witness Self, reviewing the witnessing practice on page 279 if needed. Each line below represents a continuum from strongly Piscean on the left to strongly Aquarian on the right. Place an X along the line in the spot that most closely matches your behavioral tendencies while in a leadership role. For example, if you feel that as a leader

	Piscean Values	Aquarian Values
1.	I value having authority invested in me as a leader.	I honor the inner knowing of those I lead.
2.	As a leader, I practice making hierarchical decisions.	As a leader, I encourage shared decision making.
3.	I depend on outer leaders.	I rely on my Inner Leader.
4.	I encourage competition.	I encourage cooperation.
5.	I am concerned with my immediate environment.	I am concerned with global need.
6.	I lead with an ego-led personality.	I lead with a soul-infused personality.
7.	I give priority to the welfare of humans.	I give equal care and consideration to humanity and nature.
8.	I see the world as win/lose and black/white.	I see the world as win/win.
9.	I live in the past.	I live in the present moment.
10.	I believe something is true based on faith.	I know what is true based on firsthand experience and knowledge.
11.	I embrace God the Father.	I embrace God, Goddess, All That Is.
12.	As a leader, I feel separate from group members.	As a leader, I feel in partnership with group members.
13.	When in a group, I feel separate from leaders.	When in a group, I feel in partnership with leaders.
14.	When in a group, I prefer men leaders.	When in a group, I prefer equal numbers of women and men leaders.

you prefer to have your group members depend on you as the authority, you would place an X on the far left of the line under number one. Mark your tendencies in general, even though your preference may differ for different groups you lead. After you have marked your tendencies from a leader's perspective, write a summary of your observations about your Piscean and Aquarian values.

B. Desensitization Exercise

Objective: To release the negative emotional energy propelling fears about being an Aquarian leader

Directions: Center and engage your Witness Self, referring to page 279 for clarification if needed. Write your response to each question below and/or share your responses with a trusted partner who can listen with emotional presence and with no interruptions or comments.

- What are my fears and issues about being an Aquarian leader?
- When I am a member of a group, what are my fears and issues about relating to an Aquarian leader?
- Am I willing to strive toward becoming an Aquarian leader? If yes, why? If no, what is holding me back?

C. Exploring Psychospiritual Readiness

Objective: To explore your readiness for practicing Aquarian leadership as a classroom of the soul

Directions: Study Chapters Four, Five, and Six for clarification of terms and descriptions of soul development, tri-leadership, and spiritual awakening. Center and engage your Witness Self before writing responses to each question.

1. What in my personal history (childhood, teens, young adult, adult) has most prepared me to be an Aquarian leader?
2. As a leader, what is my stage of soul development?
3. What are my soul lessons as a leader? (Select only one or two soul lessons.)
4. What is the story of my spiritual awakening?
5. How do I think others view me as a leader—my style, my strengths and weaknesses? What feedback have I received about my leadership? What would I like others to know regarding the kind of leader I am striving to be?
6. What are my leadership shadow tendencies? What part of my inner life am I not attending to that is holding me back from my leadership potential? What am I trying to satisfy within myself as a leader? What positive and negative qualities have I projected onto other leaders?
7. How would I describe my relationship to groups and their relationship to me as their leader? What is the relationship between being a good group member and being a good leader?
8. After reviewing my answers to the above questions, how would I describe my psychospiritual readiness for practicing Aquarian leadership?

Preparing for Aquarian Leadership: Practices

A. Preparing for My Aquarian Leadership Classroom

Objective: To personally and professionally prepare for Aquarian leadership

Directions: Before responding to the following inquiry questions in your journal, reread Chapters Four, Five, and Six and refer to their content as needed. Center and engage your Witness Self before writing your answers.

1. What within me is calling me to be an Aquarian leader?

2. What is the nature of my relationship to my Inner Leader?
3. What specific Piscean leadership values would I bring forward as valuable to my Aquarian leadership?
4. What are my three major leadership strengths and three major leadership challenges in the Aquarian Era?
5. In what ways does my style of leadership match Aquarian values? For example, how do I express the synthesis of feminine and masculine principles in Aquarian leadership?
6. What role could tri-leaders have in the Aquarian Era? Do I feel prepared to assess whether tri-leadership is appropriate to my group/organization? How do I feel about implementing and participating in such a model?
7. What Piscean aspects are visible in my group relationships? What aspects are Aquarian?
8. The shift from Piscean to Aquarian asks leaders to recognize, affirm, and elicit the inner knowing of the group through shared decision making. What qualities and skills will be required on my part to promote this happening? What qualities and skills will be required of group members in order for them to grow as a group and be empowered?
9. After reviewing my answers to the above questions, how would I describe my preparedness for an Aquarian leadership classroom?

B. Centering Practice

Objective: To expand your psychological space for leadership by connecting with inner strength and wisdom

Directions: Practice centering throughout the day so it becomes second nature. Centering is helpful at any time and especially in any anxious, fearful, angry, or confused situation. Sit in a relaxed position with your feet flat on the floor. Gently close your eyes.

1. Breathe slowly and consciously. Breathe in, breathe out; breathe in, breathe out.
2. Notice the body breathing by itself.
3. Now, take a deep relaxing breath and breathe out any tension in the body.
4. Breathe in, bringing energy up from the earth into your feet, legs, and body. Breathe out, bringing the energy down through your feet into the earth.
5. Feel your body firmly planted on the earth.
6. Gently inhale, bringing the energy up from the earth, filling and refreshing the body. Exhale, releasing into the earth any thoughts or feelings you may be experiencing.
7. Breathe in, allowing energy to flow through your body; breathe out, dropping your attention to your belly, your center of gravity, about two inches below your navel.
8. Now continue to breathe in and out in your own natural rhythm with your attention focused in your belly.
9. If any feelings or thoughts come up, breathe them down into the earth and return your focus of attention to the belly.
10. Fully experience yourself centered in your belly.
11. Allow yourself to fully experience the center of yourself.
12. Holding your attention in the belly, gently open your eyes.

– Written by Karen Watt, published in *Born To Serve*, pages 245-248.

C. Witnessing Practice

Objective: To develop the awareness of the part of the psyche that observes without judgment

Directions: Witnessing is helpful at any time, particularly when there is a need to see the bigger picture of a situation or experience. Plan to practice witnessing throughout the day until it becomes second nature. For this exercise, sit in a comfortable and relaxed position. Slowly take a few deep breaths and center yourself. Then make the following affirmations, slowly and thoughtfully.

I have a body, but I am not my body. I am more than my body.
My body may be in different conditions of health or sickness.
It may be rested or tired, but it is not my real "I."
My body is my precious instrument of experience and of action, but it is not my self.
I have a body, but I am not my body.
I am more than my body.
I am the constant and unchanging Self. I am the Self.

I have emotions, but I am more than my emotions.
My emotions are countless, contradictory, changing.
Yet I know that I always remain I, my self, in a state of irritation or calm.
Since I can observe, understand, and judge my emotions,
and then increasingly dominate, direct, and utilize them,
it is evident that they are not my self.
I have emotions, but I am not my emotions.
I am more than my emotions.

I am the constant and unchanging Self. I am the Self.

I have an intellect, but I am more than my intellect.
My intellect may be quiet or active.
It is capable of expanding, letting go of limiting beliefs, and learning new attitudes.
It is an organ of knowledge in regard to the inner world as well as the outer.
But it is not my self.
I have an intellect, but I am not my intellect.
I am more than my intellect.
I am the constant and unchanging Self. I am the Self.

I am a center of pure self-awareness.
I am a center of will,
capable of mastering and directing all my energies:
physical, emotional, mental, and spiritual.
I am the constant and unchanging self.
I am the Self.

Abbreviated Version of the Witnessing Practice

I have a body, but I am not my body.
I am more than that.
I am the constant and unchanging Self.
I am the Self.

I have emotions, but I am not my emotions.
I am more than that.

I am the constant and unchanging Self.
I am the Self.

I have an intellect, but I am not my intellect.
I am more than that.
I am the constant and unchanging Self.
I am the Self.

I am the center of pure self-awareness and will.
I am the constant and unchanging Self.
I am the Self.

– Based on Roberto Assagioli, *The Act of Will*, pages 214–215

D. Strengthening Contact with My Inner Leader

Objective: To establish greater sensitivity to the awareness of guidance, direction, and protection of your Inner Leader (also called Soul, Higher Self, Solar Angel, Guardian Angel)

Directions: Incorporate the following four essential practices and principles in your daily inner work and spiritual discipline.

MEDITATION
Description: Meditation is an uplifting spiritual practice that strengthens your ability to sustain an inner connection to the sacred while living in a world of intense activity and distraction.

EVENING REVIEW
Description: Clearing energies in your aura removes any static between yourself and your Inner Leader. Before sleep, review and acknowledge

thoughts and actions of the day that were negative or that did not match your values.

HARMLESSNESS
Description: With gentleness and compassion, strive to do no physical, mental, or emotional harm to yourself, others, or nature.

APPRECIATION
Description: Appreciation is a quality of the heart, a felt sense of valuing yourself, others, events, experiences, and nature. A felt sense is an internal bodily awareness that provides answers aside from mental reasoning. A felt sense of appreciation brings your heart into coherence with your mind, allowing greater access to intuition and the sacred.

E. Inner Leader Meditation

Objective: To align with the Inner Leader who protects, guides, teaches, and inspires you throughout your lifetime

Directions: Do this meditation either before or after your regular morning and evening meditation. Sit in a relaxed position and close your eyes after reading each step.

1. I acknowledge the specific times, yesterday or today, when I have acted against my values in my personal life and in my leadership.
2. To my Inner Leader, I declare that I will do my best not to act against my values again.
3. For two to three minutes, I visualize my Inner Leader enveloping my body in purifying ruby colored light that radiates outward five to seven feet. The ruby light cleanses my energy field of obscurations and negative energy.

4. To protect myself from negative energy, I use the palm of my right hand and pat my solar plexus as if patching a hole in it.
5. For two minutes, I visualize my entire body enveloped by the Light.
6. I sit in silence for two to three minutes.

– Based on Torkom Saraydarian, *The Solar Angel,* Volume II, pages 208-209

F. Self-Care Inventory

Objective: To establish support for care of physical, mental, emotional, and spiritual health during the transition between Piscean and Aquarian styles of leadership

Directions: Center and engage your Witness Self, referring to page 279 if clarification is needed. Set an intention for the next step in self-care as an Aquarian leader. Contemplate the following questions:

1. What is the status of my physical health? What steps do I need to take to support my health? Consider: exercise, diet, energy balancing, environment.
2. What is the status of my emotional health? What steps do I need to take to support my emotional health? Consider: boundaries, shadow work, communication skills.
3. What is the status of my mental health? What steps do I need to take to support my mental health? Consider: working with the will, balancing knowledge with experience.
4. What is the status of my spiritual health? What steps do I need to take to support my spirituality? Consider: meditation, contemplation, and other spiritual practices.
5. What person who is a step ahead of me in leadership could I ask to be

my mentor, to support and guide me? What do I need to work on and strengthen?

6. In what ways can I evaluate the success or failure of my self-care?

G. Challenges in the Aquarian Era

Objective: To identify possible leadership challenges in the Aquarian Era

Directions: Study Chapter Three. Center and engage your Witness Self, referring to page 279 if clarification is needed. As an Aquarian leader, (1) prioritize this list of areas of challenge from your greatest strength to the area in which you are weakest, (2) select one area of lesser strength you would like to improve, and (3) explore ways you could use an area of greater strength to do this.

1. Fear of change
2. Polarized thinking and behavior
3. Evolutionary transition from the water element to the air element
4. True partnership of feminine and masculine energies
5. Arrival of the Millennial Generation
6. Paradox of technology

Living Aquarian Leadership: Applications

A. Developing a Philosophical Container for a Group/Organization

Objective: To guide the development of a philosophical container for the practice of Aquarian values and structures in a group/organization

Definition: A philosophical container is a context and structure within which a group/organization maintains coherence among the many functions of its leadership, teams, triangles, management, programs, departments, projects, divisions, and customers. The container is the "glue" that keeps the members focused and on purpose while carrying out the group's or organization's vision and mission.

Disciplines: Leaders are responsible for guiding their group/organization through the logistical process of developing a philosophical container.

The following disciplines support leaders in their ability to fulfill this function:

1. Practice the three major roles of leadership: educator, organizational designer, and steward of the vision. To inspire, the leader must be inspired.
2. Teach communication guidelines and skills needed to guide all interpersonal, team, and group interactions. Considerable time is saved and conflict is reduced when a leader takes an educational approach and teaches a group how to practice deep heart listening, inquiry, reflection, and shared decision making. In addition, the leader demonstrates use of the Witness Self as a tool for suspending judgment and identifying assumptions.
3. Formulate and introduce one or two components at a time that are basic to the organization's philosophy and easiest to address, such as vision and mission statements and communication guidelines.
4. Establish groups of two to three people to explore a specific component and prepare a written draft before asking for feedback and discussion in the entire group. A written draft offers the group a place to begin and saves time. With the draft in hand, the group can clarify the content, provide feedback and perspective, and explore word definitions and other variables.

5. Educate the group about holographic organizational design and tools needed to implement and develop it.
6. Select the leadership style that will match the need of the group in any given situation. For example, deciding whether the people and situation require direction or need their input solicited through shared decision making.
7. Reflect on ideas during and between meetings before making any major decision. Sometimes critical information and intuitive wisdom come after meetings. Honor the adage: It takes time to save time.
8. Exemplify healthy boundaries in work relationships. Beginning and ending meetings on time builds trust for the leader and among group members.
9. Prepare a written agenda for every meeting with purpose and time allotment for each agenda item. Share this agenda ahead of time with group members.

Recognize that developing a philosophical container requires effort and time. All components of the container need to be revisited and updated annually.

Directions: Study Chapters One through Six before developing responses to the following outline of the components of a group/organizational philosophical container. The container evolves over time, guided by the leader with the ongoing participation of group members in all roles and throughout all activities within the group/organization—board of directors, staff, and members.

Seven Components of a Philosophical Container

1. PURPOSE, VISION, AND MISSION STATEMENTS

Description: Purpose represents the group's spiritual intent, vision states what the group reaches for as it moves toward that intention, and mission reflects how the vision and purpose are manifested in group activities and in the group's service.

2. PHILOSOPHICAL FOUNDATION

Description: The philosophical foundation, sometimes called a school of thought, upon which the group/organization is based determines the context in which the group evolves and assures that the group stays focused on its purpose, vision, and mission. The philosophical foundation permeates all group structures and activities.

3. THE OVERARCHING PRINCIPLES OF HOLOGRAPHIC LEADERSHIP AND GROUP LIFE

Description: Any one part of the organization—specific program, activity, or person—is a living reflection of the organization's philosophy. Each member's perspective of the vision of the whole is unique. What is true for an individual member is reflected in the organization. Each member shares responsibility for the coherent whole, not just for her or his piece.

4. COMMUNICATION GUIDELINES AND SKILLS

Description: Explicit communication guidelines for teams, meetings, and one-on-one conversations support self-responsibility and inner growth. These guidelines and skills reduce conflict and misunderstandings in the shared decision-making process. Communication skills include deep heart listening, inquiry, reflection, suspension of judgment, and identification of assumptions.

5. TEAM LEARNING AND SMALL GROUP LEADERS
Description: Teams learn to cooperate through reflection, shared meaning, shared decision making, and taking action. Their work honors the organization's purpose, vision, mission, philosophical foundation, holographic principles, healthy boundaries, standards and ethics, and communication guidelines. Leaders of small groups make effective presentations, facilitate dialogue, and give clear and purposeful directions.

6. HEALTHY BOUNDARIES
Description: Right relations among group members and with leaders develop when each person assumes responsibility for his or her actions and for practicing healthy physical, emotional, mental, and spiritual boundaries.

7. INTEGRITY: STANDARDS AND ETHICS
Description: Standards and ethics ensure that the actions of members and leaders remain coherent with the organization's ideals, values, and purpose, vision, and mission. Standards and ethics are maintained through shadow work and evaluation of competencies.

B. Setting Intention and Attention

Objective: To clarify a goal in order to select meaningful actions for self-development and for service to the group

Directions: Center and engage your Witness Self. Refer to page 279 if clarification is needed. Write your responses to the following questions or discuss them with a trusted partner. These self-inquiry questions can be used in a general way or for a specific task or issue.

1. What specifically do I want to achieve as an Aquarian leader? Or what specifically do I want to achieve with (*a certain aspect or value of Aquar-*

ian leadership)?

2. What inner work do I need to do to support myself in achieving this intention?
3. What specific action steps in my leadership and/or my relationship with the group do I need to attend to in order to achieve this intention?

C. Soul Lesson Reflection

Objective: To identify **one** or **two** of the first four leadership soul lessons and their sublessons to study and practice for mastery

Directions: Set aside a regular time for reflection and contemplation of the status of growth in your soul lessons of leadership. Document progress by writing your responses over time. Refer to Chapters Three, Four, and Five for clarification prior to responding.

Vision

Learning to formulate, sustain, and ground a **vision** is the bedrock underlying all soul lessons of leadership. This lesson gifts you with sustained energy and commitment to manifest your vision in the world.

The curriculum for soul lessons of vision includes the ability to:

1. Learn about vision
2. Formulate a vision
3. Ground the vision through the mission and organizational structure
4. Acquire skill in the practical, day-to-day operations that ground the vision
5. Translate personal vision into the slow, step-by-step creation of a shared vision
6. Create shared vision with members of the organization while maintaining healthy working relationships with staff and with the population served

7. Work with and appreciate diverse points of view while maintaining objectivity
8. Maintain constant vigilance for needed organizational change in direction or structure

Right Relations

When you neglect your physical, emotional, or spiritual wellbeing and do not engage in continuous self-development, you are a prime candidate to learn the second soul lesson, **right relations**. Learning how to be in proper relationship with self and others assures you that the highest good is served for all.

The curriculum for soul lessons of right relations includes the ability to:

1. Acquire self-knowledge and identify obstacles to personal growth
2. Attend to shadow issues
3. Study the nature of the human psyche and healthy boundaries and implement this understanding in the workplace
4. Apply communication skills and reframe mistakes as learning opportunities
5. Seek and use wise counsel from helping professionals, mentors, and spiritual advisors

Analysis

Learning the soul lesson of **analysis** helps us distinguish between criticism and the ability to analyze. The energy of analysis promotes fairness and a nonjudgmental attitude. The energy of criticism is judgmental, accusatory, harsh, and attacking.

The curriculum for soul lessons of analysis includes the ability to:

1. Assess a problem to determine accountability and address the solution without blame or condemnation

2. Apply systems thinking by recognizing that a system is made up of dynamic interactions between parts that form a complex whole
3. Appraise mistakes as opportunities to learn and to do a better job next time

Synthesis

Through the soul lesson of **synthesis**, you learn how to see the bigger picture or destiny of your organization. You examine your willingness to serve as the "glue" that creates cohesiveness within your organization.

The curriculum for soul lessons of synthesis includes the ability to:

1. Recognize every piece of the organization—person, information, idea, task, program, or event—as contributing to the creation of a shared vision and mission
2. Perform all tasks in the spirit of service and maintain a holographic team and a holographic organization
3. Apply both/and thinking and avoid polarization into right/wrong, black/white, either/or
4. Engage intuition and imagination for problem solving
5. Employ the Witness Self, that part of the mind that can stand back and observe without judgment

To Stand Alone

The ultimate soul lesson of leaders is to learn **to stand alone**. You achieve this lesson when you learn to unconditionally love humanity and after you have mastered the four soul lessons of vision, right relations, analysis, and synthesis.

The curriculum for soul lessons of to stand alone includes the ability to:

1. Express self-confidence based on feeling connected to your spiritual essence
2. Embody the spaciousness that comes with accepting life as it is

3. Face ambivalence about being a leader
4. Discern attempts to compensate for ambivalent feelings about leadership by misplacing trust
5. Acknowledge that you can stand alone only when you learn to love enough, regardless of the challenges and dangers experienced in the leadership role

D. Presentations: Self-Inquiry Questions

Objective: To prepare an effective presentation that considers the impact of the leader on the group field

Directions: Center and engage your Witness Self, referring to page 279 if clarification is needed. Write your responses to these questions in preparation for making a group presentation.

1. What does it mean to "assume the role of leader as presenter"?
2. How do I emanate an energy that participants recognize as leadership?
3. How does my nonverbal language communicate my leadership?
4. What does it look like when I, as a leader, assume a participant role? What are the risks for the participants?
5. How do I enliven the presentation without losing the content?
6. How do I choose the method of delivery and, when appropriate, the exercises to match the content of the presentation?
7. How do I encourage group members to share their inner knowing?
8. What is at risk in the group energy when I ask participants for an evaluation immediately after my presentation?
9. What are the risks for participants when I do not attend to group structures (i.e., supplies, boundaries, format, time)?

E. Feminine-Masculine Synthesis

Objective: To reflect on your leadership manner and style and determine how you are applying and living a synthesis of feminine and masculine principles

Directions: Center and engage your Witness Self, referring to page 279 if clarification is needed. Write specific examples of how you are applying a synthesis of the following feminine and masculine principles in your leadership.

STEP ONE: List examples for each heart-mind comparison. The examples given for 1) and 2) are provided to clarify ways of thinking about your own experiences as you address each of the items.

1. Idealism (heart) combines with practicality (mind) to bring higher values into reality.

   EXAMPLE: As a leader, I have an idealist view of communication. To avoid making assumptions and causing unnecessary conflict, I wish members of my organization would ask more inquiry questions. So I made a decision to have inquiry taught in our organization and to have practice sessions using inquiry. This practical decision has increased our use of inquiry and reduced the number of our conflicts. We are realizing a higher level of interpersonal communication.
2. Intuition (heart) joins with intelligence (mind) to emanate a coherent light that shows others the way to their inner light.

   EXAMPLE: I am a very intuitive leader and sometimes I cannot translate my intuition into words that convey with clarity for others to hear and see. Recently I wanted to explain my intuitive sense that a particular idea one of our committees proposed was limiting. Once I selected words that matched my heart and still respected their different view, I noticed their eyes widen with relief. It seemed they appreciated hearing an explanation that took them out of a right-wrong view into one that was a win/win for all involved.

3. Synthesis (heart) and analysis (mind) develop together to form interdependence between task and relationship.
4. Sensitivity (heart) combines with creativity (mind) to manifest artistic expression in the world.
5. Feelings (heart) desire to be verbally explained (mind).
6. All-giving (heart) joins discernment (mind) to take the right action.
7. Freedom and possibilities (heart) help resolve limitations (mind) to result in greater energy, efficiency, and improved physical, emotional, and mental health.
8. Inner security (heart) is visible in outer security (mind) to enhance living one's core values with integrity at home and at work.
9. Beauty (heart) asks knowledge (mind) to be used for the good of humanity and planet Earth.
10. Identifying the needs of humanity (heart) requires action (mind) to find ways to meet these needs.
11. Wisdom and intuition (heart) give the command to select the proper words and manner (mind) to match the heart's intent and create congruence between inner and outer realities.
12. Experience (heart) is integrated with knowledge (mind) to create one coherent voice, enabling me to apply what I know.

– Based in part on Torkom Saraydarian, *The Flame of the Heart,* pages 101-108.

STEP TWO: Synthesize your answers to the above by writing the following summaries and intentions:

1. A summary of my strengths in synthesizing the feminine and masculine

principles in my leadership

2. A summary of my challenges in synthesizing the feminine and masculine principles in my leadership
3. Three intentions I wish to accomplish that will result in my achieving a truer synthesis of the feminine and masculine principles in my leadership

F. What Holds Me Back Exercise

Objectives: 1) To explore personal obstacles that create a gap between your vision of expressing Aquarian values in leadership and the current reality of how you are or are not able to manifest these values
2) To identify specific actions to reduce the discrepancy between your vision and the current reality of that vision

Directions: When discouraged or concerned about the lack of progress in becoming an Aquarian leader, center and engage your Witness Self, referring to page 279 if clarification is needed. Contemplate each question. Write down insights and action ideas that arise.

1. What is my vision for an Aquarian leader? State clearly in one sentence.
2. What personal obstacles are holding me back from achieving that vision? Be specific.
3. What action can I take to bridge the gap between the kind of leader I want to be and the kind of leader I am? Be specific. Identify one action you are ready to take today.

G. Working with the Dangers of Leadership

Objective: To engage in inner work that supports my healing after an experience of projection, threat, or betrayal

EXAMPLES OF DANGERS: Someone engages in extreme oppositional behavior towards the leader; the leader is the target of someone's anger or rage; someone is codependent with the leader; someone opposes the leader's or organization's vision; the leader is betrayed by a board member/officer or staff member; the leader is psychically attacked with a negative projection.

Directions: Center and engage your Witness Self, referring to page 279 if clarification is needed. Write your responses to the following steps to explore your personal learning in the situation and delineate steps toward healing.

STEP ONE: Describe the situation.
STEP TWO: What are my vulnerabilities in this situation?
STEP THREE: What self-effort do I need to make?
STEP FOUR: What beneficent support do I need?
STEP FIVE: What soul lesson does this situation represent?
STEP SIX: What correction do I need to make?
STEP SEVEN: What action or communication do I need to undertake?

H. Shadow Trigger Exercise

Objective: To examine your shadow when you have reacted instead of responded to an interaction or situation

Directions: After experiencing an emotional upset, center and engage your Witness Self. Refer to page 279 if clarification is needed. Write your responses to the following questions.

1. What are the details of the event or interaction in which I reacted with an emotional upset?
2. What are my feelings and needs around the upset?
3. Who or what from my past does the theme of the event or interaction remind me of? When was it and how old was I? What happened?
4. What painful aspect of myself might I be projecting onto the present situation or interaction?
5. What underlying attitudes or outmoded beliefs might be operating?
6. What is the message of the conflict?
7. How have I, at a different time and with a different person, played the opposite side of this conflict over the same issue? (For example, if I am upset over a member who is late to a meeting, when have I been late to a meeting, class, or other scheduled event?)

– Based on Charles Whitfield, *Boundaries and Relationships*, pages 96–99

CHAPTER ELEVEN
LIVING AQUARIAN GROUP LIFE

Introduction

To shift from Piscean to Aquarian values and practices, organizations and groups must identify and bring forward relevant Piscean group skills while simultaneously creating innovative approaches to group life that embody values of the Aquarian Era. This shift invites groups to make a commitment to a steep learning curve. Groups that choose consciously to engage in the Piscean-Aquarian transition endeavor to combine knowledge with practice. By applying what they learn and inwardly know, they acquire a new set of skills that foster cooperation, group consciousness, and shared decision making.

Aquarian group life requires an exploration of readiness, preparation, and applications supported by experience, inner strength, knowledge, and creativity. The following suggestions are designed to support those of you who have heard the clarion call to learn and practice an Aquarian style of group life and who are willing to accept the responsibility this call requires.

Exploring Readiness for Aquarian Group Life

A. Identifying Piscean and Aquarian Values

Objective: To assess the willingness to bring forth relevant Piscean skills into groups based on Aquarian values

Directions: Each line below represents a continuum from strongly Piscean

	Piscean Values	Aquarian Values
1.	I value having authority invested in the leader.	I value having authority invested in the inner knowing of the group.
2.	I prefer hierarchical decisions made by the leader.	I prefer the group to engage in shared decision making.
3.	I depend on the outer leader.	I rely on my Inner Leader.
4.	I am encouraged by competition.	I am encouraged by cooperation.
5.	I am concerned with my immediate environment.	I am concerned with global needs.
6.	I participate in groups with an ego-led personality.	I participate in groups with a soul-infused personality.
7.	I give priority to the welfare of humans.	I give equal care and consideration to humanity and nature.
8.	I see the world as win/lose and black/white.	I see the world as win/win.
9.	I live in the past.	I live in the present moment.
10.	I believe something is true based on faith.	I know what is true based on firsthand experience and knowledge.
11.	I embrace God the Father.	I embrace God, Goddess, All That Is.
12.	When in a group, I feel separate from leaders.	When in a group, I feel in partnership with leaders.
13.	When in a group, I feel separate from group members.	When in a group, I feel in partnership with group members.
14.	When in a group, I prefer men leaders.	When in a group, I prefer equal numbers of women and men leaders.

on the left to strongly Aquarian on the right. Place an X along the line in the spot that most closely matches your behavioral tendencies while a member of a group. For example, if you feel that you prefer a group in which the leader makes unilateral decisions, you would place an X on the far left of the line under number two. Mark your tendencies in general, even though your preferences may differ for different groups of which you are a member. After you have marked your tendencies, write a summary of the observations of your tendencies toward Piscean and Aquarian values. Center and engage your Witness Self as you complete this inventory from a group member's perspective. Refer to page 279 for directions on using the Witness Self.

B. Desensitization Exercise

Objective: To release negative emotional energy fueling fears about being a member of an Aquarian group

Directions: Before beginning the exercise, center and engage your Witness Self, referring to page 279 if clarification is needed. Write your responses to each question or share your insights with a trusted partner who can listen with emotional presence and without interruptions or comments.

- What are my fears and issues about being in an Aquarian group?
- As a group member, what are my fears and issues about relating to an Aquarian leader?
- Am I willing to strive toward becoming an Aquarian group member? If yes, why? If no, what is holding me back?

C. Exploring Our Psychospiritual Readiness

Objective: To explore readiness for practicing Aquarian group life as a classroom of the soul

Directions: Study Chapters Seven, Eight, and Nine for clarification of terms and descriptions. Before beginning the exercise, center and engage your Witness Self, referring to page 279 if clarification is needed. Individually write your responses to the following nine questions. Over a period of weeks and months, the group is to select one or two questions at a time for discussion until all have been reviewed.

1. What in my personal history (childhood, teens, young adult life, adult life) has most prepared me to participate in an Aquarian group?
2. As a group, what is our stage of soul development?
3. What is our group's soul lesson? (Select only one or two group soul lessons.)
4. How would we, as a group, describe our relationship to the Group Soul?
5. How far have we journeyed on the path of spiritual awakening?
6. What are the shadow tendencies of our group? What positive and negative qualities do we project onto one another? What shadow tendencies do we project onto the leader? How do I and other group members hold back from contributing to the group's potential?
7. How do I think others view our group—its style, its strengths and weaknesses, and its shadow? What feedback has the group received?
8. What would I like others to know regarding the kind of group member I am striving to be?
9. After reviewing my answers to the above questions, how would I describe the psychospiritual readiness of our group for practicing Aquarian group life?

Preparing for Aquarian Group Life: Practices

A. Preparing for Our Aquarian Group Life Classroom

Objective: To individually and as a group prepare for the practice of Aquarian group life

Directions: Study Chapters Seven, Eight, and Nine so that you can refer to their content as you proceed. Center and engage your Witness Self before individually writing your responses to the following inquiry questions. Refer to page 279 to clarify the witnessing practice, if needed. Over a period of weeks and months, the group selects one or two questions at a time for discussion until all have been reviewed.

1. What within me is calling me to be in an Aquarian group?
2. What specific Piscean values do I identify in our group that we can bring forward to support our Aquarian group life?
3. In what ways does the style of our group currently match Aquarian values?
4. What do I identify as our group's three major strengths and three major challenges in the Aquarian Era?
5. What qualities and skills does our group need in order to practice the Aquarian values of cooperation, group consciousness, and shared decision making?
6. What role could the Energy Triangle Model have in our group? How prepared are we to incorporate this model into our group?
7. The shift from Piscean to Aquarian asks leaders to recognize, affirm, and elicit the inner knowing of the group. What is our group responsibility in making the practice of inner knowing a reality? What qualities and skills does our group need in order to grow together and be

empowered?

8. How would I describe the partnership of an Aquarian group with its leader?
9. After reviewing my answers to the above questions, how would I describe our group's preparedness for an Aquarian group life classroom?

B. Focus Groups on Group Consciousness

Objectives: 1) To set up focus group(s) to study and explore group consciousness
2) To formulate specific actions the group can take to apply and practice group consciousness

Directions: Meet in small groups of no more than six people to read and study Parts Two and Three of *The Clarion Call* and *The Psychology of Cooperation and Group Consciousness* by Torkom Saraydarian. Bring the material alive by applying the concepts directly to the needs of your group.

C. Centering Practice

Objective: To expand the group's psychological space for group life by connecting with inner strength and wisdom

Directions: Practice centering as a group and/or individually throughout the day so it becomes second nature. Centering is helpful at any time and during any anxious, fearful, angry, or confused situation. Refer to directives in Chapter Ten, page 277.

D. Witnessing Practice

Objective: To develop the awareness of the part of the psyche that observes without judgment

Directions: Practice witnessing to begin your day. You may want to use the abbreviated version during the day when in tense situations. Focus on seeing the bigger picture of a situation or experience. Refer to directives in Chapter Ten, page 279.

E. Strengthening Sensitivity to the Group Soul

Objective: To strengthen your sensitivity as a group member to the impressions and teachings of the Group Soul by incorporating four practices and principles into your personal inner work and spiritual disciplines

MEDITATION
Description: Meditate daily to strengthen the ability to sustain an inner connection to the sacred.

EVENING REVIEW
Description: Clearing energies removes any static between group members and the Group Soul. Before sleep, review and acknowledge thoughts and actions of the day that were negative or that did not match your values.

HARMLESSNESS
Description: With gentleness and compassion, strive to do no physical, mental, or emotional harm to yourself, others, or nature.

APPRECIATION

Description: Appreciation is a quality of the heart, a felt sense of valuing the self and others, events, experiences, and nature. When you express appreciation, your heart is brought into coherence with your mind, allowing you greater sensitivity to impressions of the Group Soul.

F. Group Soul Alignment Visualization

Objective: To align each group member with the Group Soul, which protects, guides, teaches, and inspires group members

Directions: This visualization is particularly helpful when done before a meeting of a team, class, or other group. It also benefits individuals. If done in a team or group, the leader of the exercise explains to those new to this visualization that the human soul (small "s") is located in the heart. Therefore, in the visualization, the words heart and human soul are used interchangeably. Each individual's Soul (capital "S") is located about eight inches above the head. The Group Soul can be visualized at an elevated level in the center of the group. Pause at least ten seconds between each step.

1. Take a deep breath to calm your physical body (pause), then your emotional body (pause), and then your mental body (pause).
2. Focus your awareness in your heart.
3. Visualize a line of energy extending from your heart down to the heart of Mother Earth.
4. Visualize a line of energy from your heart to your Soul located above your head.
5. Visualize the energy extending from your Soul to the Group Soul, which is elevated above the center of the group.
6. Visualize the energy extending from each member's Soul, located

above the head, to the Group Soul.

7. Visualize the energy extending from the Group Soul to Divine Source.
8. Sit in silence for a few moments as you hold this alignment from the heart of Mother Earth to Divine Source. See the energy of Source moving down the alignment to the heart of Mother Earth and then back again to Source, creating a circuit of energy.

G. Group Meditation and Contemplation

Objective: To regularly engage in group meditation and contemplation

Directions: As a group, set aside regular times to meditate silently and to contemplate on questions, concepts, issues, and inspired thoughts. After contemplation, members can share their individual insights and intentions with the group as a whole.

Description: Regular meditation, either when together as a group or at designated times when apart, raises the group members' awareness of their inner states so that they are increasingly able to hold an attitude of meditation in their group activities. Stilling the mind allows them to consciously connect to the Group Soul, enhancing their awareness of a higher plan and honing their intuition as a source of information and direction. Meditation leads to contemplation in which the group enters into silence that allows them to discover the faculties and powers of the mind, eventually tapping truth at its source and entering One Mind.

Suggestions for Contemplation:

1. Why is it so difficult to work together as a group?
2. What are some of our illusions as individuals within the group, i.e., some of the ways we justify feeling separate from other group members?

3. How do we move, as individuals, from feeling separate as a group member to knowing that as a collective, we have formed a *conscious* group?
4. What does "yes" from every member to every other member of the group look like?
5. What is every member saying "yes" to?

H. Group Contemplation on Self-Care

Objective: To contemplate the status of group members' physical, mental, emotional, and spiritual health during the Piscean–Aquarian transition

Directions: The group can select any of the following questions for contemplation and for setting an intention for the wellbeing of its members. Afterwards, members can share their insights and intentions with the group.

1. What is the status of my physical health? What intention do I need to set to support my health? Consider: exercise, diet, energy balancing, and environment.
2. What is the status of my emotional health? What intention do I need to set to support my emotional health? Consider: boundaries, shadow work, communication skills.
3. What is the status of my mental health? What intention do I need to set to support my mental health? Consider: working with the will, balancing knowledge with experience.
4. What is the status of my spiritual health? What intention do I need to set to support my spirituality? Consider: meditation, contemplation, and other spiritual practices.
5. In what ways can I evaluate the success or failure of my self-care?

I. Challenges in the Aquarian Era

Objective: To identify possible group challenges in the Aquarian Era

Directions: Read and study Chapters Two and Six. As an Aquarian group, describe potential vulnerabilities in each area of challenge. Propose ways to handle these areas of greatest challenge. Propose ways to capitalize on areas of greatest strength.

Some possible challenges are:

1. Fear of change
2. Polarized thinking and behavior
3. Evolutionary transition from the element of Water to the Air
4. True partnership of feminine and masculine energies
5. Influence of the Millennial Generation
6. Paradox of technology

Living Aquarian Group Life: Applications

A. Developing a Philosophical Container for Aquarian Group Life

Objective: To partner as group members with leaders in building a philosophical container for the practice of Aquarian values and structures in a group/organization

Definition: The philosophical container is a context and structure within which a group/organization maintains coherence among the many functions of its leadership, management, programs, departments, projects, divisions, and customers. The container is the "glue" that keeps the members focused and on purpose while carrying out the group/organization vision and mission.

Disciplines: Individuals are responsible for cooperating with one another through the logistical process of developing a philosophical container for their group. The following disciplines support groups in their ability to fulfill this function. Use of these disciplines also supports teams formed to do specific tasks as part of a group.

1. Develop and use communication guidelines and skills to guide all interpersonal, team, and group interactions. Considerable time is saved and conflict is reduced when groups and teams learn to practice deep heart listening, inquiry, and reflection, and to use the Witness Self as a tool for suspending judgment and identifying assumptions.
2. Practice healthy boundaries with one another and with the group. Devote group time to learning about healthy and unhealthy boundaries and how both impact the wellbeing of a group. Study the Group Soul lesson on right relations in *The Clarion Call* on page 207-209 and the book *Boundaries and Relationships*, by Charles Whitfield.
3. Healthy boundaries include honoring time. Arriving on time, beginning and ending sessions on time, and doing what one agrees to do are essential for building trust among group members.
4. Group members are responsible for the quality of their inner state and for continuously engaging in self-development.
5. Begin by formulating one or two components that are basic to the group's philosophy and easiest to address, such as vision and mission statements and communication guidelines.
6. Establish group structures and accountabilities, such as defining the role and responsibilities of the group leader or coordinator.
7. Establish groups of two to three people to explore a specific component. Prepare a written draft before asking for feedback and discussion from the entire group. A written draft offers the group a place to begin

and saves time. With the draft in hand, the group can clarify the content, provide feedback and perspective, and explore word definitions and other variables.

8. Learn and practice shared decision making in which every perspective is heard and the focus is on what really matters.
9. Take time to reflect on ideas during meetings and between meetings before making any major decision. Sometimes critical information and intuitive wisdom come after meetings.
10. Honor the adage: It takes time to save time. A group saves time when it applies what it learns about group life.
11. Have a written agenda for every meeting with a purpose and time allotment for each agenda item. Share this agenda ahead of time with group members.
12. Recognize that developing a philosophical container requires effort and time. All components of the container need to be periodically revisited and updated.

Directions: Study Chapters One through Six before developing responses to the following outline of the components of a group/organizational philosophical container. The container evolves over time through the ongoing participation of persons in all roles within the group/organization— board of directors, executive director, staff, and members.

Seven Components of a Philosophical Container

1. PURPOSE, VISION, AND MISSION STATEMENTS

Description: Purpose represents the group's spiritual intent, vision states what the group is reaching for as it moves toward that intention, and mission reflects the vision and purpose in the group's activities.

2. PHILOSOPHICAL FOUNDATION

Description: The philosophical foundation, sometimes called a school of thought, upon which the group/organization is based determines the context in which the group evolves, and it assures that the group stays on purpose with its vision and mission. The philosophical foundation permeates all group structures and activities.

3. THE OVERARCHING PRINCIPLES OF HOLOGRAPHIC LEADERSHIP AND GROUP LIFE

Description: Any one part of the organization (any specific program or activity, any person) is a living reflection of the organization's philosophy. Each member's perspective of the vision of the whole is unique. What is true for an individual member is reflected in the organization. Each member shares responsibility for the coherent whole, not just for her or his piece.

4. COMMUNICATION GUIDELINES AND SKILLS

Description: Explicit communication guidelines for teams, meetings, and one-on-one conversations support self-responsibility and inner growth. These guidelines and skills reduce conflict and misunderstandings in the shared decision-making process. Communication skills include deep heart listening, inquiry, reflection, suspension of judgment, and identifying assumptions.

5. TEAM LEARNING AND SMALL GROUP LEADERS

Description: Teams learn to cooperate through reflection, shared meaning of words, accountability, shared decision making, and taking action. Their work honors the organization's purpose, vision, and mission, philosophical foundation, holographic principles, healthy boundaries, standards and ethics, and communication guidelines. Leaders of small groups make effective presentations, facilitate dialogue, and give clear and purposeful directions.

6. HEALTHY BOUNDARIES

Description: Right relations among group members and with leaders develop when each person assumes responsibility for his or her actions and for practicing healthy physical, emotional, mental, and spiritual boundaries. Boundary work requires continuous self and group evaluation and practice.

7. INTEGRITY: STANDARDS AND ETHICS

Description: Standards and ethics ensure that the actions of members and leaders remain coherent with the organization's ideals, values, and purpose, vision, and mission. Standards and ethics are maintained by continuous shadow work and evaluation of competencies.

B. Group Life Soul Lessons Inventory

Objective: To identify one or two of the first four leadership soul lessons and their sublessons to study for mastery

Directions: Study Chapter Seven. Set aside time on a regular basis to reflect and contemplate on the status of and growth in your group's soul lessons—shared vision, greater good, right relations, and service. Remember that the fifth soul lesson—to stand strong in group consciousness—can only be learned after mastering the first four. Ask one group member to document the group's progress over time.

Shared Vision

The **shared vision** soul lesson serves as the foundation that supports all other soul lessons of group life. A group successfully creates and manifests a shared vision when they learn how to translate personal vision into shared vision; to develop, ground, and sustain a shared vision; and to evolve a shared holographic philosophical framework.

The curriculum for the group soul lesson of shared vision includes:

Translating Personal Vision into Shared Vision

1. Learn how to define a personal vision
2. Define personal vision and monitor its alignment with the group's shared vision
3. Ensure the shared vision is understood by all group members

Developing, Grounding, and Sustaining a Shared Vision

1. Know the definition of shared vision and how the shared vision will be actualized
2. Develop shared vision from dependence on the leader to interdependence between the leader and the group
3. Cocreate shared vision with the leader and members of the organization while maintaining healthy working relationships with staff or with the population served
4. Ground shared vision by holding its energy all the way from conception to realization
5. Use creative tension to ensure shared vision expands and reveals itself over time
6. Ground shared vision through the mission, group/organizational structure, and application of skills in practical day-to-day operations
7. Use appropriate skills and competencies to perform tasks and relate effectively and creatively on teams
8. Recognize that a group is inclusive when it consists of members who share both the vision and how the vision will be actualized
9. Monitor the direction or structure of the group
10. Resolve group conflicts about shared vision through self-development, inner work, and effective communication

11. Develop the Aquarian value of cooperation as integral to manifesting shared vision
12. Create shared vision by encouraging one another to make every effort to do their part in bringing the vision closer to realization

Evolving a Shared Holographic Philosophical Framework

1. Perceive each piece of the organization—a person, information, idea, task, program, and event—as contributing to the shared vision and mission
2. Permeate all activities, structures, and member actions with the philosophy
3. Hold the higher ideal of the organization's destiny
4. Think systemically, thereby enhancing the skill of analysis
5. Apply intuition and imagination to problem solving
6. Practice continual use of the Witness Self

Greater Good

To understand and apply the concept of a group's **greater good** is a complex and profound group soul lesson. The soul lesson of greater good depends on the group members' emotional, mental, and spiritual maturity, development of intuition and will, and the ability to synthesize.

The curriculum for the group soul lesson of greater good includes:

Seeking Emotional, Mental, and Spiritual Maturity

1. Set aside personal agendas for the greater good of the group
2. Monitor personality obstacles that disrupt the practice of greater good
3. Relinquish dualistic thinking
4. Maintain self-responsibility for behavior, reactions, and inner work that impede the greater good

Developing Intuition and Will

1. Define the Aquarian value of greater good as meaning that the greater good for the individual is the greater good for the group and vice versa
2. Use intuition as the key mechanism to identify greater good in a group
3. Practice head/heart coherence to determine greater good
4. Connect to Group Soul and greater good through regular group meditation and contemplation
5. Identify greater good and accessing appropriate action by connecting to Group Soul
6. Practice inner knowing as an asset to greater good
7. Use will and intentionality to practice greater good

Practicing Synthesis

1. See the bigger picture and select appropriate actions for the greater good of a group by synthesizing opposites (nonduality), partnering feminine and masculine energies, and partnering science and spirituality
2. Study Aquarian values of group cooperation and group discovery
3. Share the practice of greater good by being sensitive to the role of leader

Right Relations

When groups neglect their physical, emotional, and spiritual wellbeing and do not engage in continuous self-development, they are prime candidates to learn the soul lesson of **right relations**. The right relations group soul lesson includes self-realizing three values: healthy boundaries, friendship, and integrity. All three values are spiritual principles that create cooperation and group consciousness among group members.

The curriculum for the group soul lesson of right relations includes:

Healthy Boundaries

1. Study the nature of the human psyche and healthy boundaries and implement this understanding in the group
2. Develop and practice explicit guidelines in order to establish healthy boundaries between group members and with leadership
3. Write explicit descriptions of the accountability of each role on every team or group
4. Establish appropriate guidelines to acknowledge and handle the complexity of dual relationships
5. Recognize when the personal history of an individual triggers projections that impact the group
6. Use inquiry to check out assumptions and understandings of others' points of view and behaviors
7. Relate to members and leader with respect, avoiding discounting, critiquing, or negating
8. Establish guidelines for handling group conflict and assure that all group members understand and support these written guidelines and policies

Friendship

1. Encourage group friendships, defined as a context in which members support one another's spiritual development, transformation, self-knowledge, and creativity
2. Honor one another's authentic specialness at the level of soul while seeing one another's divinity and peculiarities
3. Work together with a spirit of cooperation, inner knowing, partnership, and consciousness, striving for integration of the group personality

Integrity

1. Value and respect communication and boundary guidelines, orderliness, timeliness, partnership, and all forms of life
2. Practice shared vision, greater good, right relations, service, group cooperation, and consciousness
3. Observe group process without judgment
4. Practice a synthesis of a diversity of views
5. Reframe mistakes as learning opportunities
6. Receive guidance through intuition by aligning with the Group Soul
7. Identify and implement the wise counsel received from helping professionals, mentors, and spiritual advisors
8. Respect Aquarian values
9. Understand and practice group soul lessons and "walk the talk" through behavior that matches inner qualities and motivations
10. Perceive and experience the gifts and lessons of feedback regardless of the form in which it is given

Service

The Group Soul lesson of **service** is unique in that it integrates the previous soul lessons of shared vision, greater good, and right relations. This integration occurs when groups learn to see the bigger picture and practice True Service.

The curriculum for the group soul lesson of service includes:

Seeing the Bigger Picture

1. Express Aquarian values of cooperation and consciousness as they relate to the group's service
2. Recognize an unfolding destiny of the group

3. Live from the perspective of universal truths and principles
4. Acknowledge that personal will and its strength, skill, and goodness reflects the Will of Source and thus serves the greater good

Practicing True Service

1. Establish a written definition of True Service
2. Determine and study the stage of the group's soul development through the eyes of service
3. Explore how the group's stage of soul development relates to its view of service as a classroom for spiritual development and self-transformation
4. Maintain self-responsibility for monitoring motivations for service and engage fully in psychological and spiritual wellbeing
5. Acknowledge and work with individual and group shadow tendencies of service
6. Experience the lesson of shared vision through the eyes of service
7. Experience the soul lesson of greater good through the eyes of service
8. Experience the soul lesson of right relations through the eyes of service
9. Integrate the first four soul lessons through the eyes of service
10. Receive intuitive impressions about group decisions related to True Service by aligning with the Group Soul

To Stand Strong in Group Consciousness

As groups master the four group soul lessons of shared vision, greater good, right relations, and service, they stand strong in the face of adversity and are open to fusion of Group Soul and group personality. They attain the Aquarian values of partnership, cooperation, and group consciousness.

The curriculum for the group soul lesson of **to stand strong in group consciousness** includes:

Fusing Group Soul and Group Personality

1. Welcome oversight of the Group Soul as it guides the group in learning Aquarian values of cooperation, consciousness, and shared decision making
2. Recognize that, as One Mind, the group does the right thing in the right way for the right reason, and expresses the group's shared vision and mission with steady wisdom
3. Develop self-confidence that emerges when the group feels connected to its spiritual essence and when it experiences the spaciousness that comes with accepting life as it is

Standing Strong in the Face of Adversity

1. Face ambivalence about being in a conscious group with Aquarian values
2. Discern when trust is misplaced in an attempt to compensate for ambivalent feelings about the group's purpose, vision, and mission
3. Learn to stand with steady wisdom when conflicts occur with other groups and when the general public projects negative thoughts and opinions onto the group
4. Acquire knowledge that, regardless of the challenges and dangers experienced by an Aquarian group, members can stand alone only if they learn to love enough

C. Practice of Accountability on Teams and in Groups

Objective: To practice being accountable in roles as team or group members

Description: Being accountable on a team or in a group asks you to hold yourself and others responsible for doing what you/they say you/they will do.

Directions: All roles and responsibilities are explicitly stated and written down on any team or in any group. Each member keeps a written copy. Responsibilities are what you do and are written using "ing" verbs. EXAMPLES: "I am typing the draft of the agenda." "I am arriving on time for team meetings." "I am sending my handouts to the team members for review three days before the next team meeting." Each member keeps a written copy of all roles and responsibilities.

Process One. Establishing Responsibilities

State the specific responsibility in question. Examples: "team teaching a class" or "recruiting enrollment" or "care of the physical facility." Individual team or group members respond to the following inquiry questions, share their answers, and mutually agree with all explicitly stated responsibilities.

1. What am I accountable for? (Not to whom am I accountable?)
2. What do I count on others for?
3. What do others count on me for? (Ask others, "What do you count on me for regarding the specific responsibility in question?")

Process Two: Clearing Unmet Expectations

Unmet expectations occur in two situations: 1) a member does not perform the responsibility that he or she agreed to, and 2) members misinterpret and make assumptions about a responsibility on the list. The situations are resolved in different ways.

1. When a member does not perform the responsibility that he or she agreed to:

   a. The member who has not met the expectation meets with the group face-to-face, reads aloud the relevant responsibility from the original list, and shares issues with meeting his or her commitment.
   b. The group processes the issue until it is clarified for all members using communication guidelines, inquiry, shared meaning of words, and shared decision making.
   c. Once the issue is clear, the member either recommits to his or her responsibility, or asks to negotiate the task.
   d. If the task is renegotiated, the responsibility is rewritten to the agreement of all members.
2. When members misinterpret and make assumptions about a responsibility on the list:
   a. The group meets face-to-face to explore the misinterpretation while referring to the original written list and while using communication guidelines, inquiry, shared meaning of words, and shared decision making.
   b. Once the misinterpretation is clarified, the responsibility is rewritten and agreed upon.

D. Shared Decision-Making Practice

Objective: To practice the process of shared decision making in groups and on teams

Definition: Shared decision making is a holographic and organic process in which a decision emerges from within the group or team as it focuses on what really matters and allows every perspective to be heard. This practice enables groups and teams to make decisions that convey saying and doing the right thing in the right way for the right reason at the right time.

Directions: With one individual designated to guide the process, groups and teams proceed through the following decision-making steps. For this practice to be successful, the person guiding the process needs to remind the group or team to **focus only on what really matters** and to always keep the decision under question in the forefront.

1. Do the Group Soul Alignment Visualization on page 305.
2. Pose the question, concern, or idea as clearly and succinctly as possible. Write it for everyone to see.
3. When a group or team is revisiting a previous decision, it is helpful to first address these two questions:
    a. What successes can we bring forward?
    b. What no longer serves us or needs to be acknowledged so it can be left behind?
4. Together affirm the intention to allow the highest possible resolution or response to the subject at hand to emerge from within the group or team.
5. In silence contemplate the question, concern, or idea for five minutes.
6. As each team or group member expresses his or her perspective, the other members listen with focused attention in the present moment without interrupting.
7. After the initial sharing is complete, the communication guidelines and skills are used to continue the process. The practice of suspension of judgment, observation, reflection, deep heart listening, identification of assumptions, inquiry, and advocacy is essential for successful decision making.
8. A synthesis of individual perspectives organically emerges as a shared decision is made that reflects an integration of the soul lessons of shared vision, greater good, right relations, and service.

E. Identifying and Working with Variables that Influence the Group's Energy Field

Objective: To determine what variables enhance (raise) or disrupt (lower) the flow of energy in the group

Directions: Read and study Chapters Seven, Eight, and Nine. Center and engage your Witness Self before doing the following four steps, referring to page 279 if clarification is needed.

STEP ONE: Under each variable, list what you individually bring with you into the group.

STEP TWO: Share as a group what variables you feel enhance or raise the group's energetic vibration.

STEP THREE: Share as a group what variables disrupt or lower the group's energetic vibration.

STEP FOUR: Set three intentions or goals you feel would enhance the energy flow in the group.

Variables Influencing Group Energy

1. Generation
2. Age
3. Gender
4. Size of group
5. Helpful beliefs and behaviors in First Group (family of origin)
6. Problematic beliefs and behaviors in First Group
7. Inner work practices and attainments
8. Healthy boundaries
9. Unhealthy boundaries

10. Spiritual practice
11. Awareness of Group Soul
12. Nature of previous experience with groups
13. Balance of natural elements
14. Healthy feminine (heart) and masculine (head) energies
15. Unhealthy feminine (heart) and masculine (head) energies
16. Stage of members' personal soul development
17. Awareness of group soul lessons
18. Awareness of group structures

F. Identifying and Working with the Universal Principles of Group Energy

Objective: To determine how the Universal Principles of Group Energy influence the nature and quality of the group's energy field

Directions: Read and study Chapters Seven, Eight, and Nine. Review the Universal Principles of Group Energy on page 176. Center and engage the Witness Self before doing the following four steps, referring to page 279 if clarification is needed.

STEP ONE: Write about your experience of each energy principle in the group context.

STEP TWO: Share with the group what principles you feel increases the energy flow of the group.

STEP THREE: Share with the group what principles decrease the energy flow of the group.

STEP FOUR: Set three intentions or goals you feel would support the group's awareness of the energy principles while in the group.

G. Group Shadow Work: First Group Exercise

Objective: To identify First Group (family of origin) beliefs, qualities, and behaviors that influence how you personally experience subsequent groups are experienced

Directions: This exercise can be done alone or while in a group setting. Center and engage the Witness Self before following the five steps of this writing exercise. Refer to page 279 to clarify the witnessing practice if needed.

STEP ONE: List five to ten positive beliefs, qualities, and behaviors, and five to ten negative beliefs, qualities, and behaviors you observe in yourself when you are in a group *at this time* in your life.

STEP TWO: Draw a circle that represents your Parent Shadow Pie. Draw a line dividing the circle in half, with one half representing your biological mother, the other your biological father. Use your biological parents even if they did not raise you. Draw an additional shadow pie if other individuals served as your parent figures.

Write qualities and behaviors you observed for each parent in their space in the circle. Note if your parents have similar or opposite qualities and behaviors. For example, both parents may have had a strong work ethic, or one parent had a strong work ethic and the other was a free spirit. Or, one was extroverted and social and the other was introverted and preferred to be alone.

STEP THREE: Draw a blank circle that represents the Shadow Pie of you and your siblings. Divide the circle into equal parts to represent yourself and each sibling, whether the sibling is living or has died (even if at or before birth).

Write qualities and behaviors for each sibling in his or her section of the circle, noting who has similar or opposite traits. Note if one or more siblings represents a certain archetypal trait, such the Artist, the Athlete, the Rebel, the Intellectual, the Golden Child, the Scapegoat, etc.

STEP FOUR: Compare the Parent and Sibling Shadow Pies. What beliefs, qualities, and behaviors are you bringing from your Parent or Sibling Shadow Pies into groups *now*? For example, if you were the rebellious one who went against any hint of authority, are you doing that now in a group? If you were the silent one in the family or felt your contributions were overlooked, do you hesitate to express your views in a current group or do you overcompensate by monopolizing group time when sharing your views? Or if your parents did not teach you healthy boundaries, you may not have healthy boundaries in a current group. Also, be aware that an aspect of the family or sibling shadow can erupt unexpectedly in a group. For example, you might project your mother or father onto the leader and react with oppositional behavior if something the leader says or does reminds you of your parent.

STEP FIVE: Personal Shadow Work
Excellent resources for approaches to personal shadow work include:

- Part Three: Unveiling the Soul in *Born to Serve* by Susan Trout
- *Romancing the Shadow* by Connie Zweig
- *Boundaries and Relationships* by Charles Whitfield
- *The Wisdom of the Enneagram* by Don Riso and Russ Hudson

H. Group Structures and Skills

Objective: To develop, establish, and implement structures that, when used together, provide a safe and vibrant psychological space for group learning and growth in cooperation and consciousness

Carefully study the following group structures and skills. Make a group intention to master these structures on behalf of your group's physical, emotional, mental, and spiritual wellbeing.

Five Components of Group Structures and Skills

1. COMMUNICATION GUIDELINES

Description: Guidelines for communication serve as the foundation for all group structures and skills. They provide healthy boundaries for conversation and dialogue among group members. Guidelines should be read aloud and explained in every group until they are mastered.

2. COMMUNICATION SKILLS

Description: The mastery of communication skills creates a meaningful and nurturing structure for group conversation and dialogue.

These nine skills include:

- Suspension of judgment
- Observation
- Reflection
- Deep heart listening
- Identification of assumptions
- Inquiry
- Advocacy
- Delivering communications
- Shared decision making

3. GROUP BOUNDARIES

Description: The practice of three guidelines ensures healthy boundaries within a group: creating a safe space, honoring the process, and staying on purpose.

4. GROUP MEETINGS

Description: Clearly outlined agendas ensure productive and creative group meetings. Agendas include items to be addressed and time needed for each. To be effective and respectful, all group structures need to be practiced in group meetings.

5. STANDARDS AND POLICIES

Description: Explicitly stated standards and policies provide a system or code of ethical boundaries for the group. They create an environment that supports the emotional and spiritual wellbeing of the group with integrity and respect.

I. Team Structures and Skills

Objective: To develop, establish, and implement structures that, when used together, provide a safe and vibrant psychological space for team learning and for growth in cooperation and group consciousness

Directions: Carefully study the following five team structures and skills. Make a team intention to master these structures on behalf of your team's physical, emotional, mental, and spiritual wellbeing.

Description: The most effective teams consist of no more than three individuals who come together for a common purpose. Typically, teams are members from a larger group that perform a specific function.

Five Components of Team Structures and Skills

1. PERSONAL PREPARATION

Description: Preparation is important before joining a team. Effective and creative team members formulate an intention and identify soul lessons, shadow tendencies, support needs, and methods for self-evaluation.

2. TEAM MEETINGS

Description: Establishing a format for team meetings ensures that roles and responsibilities are explicitly stated, agendas and materials are prepared, and a structure is followed that balances task with team relationships. Centering before the team meeting begins assures that the energy of team members is focused in the present moment.

3. COMMUNICATION GUIDELINES AND SKILLS

Description: The mastery of team communication guidelines and communication serves as the foundation for all group structures. Communication guidelines and skills provide healthy boundaries for conversation and dialogue among group members. Guidelines should be read aloud at all team meetings until they are mastered.

The nine skills include:

- Suspension of judgment
- Observation
- Reflection
- Deep heart listening
- Identification of assumptions
- Inquiry
- Advocacy
- Delivering communications
- Shared decision making

4. TEAM LEARNING

Description: Team learning begins with self-knowledge and looks out-ward to develop knowledge of and alignment with others on the team. Team learning goes beyond traditional team building such as bonding, communicating, and supporting one another. Self-responsibility is key to team learning.

Teams learn cooperation when they have a structure that supports different learning styles. Teams honor the diverse strengths of members, such as abilities to reflect, form connections, make decisions, and take action. Teams practice group communication guidelines and skills and learn to balance task and relationship, build shared vision, practice shared decision making, self-evaluate, and give and receive helpful feedback.

5. TEAM BOUNDARIES

Description: The following three guidelines ensure the practice of healthy boundaries within a team: creating a safe space, honoring the process, and staying on purpose.

J. The Energy Triangle Model

Description: The alignment of teams of three brings more energy to the team, their group, and those they serve. The wisdom of the team is greater than the wisdom of one individual. Teams of three share the workload and model interpersonal relationships. Together, they hold the space, honor the process, and stay on purpose. Teams of three successfully implement the Energy Triangle Model when their members are at a Stage Five level of soul development and personality integration.

Those comprising the triangle must be capable of:

1. Setting aside personal interests on behalf of their service
2. Honoring healthy boundaries, keeping time commitments, and following through on tasks
3. Engaging in their inner work with dedication and persistence

4. Promoting goodwill
5. Building friendships that are a source of inspiration
6. Functioning as an energetic unit, circulating three elements of spiritual energy—Light, Love, and Willpower—through the three linked focal points of the triangle

K. Group Cooperation

Objective: To develop four components of group life that foster cooperation among members and with leadership and that encourage a commitment to manifest the group's shared vision

Directions: Center and engage your Witness Self, referring to page 279 if clarification is needed. Carefully study each component. Determine how each component can be developed and effectively expressed in your group.

Four Components of Group Cooperation

1. SETTING INTENTIONS AND ATTENTIONS

Objective: To clarify an aim or goal in order to help the group select meaningful actions for self-development and for service to the group

Directions: Contemplate, write, or discuss the following self-inquiry questions. The questions can be used in a general way or related to a specific task or issue.

a. What specifically do I want to achieve as an Aquarian group member? Or, what specifically do I want to achieve with *(a certain aspect or value of Aquarian group life)*?
b. What inner work do I need to do to support me in achieving this intention?

c. What specific action steps in my relationship with the group do I need to attend to in order to achieve this intention? In my relationship with the leader?

2. FEMININE-MASCULINE SYNTHESIS

Objective: To reflect on the group's manner and style and determine how its members can apply and live a synthesis of feminine and masculine principles

Directions: The examples given in c) and d) below are provided to clarify ways of thinking about your own experiences as you address each of the items.

Center and engage your Witness Self, referring to page 279 if clarification is needed. Write specific examples of how you are applying a synthesis of the following feminine and masculine principles in your group.

a. Idealism (heart) combines with practicality (mind) to bring higher values into reality.
b. Intuition (heart) joins with intelligence (mind) to emanate a coherent light that shows others the way to their inner light.
c. Synthesis (heart) and analysis (mind) develop together to form interdependence between task and relationship.
   EXAMPLE: I work at a publishing company that strives to maintain a healthy relationship among its workers while getting the task done. We work in teams whose responsibility is to create ways to design pictorial communication cards that can be used by anyone in foreign countries. This idea was born out of a need for servicemen to communicate in Iraq. Not only does the work itself focus on purposeful communication, we do as well. Before we begin working, we check in with one another, briefly acknowledging how we are doing in our

lives. Practicing the language cards with one another also strengthens our relationships.

d. Sensitivity (heart) combines with creativity (mind) to manifest artistic expression in the world. Feelings (heart) desire to be verbally explained (mind).

   EXAMPLE: I am a member of a group of people whose intent is to create a healthy nonprofit service organization. We view our intent as an art form. To develop a healthy organization requires a sensitivity to the minds and hearts of others and considerable creativity to bring it about. It has taken us many years to develop a philosophy that honors ourselves and those we serve.

e. All-giving (heart) joins discernment (mind) to take the right action.

f. Freedom and possibilities (heart) help resolve limitations (mind) to result in greater energy, efficiency, and improved physical, emotional, and mental health.

g. Inner security (heart) is visible in outer security (mind) to enhance living one's core values with integrity at home and at work.

h. Beauty (heart) asks knowledge (mind) to be used for the good of humanity and planet Earth.

i. Identifying the needs of humanity (heart) requires action (mind) to find ways to meet these needs.

j. Wisdom and intuition (heart) give the command to select the proper words and manner (mind) to match the heart's intent and create congruence between inner and outer realities.

k. Experience (heart) is integrated with knowledge (mind) to create one coherent voice, enabling me to apply what I know.

– Based in part on Torkom Saraydarian, *The Flame of the Heart,* pages 101-108

Individually synthesize your answers to the above by writing the following summaries and intentions:

- A summary of my strengths in synthesizing the feminine and masculine principles in the group
- A summary of my challenges in synthesizing the feminine and masculine principles in the group
- As a group, list three intentions that will result in the group achieving a truer synthesis of the feminine and masculine principles in its group life

3. FRIENDSHIP

Objective: To explore ways in which group members can consciously support the soul development of one another and honor the value that each member contributes to the whole of the group

Directions: After centering and engaging the Witness Self, individually write responses to the following inquiry questions. When all your members have completed the inquiry, share your insights with the group, concluding by forming a group intention to foster friendships in the group.

a. How would I describe the single value of the group when viewed as a whole, undivided unit?
b. If I view each group member as being an essential piece of a puzzle, what piece do I see each group member being? (It could be a physical, emotional, mental, or spiritual piece.)
c. What is my piece of the puzzle and how does it relate to the other pieces?
d. What is my vision for friendship and what is my commitment to this vision?
e. What obstacles do I need to dissolve within myself in order to contrib-

ute to the health, happiness, prosperity, and soul development of the members of the group?

f. How can I specifically contribute to the health, happiness, prosperity, and soul development of my fellow group members?

4. INTEGRITY

Objective: To develop a group Code of Integrity that supports doing and being what is espoused

Directions: Read this purpose of a Code of Integrity aloud to the group: *"Qualities and motivations conveyed on the outside must match the qualities and motivations possessed on the inside. The congruence of inner to outer and being to doing creates self-confidence in group members. An aura of honesty, sincerity, authenticity, ease, and appreciation surrounds the group. A Code of Integrity is kept alive and purposeful by integrating it into group discussions and by using it as a group self-evaluation."*

Center and engage the Witness Self, referring to page 279 if clarification is needed. Individually write responses to the following inquiry questions. Share your insights within the group. Write a joint Code of Integrity for your group.

a. How can the group ensure that all forms of life energy—physical, emotional, mental, and spiritual—have equal value and are not wasted and misused?
b. In what ways can the group foster orderliness as a container that holds the purpose, vision, and mission of the group?
c. How can the group accomplish tasks with efficiency and competence while having time and energy for maintaining right relations?
d. What are specific ways the group values and respects time?
e. How can change be conveyed in a way that honors each member's role

so that change invigorates the spirit of the group?

f. In what ways can partnership in "getting the job done" support unity of purpose and shared vision?
g. What guidelines need to be put into place so members view mistakes as learning opportunities and not as judgments on their personal value?
h. How can genuine appreciation and gratitude be expressed to other group members through thoughts, words, and actions?

L. Group Contemplation

Objective: To explore the group's understanding and application of group cooperation and consciousness using contemplation

Directions: The group proceeds through the following ten steps as a group:

1. Select one of the statements for contemplation.
2. Center and engage the Witness Self, referring to page 279 if clarification is needed.
3. Align with the Group Soul using the Group Soul Alignment Visualization on page 305.
4. Contemplate the question or statement for ten minutes.
5. Individually write down insights and awarenesses.
6. Share the contemplation experience with a partner in the group or with the entire group.
7. As a group, glean the essential message(s) of the contemplation.
8. Set an intention.
9. Decide whether to act on the intention.
10. Act on the intention.

Statements:

- "Every time we think we have to decide between our interests and the interest of the group, it is an illusion."
- "Groups show us exactly our point of development, our needs, our group-wounds. Groups challenge us exactly in the way we need to free and use our gifts. So, the biggest problems in our groups are leading us to our biggest gifts."
- "The more individual group members are in contact with their hearts and souls, the more conscious they become. More and more light can then flow in and support the group's vision. The group radiates light and the power to manifest grows."
- "In a developed group, people still have their special gifts and tasks and there are still differences of competence and differences in consciousness development in different areas. But, the knowing about the group 'I' becomes so powerful that the differences can be welcomed as an abundance of possibilities and choices."
- "A group is conscious when each member of a group cares about, nurtures, and supports the soul development of every other member. A group practices group consciousness when group members care about, nurture and support the soul development of the group leader. A group that practices group consciousness is a healed group."

– Ludger Scholl, "Structures of Group Energy"
Used with permission

M. Group Self-Evaluation: What's Holding Us Back?

Objective: 1) To identify personal obstacles that create a gap between the group's vision to manifest Aquarian values in group life and the current reality of how the group is or is not able to express these values.

2) To identify specific actions to reduce the discrepancy between the group's vision and the current reality of that vision.

Directions: When individuals or the group become discouraged or concerned about the lack of progress in becoming an Aquarian group, follow these steps. Center and engage your Witness Self, referring to page 279 if clarification is needed. Contemplate the following questions. Write insights and action ideas that arise. Share these insights and ideas with the group as a whole.

1. What is my vision for our Aquarian group? State clearly in one sentence.
2. What personal obstacles are holding me back from achieving that vision? Be specific.
3. What action do I feel we can take to bridge the gap between the kind of group we want to be and the kind of group we are? What one action do I think we are ready to take today?

Epilogue

True Groups consist of members
who practice the Universal Principles
of Group Energy and whose consciousness
blends to form One Mind.

Susan S. Trout

EPILOGUE

When you move into the pillar, the pillar moves into you.
– Master Chang

While writing *The Clarion Call*, I walked cautiously into the uncharted territory of the unstable years between 2008 and 2025 of the early Aquarian Era. The year 2008 marked the midpoint between the five-hundred-year transition from the Piscean to the Aquarian eras. I selected the year 2025 and learned only later that the date holds great significance in esoteric writings as the year the Great Assembly of Masters on the inner planes will next assemble to reassess humanity's progress in world governance and world religion. The Great Masters' vision is that humanity be ready by that date to welcome the Kingdom of God on Earth as revealed through the perfection of consciousness known as Christhood and Buddhahood.

I intend *The Clarion Call* as a roadmap for navigating the vast humanitarian and planetary crises that are occurring between 2008 and 2025. Addressing these crises and the profound needs they will engender is a soul matter. I believe that the stages of soul development for individuals, leaders, groups, and organizations provide a meaningful context for such a roadmap.

Increasing numbers of people and groups have been drawn to spiritual development over the past fifty years. Many know their unique assignments during the early Aquarian and have already positioned themselves to play critical roles. I refer to these people and groups as *brilliants.*

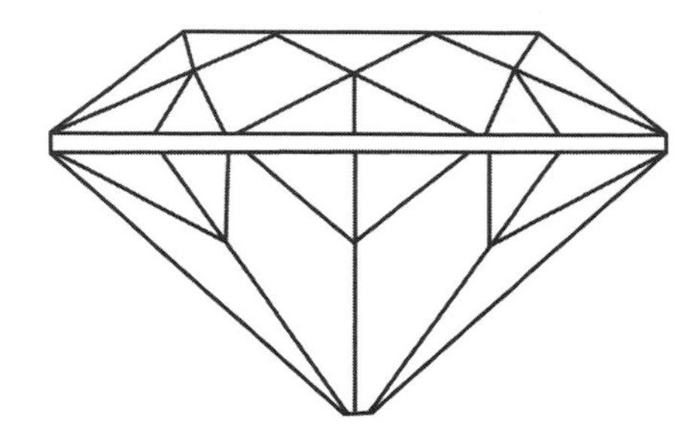

Figure 10. Brilliant, side view. Drawing by Ginger Graziano

The term "brilliant" refers both to a gem and to a specific cut shape for gems—the preferred one for diamonds. The cone-like design consists of a flat top with numerous triangular and diamond-shaped facets that maximize light return through the top. I interpret brilliant as a metaphor for an Aquarian organization, the facets being the numerous Energy Trian-

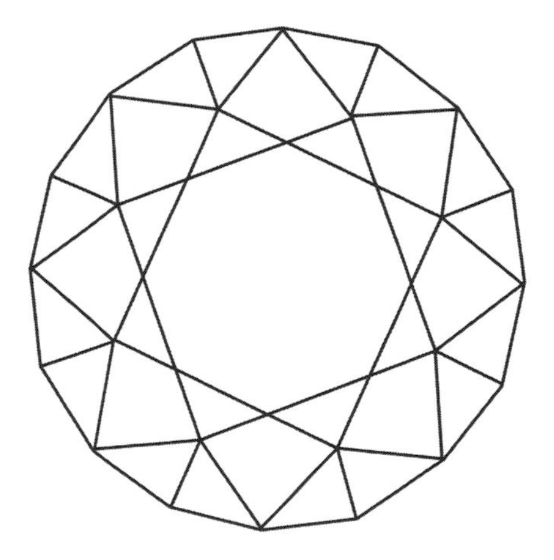

Figure 11. Brilliant, top view. Drawing by Ginger Graziano

gles and the top representing the organization's Soul through which Light pours from the Divine Source and is exchanged with all the parts and with the outer world. On an another level, each individual, leader, and group is also a brilliant and responsible for polishing their respective facets to maximize the return of Light to their unique assignment.

The world, too, is a brilliant, a gem in the form of a living organism with a vision, current reality, and creative tension. Interrelated and interdependent, the world forms a hologram whose wholeness can be viewed from different perspectives of people, cultures, and countries. Each part of the world is a microcosm of the macrocosm. When respect and appreciation prevail in any one geographic location, the heart emanates a healing energy field beyond borders to the rest of the planet. As a brilliant, the world maximizes the emanation and returns the Light. Souls hear the clarion call to join in the Light of the brilliant.

* * *

During my Piscean years, I sought to discover the voice of my True Power, although I did not refer to the search in those terms in early life. I only knew I wanted to be a writer and a poet and run an orphanage. Vivid memories of being told "no" started young and I sensed it was a "no" to quiet the voice of my many questions and teach me to obey common values of the Piscean Era, especially those of competition, faith, and rigid rules governing conventionality. I quieted my voice, until before long it changed to reflect objective masculine values and led me onto the path of rational thought, order, and practicality. But my destiny called and my Soul urged me to follow. Slowly my voice gained strength and clarity. Now, my True Voice sounds a herald of triumph, resounding as a creative flow. True Power reverberates through my total being, blending the harmonious energies of my heart, the feminine, with my head, the masculine.

On the cusp of the Aquarian Era, I invite you to join me in answering the clarion call to rediscover and reclaim your True Voice. With a True Voice, an Aquarian voice, we are willing trumpets and messengers of the energy that flows from the Divine through the Soul to be welcomed into a soul-infused personality. WE STAND STRONG IN THE LIGHT, regardless of what challenges lie ahead as we move forward together.

The ancient clarion call of life—
of the Divine to the human, of the Self to the self, and of the Soul to the personality—
will yet be the last trumpet that the world will ever hear.

Susan S. Trout

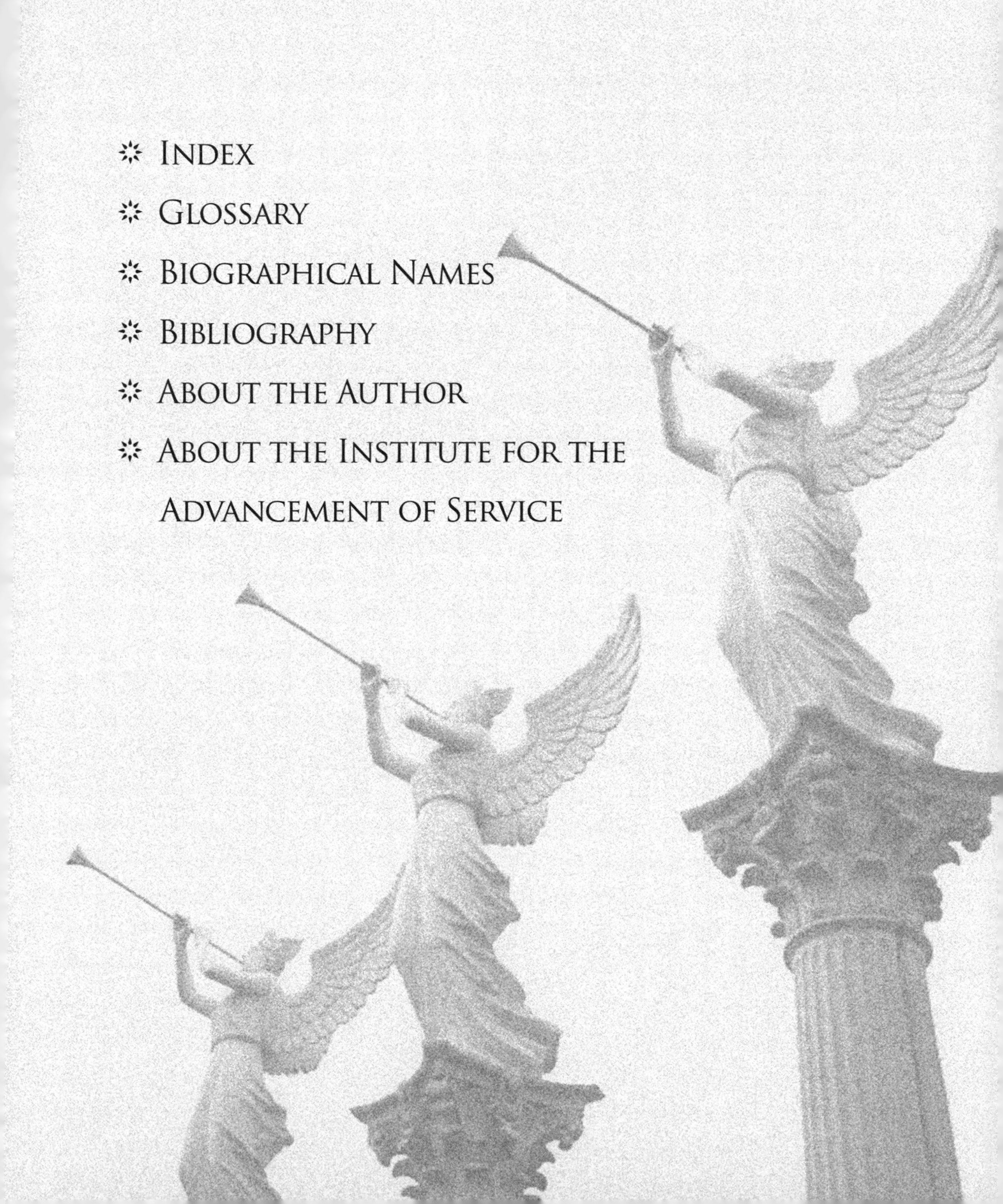

- Index
- Glossary
- Biographical Names
- Bibliography
- About the Author
- About the Institute for the Advancement of Service

INDEX

Numbers in *italics* indicate figures.

- C -

- G -

- H -

- J -

- K -

- L -

- N -

- O -

- P -

- Q -

- R -

- T -

- U -

- V -

- W -

- Y -

- Z -

GLOSSARY

Ageless Wisdom: a body of spiritual and metaphysical teachings—ideals, laws, truths—given by great spiritual masters and teachers throughout time; also referred to as Ancient Wisdom

Aquarian values: inner authority, partnership, group consciousness, and the synthesis of masculine and feminine energies

astrology: the study of celestial alignments and their influence on earth activities

astrological cycle: a span of approximately two thousand years that is the result of a precession of the equinoxes; identified by the movement of a grouping of stars called a "sign" of the zodiac

bardo: in this book, any one of many vibrational levels of different realities experienced in the intermediate state between death and rebirth; Buddhism teaches that "bardos *are occurring continuously throughout life and death,* and are junctures when the possibility of liberation, or enlightenment, is heightened" (Sogyal Rinpoche: *The Tibetan Book of Living and Dying*)

bodhisattva: in this book, the term applies to any person, regardless of spiritual tradition, who is dedicated to selfless service; traditionally, a Buddhist who postpones enlightenment in order to serve selflessly at the level of the cause of suffering

consciousness: awareness that exists in various stages of development through experience; over time, the human soul evolves in consciousness

creative tension: push-pull energy that exists between a future goal to be attained and the current reality of the level in which the goal exists, between what we want and where we are relative to what we want

cultural creatives: a global subculture identified as individuals who are leading soul-oriented lives and caring deeply about spirituality, self-actualization, self-expression, social justice, and ecology

deep heart listening: listening to another in silence with an attitude of unconditional acceptance and without judgment or need to interrupt or critique what is being spoken

dharma: the individual's practice of peace and service by following a unique duty and function in the world from a place of right attitude

Dharma: a moral law of spiritual Truth used in Eastern spiritual traditions that refers to the duty to serve God

duality: the mental process of dividing aspects of human behavior into opposites like right/wrong, good/bad, light/dark

ego: that voice of the human psyche that speaks against the soul's identity with the Divine

felt sense: an internal bodily awareness; a body-sense of meaning that provides answers aside from mental reasoning

group consciousness: the sum total of the consciousnesses of group members that have merged with One Mind

Group Soul: a spiritual presence that guides, teaches, and protects each group, communicating through the group personality that is comprised of the collective physical, emotional, and mental vibrational bodies of the members; members communicate with the Group Soul through their hearts and souls

holographic: the whole is reflected in each of the parts, though seen from a slightly different angle; the hologram suggests that life exists in an order of undivided wholeness

inner authority: a firm intuitive knowing on which an individual can confidently depend for choosing right action; as individuals develop inner authority, they no longer need to abdicate their power and responsibilities to leaders

Inner Leader: the spiritual principle and the guiding light towards which the human soul is consciously or unconsciously evolving; also called Soul, Higher Self, Transpersonal Self, Inner Guide, Solar Angel, Voice of Conscience, One Mind

inner work: the use of psychological and spiritual tools and practices to willingly explore personal motivations and mental models; doing inner work incorporates a view of life as a classroom with unlimited opportunities to heal and be healed—physically, emotionally, and mentally

inquiry: a process of asking open-ended questions to oneself (self-inquiry) or to another that inquire into the reasons behind a point of view or actions and to check out assumptions, beliefs, motives, and values

intuition: an inner knowing beyond rational thought; the heart's felt sense of which thought or action is true and right in a given situation

Lightworker: a spiritually evolved individual dedicated to serving as a conduit of Divine Light to planet Earth and all sentient beings

Master Teacher: an evolved individual who has mastered her or his physical, emotional, and mental bodies and has become Soul

mental model: an assumption, belief, or attitude about an aspect of ourselves, others, and the world that lies beneath the level of awareness and shapes behavior; a mental model escapes examination and becomes rigidly entrenched within the psyche as an absolute

mystic: a person who has totally surrendered to the Eternal Dharma of right living and to his or her dharma or duty in the world; a mystic is fully aware that his or her inner divinity is the true reality and is at one with Divine Will

One Mind: same as Soul, Group Soul, Solar Angel, Inner Leader

personality: the physical, emotional, and mental vehicles in which evolving human souls express themselves and gain experience; also referred to as self or lower self

personality integration: the harmonious bringing together of the conscious and unconscious physical, emotional, and mental bodies into wholeness so that they relate with one another as one energetic unit

philosophe: one of the deistic or materialistic writers and thinkers of the eighteenth century French Enlightenment

Piscean values: outer authority, hierarchical, masculine-energy-dominant relationships

polarity thinking: categorizing all thoughts and actions as being good/bad, positive/negative, right/wrong, victim/victimizer

shadow: the human psyche's unconscious that is not accessible to the conscious mind; the shadow holds the neglected, undeveloped, unlived, negative, and destructive aspects as well as the unrealized potentials

shared decision making: a group practice in which every perspective is heard and the focus is on what really matters

Solar Angel: an advanced being who has descended from the Higher Worlds to help the evolution of humanity; also called Soul, Higher Self, and Inner Leader

soul: the human psyche that is endeavoring to become Soul; it evolves through experience from being asleep to its true nature to awakening to its Divine Essence

Soul: the spiritual principle and guiding light towards which the human soul is consciously or unconsciously becoming; also called Inner Leader, Higher Self, Transpersonal Self, Inner Guide, Solar Angel, Voice of Conscience

Soul-infused personality: a state of being that exists after the physical, emotional, and mental bodies are purified and their energies integrated, and the human soul aligns with Soul (Inner Leader); in this state, the light of the Inner Leader radiates through the personality in full expression of Divine Light, Love, and Power

spiritual awakening: an inner experience that marks progress in the gradual expansion and unfoldment of human consciousness; points of increased awareness evolve from soul-awakening to physical, emotional, and mental purification to soul-infused personality, to release from the need to reincarnate, to being a master of wisdom on the inner planes

systems thinking: a process of looking at wholes rather than parts that stresses the role of interconnections; systems thinking questions such things as what are the patterns of events that are recurring and what structures are in place that cause these patterns

sutratma: the energetic link between the human soul in the heart and the Soul located eight inches above the head; the sutratma consists of two threads that descend from the Soul and divide, with one thread going to the pineal gland in the brain and the other going to the heart

Witness Self: the part of the mind that can observe self and others without judgment and evaluation; also called the Observer Self

BIOGRAPHICAL NAMES

Assagioli, Roberto. 1888–1974. Italian psychiatrist; founder of the psychological movement known as psychosynthesis

Aurobindo. 1872–1950. Indian seer, poet, and nationalist

Bailey, Alice. 1880–1949. Born in England, lived in the United States; writer and teacher on spiritual, astrological, Theosophical, and other religious subjects; many of her works were telepathically dictated to her by Djwhal Khul, a Tibetan Master of the Wisdom; founder of esoteric healing

Cayce, Edgar. 1877–1945. American psychic particularly adept at healing; information on his work is found at The Association of Research and Enlightenment, 215 67th Street, Virginia Beach, VA 23451, http://www.edgarcayce.org

Cedercrans, Lucille. 1921–1984. American author in the field of metaphysics and a teacher of Ageless Wisdom

Claire of Assisi. 1194–1253. Italian saint and follower of St. Francis; founder of the Order of Poor Ladies in the Franciscan tradition

Cota-Robles, Patricia. n.d. Teacher and Lightworker. Founder of the New Age Study of Humanity's Purpose, P. O. Box 41883, Tucson, AZ 85717. www.eraofpeace.org

Drucker, Peter. 1909–2005. American author of thirty-nine books; management consultant; self-described "social ecologist"; considered "the father of modern management"

Francis of Assisi. 1182–1226. Italian friar and saint; founder of Franciscan order

Greenleaf, Robert. 1904–1990. American author and founder of the servant leadership movement and The Center for Applied Ethics

John of the Cross, 1542–1591. Spanish saint, mystic, friar, priest, and reformer; joined the Discalced Carmelite Order with Teresa of Avila

The Mother. 1878–1973. French seer; joined Sri Aurobindo

Ramakrishna. 1836–1886. Hindu mystic of nineteenth century India

Sarada Devi. 1853–1920. Saint; wife of Ramakrishna

Saraydarian, Torkom. 1917–1997. Born in Armenia, lived in the US, trained in the teachings of Ageless Wisdom; his daughter, Gita Saraydarian, continues his work at TSG Publishing Foundation, P.O. Box 7068, Cave Creek, AZ 85327; www.TSGFoundation.org

Scholl, Ludger. n.d. German by birth; a resident of the Czech Republic renowned in eastern and western Europe as a speaker, teacher, and healer; integrated esoteric healing, traditional psychotherapy, and psychosynthesis

Senge, Peter. n.d. American; renowned pioneer, theorist, and writer in the field of management innovation; senior lecturer at the Massachusetts Institute of Technology; founding chair of the Society for Organizational Learning, 1280 Massachusetts Avenue, Cambridge, MA 02138, http://www.solonline.org

Teresa of Avila, 1515–1582. Spanish saint, mystic, nun, and reformer; founder of the Discalced Carmelite Order

Whyte, David. n.d. English poet and author of *The Heart Aroused: Poetry and the Preservation of the Soul in Corporate America*; associate fellow at Templeton College and Said Business School at the University of Oxford; takes his perspectives on creativity into the field of organizational development; works with European, American, and international companies

BIBLIOGRAPHY

Alder, Vera Stanley. *The Initiation of the World.* York Beach, ME: Samuel Weiser, Inc. 1939.

Arroyo, Stephen. *Astrology, Psychology, and the Four Elements.* Vancouver, WA: CRCS Publications, 1975.

Assagioli, Roberto. *The Act of Will.* New York: Penguin Books, 1982.

Bailey, Alice A. *The Soul: The Quality of Life.* New York: Lucis Publishing Company, 1974.

________. *Problems of Humanity.* New York: Lucis Publishing Company, 1964.

Bishop, Bill, coauthor of *The Big Sort: Why the Clustering of Like-Minded America Is Tearing Us Apart*; Ron Brownstein, *National Review*, and Karen Tumulty, *Time.* "Demographic, Cultural Dividing Lines Complicate '08 Race." Interview by Judy Woodruff with Bill Bishop, *The News Hour with Jim Lehrer*, PBS, May 19, 2008. Transcript at http://www.pbs.org/newshour/bb/politics/jan-june08/demographic_95-19.html (accessed June 1, 2008).

Bolen, Jean Shinoda. *The Millionth Circle: How to Change Ourselves and the World.* Berkeley, CA: Conari Press, 1999.

________. *Gods in Everyman: Archetypes That Shape Men's Lives.* New York: HarperCollins, 1989.

________. *Goddesses in Everywoman: A New Psychology of Women.* New York: HarperPerennial, 1984.

Brown, Molly Young. *The Unfolding Self: Psychosynthesis and Counseling.* San Raphael, CA: Psychosynthesis Press, 1983.

Cameron, Anne. *Daughters of the Copper Woman.* Vancouver, BC: Press Gang Publishers, 1981.

Capra, Fritjof. *The Turning Point: Science, Society, and the Rising Culture.* New York: Bantam Books, 1982.

Carr, Nicholas. "Is Google Making Us Stoopid? What the Internet Is Doing to Our Brains," *The Atlantic*, July/August 2008, 56.

Catholic Encyclopedia, Vol. IV, s.v. "Clare of Assisi." New York: Robert Appleton Company, 1908.

Cedercrans, Lucille. *Applied Wisdom.* Volumes I, II, III. Roseville, MN: Wisdom Impressions, 2007.

Childre, Doc and Deborah Rozman. *Overcoming Emotional Chaos.* San Diego, CA: Jodere Group, Inc., 2002.

Clinton, Bill. *Giving: How Each of Us Can Change the World.* New York: Knopf, 2007.

Ehrlich, Paul R., author of *The Population Bomb.* Interview "Consumption by the United States" on PBS, n.d. Quoted on http://www.mindfully.org/Sustainability/Americans-Consume-24percent.html (accessed May 19, 2008).

A Course in Miracles. Mill Valley, CA: Foundation for Inner Peace (1975) 1996.

Daniels, Patricia S. and Stephen G. Hyslop. *Almanac of World History.* Washington, DC: National Geographic Society, 2006.

Elgin, Duane. *Voluntary Simplicity.* New York: Harper, 1993.

Ferguson, Marilyn. *The Aquarian Conspiracy: Personal and Social Transformation in the 1980s.* Los Angeles: Tarcher, 1980.

Gilman, Robert. "Stages of Change: Examples from History and Ideas from Chemistry Illustrate the Process of Cultural Change." *Cultural Change* (IC39) Spring 1985. http://www.context.org/ ICLIB/IC09/Gilman1.htm (accessed May 20, 2008).

Graves, Helen. *Testimony of Light: An Extraordinary Message of Life After Death.* London: Rider, 1969.

Gurdjieff, G. I. *Views from the Real World.* New York: Dutton, 1975.

Hawkins, David R. *Transcending the Levels of Consciousness.* Sedona, AZ: Veritas Publishing, 2006.

________. *Power vs. Force: The Hidden Determinants of Human Behavior.* Carlsbad, CA: Hay House, 2002.

Heifetz, Ronald A., and Marty Linsky. *Leadership on the Line: Staying Alive Through the Dangers of Leading*. Boston: Harvard Business School Press, 2002.

Howe, Neil, William Strauss, and R.J. Matson. *Millennials Rising: The Next Great Generation.* New York: Vintage Books, 2000.

Johnson, Robert A. *Owning Your Own Shadow: Understanding the Dark Side of the Psyche.* New York: HarperCollins, 1993.

Kidd, Sue Monk. *The Dance of the Dissident Daughter.* New York: HarperCollins, 1995.

Leonard, George B. *The Transformation.* New York: Delacorte, 1972.

May, Gerald. *The Dark Night of the Soul.* San Francisco: Harper. 2005.

Olbrich, Bill. "Fraternal and Service Organizations,"http://www.answers.com/topic/fraternal-and-service-organizations (accessed May 19, 2008).

Palmer, Parker J. *Let Your Life Speak: Listening for the Voice of Vocation.* San Francisco: Jossey-Bass, 2000.

Parker, Derek and Julia Parker. "History of Astrology." www.astrology.com/aboutastrology/overview/history (accessed May 26, 2008).

Pearce, Joseph Chilton. *The Biology of Transcendence: A Blueprint of the*

Human Spirit. Rochester, VT: Inner Traditions International, 2002.

Peay, Pythia. "Feminism's Fourth Wave." *Utne Magazine*, March-April, 2005, pp. 59-60.

________. *Soul Sisters: The Five Sacred Qualities of a Woman's Soul.* Los Angeles: Tarcher/Penguin, 2002.

Penfield, Wilder. *No Man Alone: A Neurosurgeon's Life.* Boston: Little, Brown, 1977.

________. *The Mystery of the Mind.* Princeton, NJ: Princeton University Press, 1975.

Public Papers of the Presidents, Dwight D. Eisenhower, 1960, p. 1035-1040. http://coursea.matrix.msu.edu/~hst306/documents/indust.html (accessed June 5, 2008).

Ray, Paul H. Paul H. Ray to Susan S. Trout. E-mail communication on Ray's research on the growth of the cultural creative population since the year 2000. 1 August 2008.

Ray, Paul H. and Sherry Ruth Anderson. *The Cultural Creatives: How 50 Million People are Changing the World.* New York: Harmony Books, 2000.

Rempel, Gerhard, PhD. Lecture, Western New England College.http://mars.wnec.edu/~grempel/courses/wc2/lectures/enlightenment.html (accessed May 22, 2008).

Riso, Don and Russ Hudson. *The Wisdom of the Enneagram: The Complete Guide to Psychological and Spiritual Growth for the Nine Personality Types.* New York: Random House, 1999.

Rohr, Richard. *From Wild Man to Wise Man: Reflections on Male Spirituality.* Cincinnati, OH: St. Anthony Messenger Press, 2005.

Roszak, Theodore. *Person/Planet: The Creative Disintegration of Industrial Society.* Garden City, NY: Anchor Press/Doubleday, 1978.

Saraydarian, Torkom. *Initiation: The Path of Living Service.* Cave Creek, AZ:

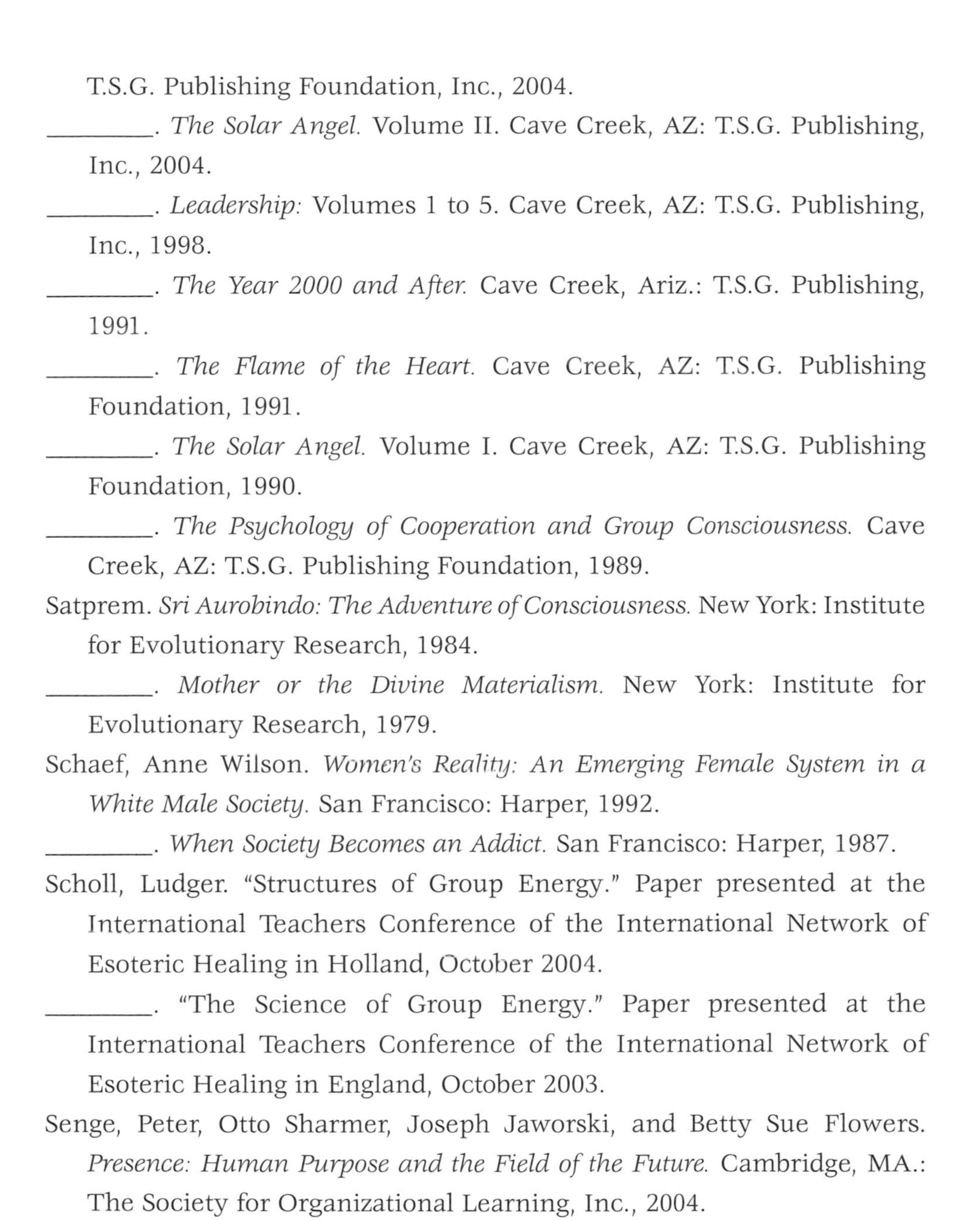

T.S.G. Publishing Foundation, Inc., 2004.

________. *The Solar Angel.* Volume II. Cave Creek, AZ: T.S.G. Publishing, Inc., 2004.

________. *Leadership:* Volumes 1 to 5. Cave Creek, AZ: T.S.G. Publishing, Inc., 1998.

________. *The Year 2000 and After.* Cave Creek, Ariz.: T.S.G. Publishing, 1991.

________. *The Flame of the Heart.* Cave Creek, AZ: T.S.G. Publishing Foundation, 1991.

________. *The Solar Angel.* Volume I. Cave Creek, AZ: T.S.G. Publishing Foundation, 1990.

________. *The Psychology of Cooperation and Group Consciousness.* Cave Creek, AZ: T.S.G. Publishing Foundation, 1989.

Satprem. *Sri Aurobindo: The Adventure of Consciousness.* New York: Institute for Evolutionary Research, 1984.

________. *Mother or the Divine Materialism.* New York: Institute for Evolutionary Research, 1979.

Schaef, Anne Wilson. *Women's Reality: An Emerging Female System in a White Male Society.* San Francisco: Harper, 1992.

________. *When Society Becomes an Addict.* San Francisco: Harper, 1987.

Scholl, Ludger. "Structures of Group Energy." Paper presented at the International Teachers Conference of the International Network of Esoteric Healing in Holland, October 2004.

________. "The Science of Group Energy." Paper presented at the International Teachers Conference of the International Network of Esoteric Healing in England, October 2003.

Senge, Peter, Otto Sharmer, Joseph Jaworski, and Betty Sue Flowers. *Presence: Human Purpose and the Field of the Future.* Cambridge, MA.: The Society for Organizational Learning, Inc., 2004.

Senge, Peter. *The Fifth Discipline: The Art and Practice of the Learning Organization.* New York: Doubleday, 1990.

Senge, Peter, Art Kleiner, Charlotte Roberts, and Rick Ross. *The Fifth Discipline Fieldbook: Strategies and Tools for Building Learning Organizations.* New York: Currency, Doubleday, 1994.

Seifer, Nancy and Martin Vieweg. *When the Soul Awakens: The Path to Spiritual Evolution and a New World Era.* New York: iUniverse, Inc., 2008.

Sinetar, Marsha. *Ordinary People as Monks and Mystics: Lifestyles for Self-Discovery.* New Jersey: Paulist Press, 1986.

Sogyal Rinpoche. *The Tibetan Book of Living and Dying.* San Francisco: Harper/Collins, 1993.

Spoto, Donald. *Reluctant Saint: The Life of Francis of Assisi.* New York: Viking Press, 2002.

State University of New York at Suffolk. "The Effects of WW II."http://www2.sunysuffolk.edu/westn/effectww2.html (accessed May 25, 2008).

Strauss, William and Neil Howe. *The Fourth Turning: An American Prophecy.* New York: Broadway Books, 1997.

Tielfoldt, Diane and Devon Scheef. "Generation X and the Millennials: What You Need to Know about Mentoring the New Generations," *Law Practice Today,* August 2004. http://www.abanet.org/1pm/1pt/articles/mgt08044.html (accessed April 7, 2008).

Tenzin Wanghal Rinpoche. *Healing with Form, Energy and Light: The Five Elements in Tibetan Shamanism, Tantra, and Dzogchen.* Boulder: Snow Lion, 2002.

Trout, Susan. *Born to Serve: The Evolution of the Soul Through Service.* Alexandria, VA: Three Roses Press, 1997.

________. *The Awakened Leader: Leadership as a Classroom of the Soul.* Alexandria, VA: Three Roses Press, 2005.

Welch, John. *Spiritual Pilgrims: Carl Jung and Teresa of Avila.* New York: Paulist Press, 1982.

Whitfield, Charles. *Boundaries and Relationships: Knowing, Protecting, and Enjoying the Self.* Deerfield Beach, FL: Health Communications, Inc., 1993.

Wilson, Marie C. *Closing the Leadership Gap: Why Women Can and Must Help Run the World.* New York: Penguin Books, 2004.

Woodman, Marion. *Conscious Femininity.* Toronto: Inner City Books, 1993.

Wright, Machaelle Small. *The Mount Shasta Mission.* Jefferson, VA: Center for Nature Research, 2005.

Yeomans, Tom. "The Corona Process: Group Work in a Spiritual Context." Unpublished paper, 1996.

Zogby, John. *The Way We'll Be: The Zogby Report on the Transformation of the American Dream.* New York: Random House, 2008.

ABOUT THE AUTHOR

Susan S. Trout, PhD, cofounded the Institute for the Advancement of Service in Alexandria, Virginia, in 1980. She served as executive director for twenty-two years. In 2008, she became director of outreach, dedicating her efforts to sharing the teachings of her seminal work, *The Soul and Service Trilogy*, with national and international leaders, groups, and organizations. *The Clarion Call* is the third book of *The Trilogy*, which includes *Born to Serve: The Evolution of the Soul Through Service* and *The Awakened Leader: Leadership as a Classroom of the Soul.*

Dr. Trout holds graduate degrees from Stanford and Northwestern universities in psychoneurology, deaf education, audiology, speech pathology, and communication disorders. She has worked as a specialist and researcher in communication and neurological disorders in Alaska, Illinois, and California. Prior to her work at the Institute, she served fourteen years as a professor, chairperson, and researcher at the University of the Pacific and University of California Medical Centers in San Francisco.

ABOUT THE INSTITUTE FOR THE ADVANCEMENT OF SERVICE

The Institute for the Advancement of Service (IAS) is an educational and spiritual organization offering classes and trainings in soul development, service, leadership, and organizational design. The foundation of IAS teachings and practices derives from the trilogy *Born to Serve: The Evolution of the Soul Through Service* with a Foreword by His Holiness The Dalai Lama; *The Awakened Leader: Leadership as a Classroom of the Soul*; and *The Clarion Call: Leadership and Group Life in the Aquarian Era* by Susan S. Trout, PhD. Three Roses Press publishes all Institute books and materials. IAS was founded in 1980 as a non-profit 501c(3).

The Institute offers:

- Trainings in leadership, organizational design, and group life for individuals and organizations
- Courses and workshops, and independent studies in psychospiritual development
- Trainings in personal development, peer support, and leadership for high school students
- Services and trainings in healing modalities that support individual health and wellbeing

Contact Information

Susan S. Trout is dedicating her efforts to sharing the transformative teachings of *The Soul and Service Trilogy* with groups, organizations, and national and international leaders who are searching for concrete ways to usher in the new world.

To contact Dr. Trout about her availability for trainings, workshops and speeches or to learn more about the programs and services of the Institute for the Advancement of Service, please use the information below:

Institute for the Advancement of Service
P. O. Box 320245
Alexandria, VA 22320

Phone: 703.706.5333
btsias@aol.com
www.ias-online.org

To purchase any or all of *The Soul and Service Trilogy* books,

Born to Serve: The Evolution of the Soul Through Service
The Awakened Leader. Leadership as a Classroom of the Soul
The Clarion Call: Leadership and Group Life in the Aquarian Era

address inquires and orders to:

Three Roses Press
P. O. Box 320245
Alexandria, VA 22320

Phone: 703.706.5333
btsias@aol.com
www.ias-online.org